9

D1124607

GHOST ARMY OF WORLD WAR II

Ghost
ARMY OF
World War II

By Jack Kneece

PELICAN PUBLISHING COMPANY
Gretna 2001

Library of Congress Cataloging-in-Publication Data

Kneece, Jack.
 Ghost Army of World War II / Jack Kneece.
  p.cm.
 ISBN 1-56554-876-0
  1. United States. Army. Headquarters Special Troops, 23rd—History. 2. World
War, 1939-1945—Regimental histories—United States. 3. World War, 1939-
1945—Western Front. 4. World War, 1939-1945—Deception—United States.
5. Disinformation—History—20th century. I. Title.

D760.25 .K54 2001
940.54'21—dc21

                                                    2001021385

Manufactured in the United States of America
Published by Pelican Publishing Company, Inc.
1000 Burmaster Street, Gretna, Louisiana 70053

For my parents, Jack Sr. and Margie

Contents

GHOST ARMY OF WORLD WAR II

Chapter One

A Top Secret Army

German Lt. Gen. Hermann B. von Ramcke picked up his big Zeiss binoculars and peered over fortifications at Brest toward the American lines 700 yards away. It was a gray, overcast day, August 24, 1944. He hoped the overcast would stop the incessant air attacks by the American and British planes, which had bombed and strafed the German-occupied French port city around the clock.

The city on the English Channel was considered vital because it was home to many German submarines and a good deep-water port. The Allies wanted badly to capture it to help keep the Normandy invasion supplied. Von Ramcke knew he was in for a tough and perhaps hopeless fight.

Von Ramcke could see a few American Sherman tanks, but more importantly, he could see many camouflage net enclosures that were designed to hide tanks, the tanks he and his men had heard grinding and clanking into position on his right during the night. Behind him, American and British ships patrolled just out of range of the big German guns aimed seaward. His radio operators had heard the Americans on their battlefield radios ordering the tanks into positions and ordering up ammunition and supplies. He and his men also had seen hundreds of artillery flashes from the right side of their fortifications. He feared that the American Gen. George Patton's tanks would attempt a thrust at fortifications on the German right.

Von Ramcke and his nearly 40,000 troops were not in the most advantageous position. They were on the end of the Brittany Peninsula in the city of Brest. His Fuhrer, Adolf Hitler, had ordered that Ramcke and his men, many of whom were SS troops, fight to the last man. If nothing else, this would tie up much of the Allied invasion force. The SS, or "Shutz Staffel" troops, were as zealous and fanatical as von Ramcke, and were used to keep the ordinary soldiers fighting to the utmost despite the desperate odds. Brest was swollen with troops seeking refuge from the Allied onslaught. Von Ramcke had dispersed the SS troops among the Second Division paratroops under his command, men who already were battle-hardened and tough.

Hitler need not have delivered such an order to von Ramcke, the hero of Crete in 1941, a clever and fanatical officer. Von Ramcke planned to fight to the last man—and that included himself. Although he knew it was a mere redundancy, he had ordered that any soldier who showed cowardice or failed to stay in position be executed on the spot by his SS troops, men who had shown the utmost loyalty to von Ramcke in other battles. If the Americans and British were going to take Brest, von Ramcke had decided it would be at a dear cost. He had decided to go down fighting himself, at least dying an honorable death.

Hitler knew that the men trapped on the tip of the Brittany Peninsula, bottled in as the Normandy invaders gained more and more ground, were in a hopeless position. But he also hoped that a suicidal stand would tie up vast numbers of Allied men and materiel that could not be used in the Allied thrust to the east. Ever the optimist, however paranoid, he also wondered if at some point von Ramcke might even break out of his position and harass the vast American and British armies from the rear, perhaps simultaneously with a German attack at Avranches, the elbow where the Allies were turning the corner onto the Brittany Peninsula.

Brest was protected by the terrain, to a certain extent, with many hills and ridges and valleys and several streams. Heavy concrete and steel pillboxes were connected by tunnels, and had withstood well the heavy Allied bombing day after day and night after night. Already von Ramcke had ordered a systematic destruction of the port so that when the inevitable came, the port would be virtually useless. Docks and wharfs were blown up. Channels were filled with debris. Mines, burned-out vehicles, and anything that would prevent easy access were shoved into the port's shipping lanes. Submarines had escaped to the North Sea.

Von Ramcke thought that the American troops on his right were more numerous, and had more armor. There also were numerous American patrols reported in the area. This, he thought, was probably where the next attack would come. He decided to concentrate his tank-busting 88mm artillery, his tank grenadiers, and as many men as he could spare from the other sectors on his right. If the Americans were foolish enough to attack on his right, then they would be in for a deadly surprise. He barked the orders and immediately his subordinates began to concentrate the anti-tank artillery in place, borrowing some of the big guns from other sectors of the front.

But what von Ramcke did not know was that the apparently heavy concentration of American troops he saw several hundred yards away, the noises heard at night of tanks on the move, and the heavy radio traffic was all part of an elaborate ruse by the Americans, members of a special army trained in the art of subterfuge. The artillery flashes were small canister bombs, not real artillery. The tank noises were broadcast by giant speakers atop half-tracks and trucks.

In actuality, there were less than a thousand men on his right front in the area where he looked through his binoculars, many of them former actors, writers, decorators, radio and camouflage experts, and even fashion designers. They were part of a top secret American army trained to dupe the Germans in order to free up other American units and freeze Germans in position. While von Ramcke fretted and worried about Patton's army at his front, Patton and his Third Army were actually far away, racing eastward, with Paris as a glittering goal in the distance.

Patton's armor *had* been on the Brittany Peninsula near Brest, but had left during the night. The armor had been replaced with fake, inflatable tanks. Had von Ramcke known that the tanks he saw were merely realistic rubber dummies, inflated with air, he could have led his men on a disruptive breakout that could have wreaked havoc in the Allies' rear. Had he timed it with the Avranches counterattack, which failed, it might have led to an Allied defeat on the peninsula. But he was convinced by the performance before him.

The artists and decorators and fashion designers were so adept that not one of von Ramcke's men had an inkling that the army was fake. And even the best binoculars could not determine at 700 yards that the tanks and the artillery pieces, the camouflage netting enclosures, and trucks and half-tracks in the distance were empty or filled with air, manufactured with great secrecy by several big American tire companies during the previous two years.

One of those men a few hundred yards away from von Ramcke was famed fashion designer Bill Blass, a young man who had already made a name for himself in the New York world of high fashion even before the war started. Blass and his world today are light years away from the muddy danger he faced more than half a century ago. He is considered one of the most sophisticated men in America. A friend once quipped that Cary Grant seemed to be an English peasant by comparison.

Blass is on a casual, first-name basis with powerful and wealthy people all over the world. But his friends also include men in rural areas with whom he served in the secret army. He founded a fashion and design empire with worldwide influence. When Blass decided to retire as the new millennium approached, he put his fashion empire—represented by the famous logo of mirror-image Bs—on the market for a reported $700 million and had no trouble finding a buyer. He now lives quietly in New York City's One Sutton Place South. His unique designs for everything from women's dresses to automobile interiors are known worldwide. People were always surprised to learn that he is from Fort Wayne, Indiana, where he was born in 1922, the son of a hardware store owner.

Blass came to New York as a young man to try to break into the world of high fashion design. After he established his company, Bill Blass Ltd., his clients later included Nancy Reagan, Barbara Bush, Barbra Streisand, Barbara Walters, Candice Bergen, and Mary Tyler Moore. His fashions were noted for their sophistication and rich fabrics, elegant simplicity, and subtle style. His work was recognized by three prestigious Coty American Fashion Critics awards and his induction into the Coty Hall of Fame. He was awarded the Lifetime Achievement Award by the Council of Fashion Designers of America in 1987. All of this color and glitter and fame were far removed from his world of olive drab in 1944.

As the new millennium approached, Blass got a call from one of his best friends, Bob Tompkins, of Gardnerville, Nevada, also an artist. While in basic training during World War II at Fort Meade, Maryland—the training facility situated between Washington and Baltimore—Blass had met Tompkins, was delighted to know that he was a fellow artist, and soon learned that he was quite an intelligent and sophisticated young man himself. Tompkins was newly married to a lovely young woman, Bunny Hart, who looked like a model and, in fact, had been offered a job by a top New York modeling agency.

The three of them had become fast friends, almost in a mode reminiscent of *Jules et Jim*, picnicking together, drinking, smoking, and planning their postwar futures.

The telephone call to Blass evoked memories of a world far removed in time and place from his life as a designer. It had been a world of olive drab and camouflage netting, burlap and canvas instead of fine brocades and silks. Blass would later say it was only a footnote to his fabulous life, but what a footnote it was.

Blass learned that the work he and Tompkins did as members of an elite top secret army unit of 1,100 men was at last declassified. The men were free to talk about it for the first time in more than fifty years. A newsman wanted to chat with him about the ultra secret part of his life. Until then, the many articles and biographies and stories about Blass had a casual mention of his war-time service, simply stating—incorrectly and incompletely, because of the secrecy—that he had served in the Army Corps of Engineers. This was Blass' cover story for all of his postwar life.

Blass had suffered a mild stroke, and, like many men who begin to look back on their lives, he thought about his war service, prompted by recent declassification of the work. Because his work had been so secret, it was not easy to suddenly discuss it in detail, even though, at long last, he was free to do so.

He was a thin, handsome young man, just twenty-four years old back then.

"I was a patriot then and I'm still a patriot," he says.

Suddenly, it seemed, he was drafted out of the sophisticated world of New York fashion and into a pup tent on the Normandy coast, sleeping in a heavy rain with his bare feet sticking out. A few hundred yards away were some of the most deadly enemy soldiers in history. Aircraft engines whined overhead—sometimes as many as 1,500 bombers at a time flew over—artillery shells fell randomly, machine guns split the air with a deadly staccato.

He often wondered whether he would ever get back to New York, where, he said, "There was a whole café society that was in its full glory. You went from El Morocco to the Blue Angel to Monte Carlo to the 1-2-3."

Even before the war, he had planned to become a fashion designer, but like many Americans, World War II interrupted those plans.

"Yes," he repeated, perhaps searching his memory of those days half a century ago, "I was a patriot then and so was everyone in America. We had a job to do, and we did it."

Blass and his fellow veterans of the Twenty-third Headquarters Special Troops—dubbed by the men in it the "Ghost Army"—were bound by orders from the Pentagon to never discuss the secret work

This is a sketch of the shoulder insignia designed and drawn by men of the Ghost Army. They were never allowed to wear it.

they did during World War II unless they were prepared for severe penalties. At last he and his comrades could talk openly about it without facing prison.

This is the story of the men who formed and operated this small, secret army and how it successfully and repeatedly duped the Germans, thereby saving thousands of American and British and even German lives. The unit was so secret that the men never once during the war wore their own insignia. *They always wore the patches and insignia of other army outfits as a cover for their work.* They did, however, later design their own insignia—one that featured a ghost hurling a lightning bolt. It now adorns the cover of this book—its first public display ever.

Blass learned that Tompkins had been in touch with the author of this book, and with Art Shilstone, another war buddy and now a well-known New York and Connecticut illustrator. A letter from Tompkins reminisced about the years he and Blass had spent together in World War II, along with George Stulter, who became a Hollywood set designer, famed painter Elsworth Kelly, whose work is on display in the National Museum of Art, renowned photographer Art Kane, and famous bird painter Art Singer.

The two men later chatted about these men, and Col. Howell Railey, who had become a newspaper editor in New York, a *New York Times* writer, and a globetrotting foreign correspondent for *Fortune* magazine. Railey was also author of the novel *Touched With Madness*. They had often marveled that their Army unit produced soldiers who would become so famous and respected in the postwar years. But then again, it was not an average army unit. In fact, it was a hand-picked outfit whose very existence was not fully declassified from "top-secret" until 1996.

How the Secret Army Came to Be

As Blass sat in his bed thinking back on his war years, he smiled as he recalled the days when he and Bob Tompkins shared the danger, shivered in the snow, trudged in the mud, smoked many cigarettes, lived on K-rations, and prayed for a quick end to the war. They also had shared a pup tent throughout the mud and snow of Europe after D-Day. They had raced to get away from rampaging Panzer divisions during the Battle of the Bulge. Blass and Tompkins laughed as they recalled trying to sleep in the small tent they shared during one particularly cold and driving rain. His and Tompkins' bare feet were sticking out of the tent.

The name they had adopted for themselves, Ghost Army, stuck. They never got to wear that ghost patch, however. Ironically, the Germans also spoke of an American Ghost Army because of its will-o'-the-wisp work, but they could never quite figure it out. The Germans also called it the "Phantom Army" because one day it was in one place and the next day it was attacking their flanks or even attacking from the rear. Some simply chalked it up to amazing American logistics, but it was far more than that.

Most other American, British, and Free French troops never knew of the existence of the Ghost Army—the Twenty-third Headquarters Special Troops—yet all were affected by it, and as many as 40,000 men probably owed their lives to it, including many German troops. The mission of this small army unit was to deceive the German Army after D-Day, representing themselves as very large units of up to a division in strength, or 14,000 to 17,000 men. On one occasion this small outfit pretended to be two divisions or about 30,000 men.

They did this in many ways: with sounds broadcast at night by huge speakers, the use of up to a thousand inflatable but realistic vehicles and aircraft, phony artillery, artillery explosions, false and misleading radio traffic, phony markings and insignia on vehicles and uniforms, simulated tank tracks in the snow and mud, phony troop movements made by a small number of men going in circles, misinformation leaked to French and Belgian spies for Germany, and a host of other tricks, including large camouflage nets that concealed nothing but that led the Germans to assume the netting covered thousands of tanks.

Each mission had special goals and all used the secret bag of tricks developed in top-secret training just for the purpose. The Ghost Army was so secret that its half-track vehicles and trucks, carrying special secret equipment, were outfitted with plastic explosives under the seats to completely destroy the equipment, so the Nazis would not discover it, should a vehicle be hit by enemy gunfire. One of them was destroyed in just this fashion by a Nazi railroad gun.

The story of this unique outfit sounds more like a wild movie plot than the real thing. The Ghost Army had an unlikely and rather oblique beginning not many months after the war began, when the Japanese attacked Pearl Harbor. One impetus for creation of the Ghost Army was the realization of just how ill prepared America was after the attack. Quite simply, if America didn't have the troop strength, it would have to simulate armies and use deception. The Ghost Army was just such a simulated army, one specifically designed for operation in Europe against the Germans after D-Day.

Within hours after the attack on Pearl Harbor, what looked to be machine guns appeared on the roof of the White House and the U.S. Capitol Building. Many people were reassured to see this sudden and tangible evidence of American resolve. Only a few people knew they were fakes—dummy wooden guns painted black. The U.S. had so few weapons that wooden training implements were put in place just to bolster the morale of Washingtonians. The situation was far more desperate than most Americans realized. Many regular troops also trained with wooden machine guns and dummy mortars while American industry cranked up its war manufacturing apparatus.

But future historians will see the Pearl Harbor attack as a pivotal point in the survival of American democracy—indeed, world democracy. Lethargic, pacifist America had been slapped hard in the face. More than 2,000 men had been killed and another 2,000 were wounded in the sneak attack, conducted while Japanese diplomats in Washington feigned negotiations to head off a war.

Few dared mention pacifism after Pearl Harbor. The national goal turned to righteous vengeance, and damn the cost. This was all the more remarkable when contrasted to a Gallup poll conducted in May 1941 that showed 80 percent of Americans opposed getting involved in an overseas war. And President Franklin D. Roosevelt had been criticized for allowing American military leaders to meet with their British counterparts to discuss war readiness and the probability of American involvement.

Adm. Bull Halsey summed up the reversal in national feeling with his first order: "Kill Japs, Kill Japs, Kill Japs!" But it was tough going in the early weeks and months. The government kept America's lack of preparedness a secret while military leaders at the highest echelons worked feverishly to prepare the country.

Genesis of the Ghosts

Less than two years after Pearl Harbor shocked the nation, an olive drab Army Chevrolet with four stars on its flag rolled up the White House driveway. It was a beautiful fall day in 1943, and autumn leaves were brilliant yellows and reds. A distinguished-looking, gray-haired general got out of the car, followed by a couple of aides, and strode purposefully into the White House. Aides to Gen. George Catlett Marshall scrambled to keep up with his deliberate stride. Marshall was chief of staff of the United States Army, America's highest-ranking soldier. A look of somber gravitas, perhaps due to a perpetual look of worry about his brow, made Marshall look older than his 62 years.

Marshall had come to the White House for one of his regular meetings with President Franklin Delano Roosevelt. Often Secretary of War Henry L. Stimson and Roosevelt's top troubleshooter and confidant, Harry Hopkins, were present at these meetings. Marshall regularly kept Roosevelt and the war cabinet abreast of the war effort in private meetings in the Oval Office. They had been meeting routinely to discuss war readiness or planning even before Pearl Harbor. Roosevelt and Marshall, unlike the average isolationist American, had seen the war coming like an unstoppable freight train. Their chief worry in the days before Pearl Harbor was America's reluctance to arm, and the nation's collective inability to see the grave danger of being unprepared.

Most Americans thought the Atlantic and Pacific oceans were sufficient to keep them out of another "foreign war." The carnage of World War I was still a fresh memory in the minds of many Americans. Americans were trying to ignore what was happening in Europe.

The situation was indeed bleak. In 1939, the Army's enlisted strength, including the Army Air Corps, was 130,000. There was not one armored division. There were only 1,175 airplanes, most of them hopelessly out of date. Many were bi-planes scarcely more airworthy than World War I models. When the Japanese attacked Pearl Harbor on December 7, 1941, the situation had not improved much. The United States was far from being on a war footing—far from the nine million men it would have in its armed services by the end of the war.

Gen. Dwight D. Eisenhower, formerly top military aide to Gen. Douglas MacArthur in the Philippines, was ordered to Washington by Marshall to help in planning the war effort. MacArthur had high praise for Eisenhower's administrative talents. Eisenhower wrote in *Crusade in Europe* of this time in America's history:

> There was no dependable defense against a modern tank or plane; troops carried wooden models of mortars and machine guns, and were able to study some of our new weapons only from blueprints. Equipment of all sorts was lacking and much of that in use had been originally produced for the national Army of World War One.

Despite all of this, British Prime Minister Winston Churchill wrote in *The Grand Alliance:*

> No American will think it wrong of me if I proclaim that to have the United States at our side was to me the greatest joy. . . . I thought

of a remark which Edward Grey had made to me more than thirty years before—that the United States is like "a gigantic boiler. Once the fire is lighted under it there is no limit to the power it can generate."

But there was scarcely a flicker in that boiler when the war began. It was against this backdrop that General Marshall found the President sitting in his wheel chair, the dark lines under his eyes making his normally worried mien appear even more grave. The two men liked and respected one another. Throughout the war they had a close and symbiotic relationship that proved a powerful force, unappreciated even today by most Americans. Roosevelt was so dependent on Marshall that he refused to let him leave to head the Allied war effort in London, and instead appointed General Eisenhower as Supreme Allied Commander. He wanted to keep Marshall near him, just a short drive from the Pentagon or Marshall's home in nearby Virginia.

Marshall also enjoyed Roosevelt's total confidence, and generally knew all that Roosevelt knew about the war and communications with foreign leaders. Roosevelt usually shared with Marshall the constant stream of secret messages he received from Winston Churchill, and, later, Josef Stalin. Indeed, Churchill, knowing how close Roosevelt and Marshall and Harry Hopkins were, often suggested that Roosevelt share his messages with Hopkins and Marshall. Churchill had developed a very close relationship with Hopkins when Hopkins came to Great Britain on a fact-finding mission for Roosevelt. Roosevelt was far closer to Marshall than he was to his own vice president, Harry Truman.

Marshall at first reflected the anger of most Americans when he rashly urged an Allied invasion of Europe as early as 1942. His and America's thirst for ending the war with a mighty effort had to be reined in by the British, who feared another Dunkirk—where the Germans almost captured a British army of 300,000 men—if the Allies acted too soon. Marshall and Roosevelt finally realized that Churchill was right—the Allies were far from ready. And Germany was a far more formidable foe than they had realized. It was so formidable that the war in the Pacific would have to rank second in America's overall effort.

On this particular day, Marshall briefed Roosevelt on the usual loss of shipping to German submarines and the progress of the war in the Pacific and Mediterranean. He saved a special treat he knew the President would especially like: a plan to create a small, top-secret, special tactical army group, one little larger than a battalion in size at just 1,100 men, and that included 300 officers. The idea had been approved by Stimson, who wrote the order officially creating it. It was a project urged by the British and even discussed briefly with Roosevelt by Winston Churchill at the Tehran Conference.

In a symbolic sense, the new Army was more of the wooden guns atop the White House, but on a far more elaborate and sophisticated scale. Some military men likened it to a gadget or trick play in football, a daring bit of theatrics that would have a salubrious effect after the invasion of Normandy and during the rest of the war far out of proportion to its small size. In fact, its results would be little short of spectacular, far exceeding the hopes of its planners. And its very existence was perhaps the last great secret of World War II.

It was so successful that, after the war, Army leaders up to Eisenhower decided to keep it secret in case its skills, equipment, and know-how should be needed again.

Marshall reminded Roosevelt that American Gen. Jacob L. Devers and several top British generals and British leaders, including Churchill, had urged that America quickly get up to speed in learning the deceptive military techniques used by the British with great success in North Africa and elsewhere. The techniques had not only saved thousands of lives, but were pivotal in Gen. Bernard L. Montgomery's spectacular victory against Rommel at El Alamein.

Churchill, in fact, told Roosevelt that the British under Montgomery had used the deceptive techniques that actually led to the victory in the Battle of El Alamein, saving many lives in the process. Some went so far as to state that the victory would not have occurred without the use of the novel deceptive tactics.

Roosevelt learned a bit about this deception first in January 1943 during his top-secret journey to Casablanca to meet with Churchill. Use of deception by British military units was one of Churchill's favorite topics, and it is highly unlikely that the subject was not raised during the many long chats between the two men in Casablanca, but even now the exact details of those conversations are not known. What is known is that Churchill enjoyed chatting about it with Harry

Hopkins and Roosevelt during these times.

Some of those tricks in North Africa had included what the British called "Chinese soldiers." This was a system in which a large group of wooden dummy soldiers, complete with pith helmets and desert uniforms, could be pulled upright out of holes in the sand with a system of ropes and pulleys to draw German fire. It also made the enemy wrongly think an attack would come from a certain area.

This accomplished several other things as well. It saved lives, wasted German ammunition, and—perhaps more importantly—pinpointed the exact location of German troops and weaponry for more effective return fire. Gen. Omar N. Bradley in the Tunisian campaign said one trick even involved having the U.S. and British military police directing road traffic wear burnooses so that they appeared to be Arabs. This confused the Germans as to which troops were in the area.

There were many more techniques, even more elaborate and intricate. As Churchill explained in *Closing the Ring:*

> General Montgomery had at his disposal three armored and the equivalent of seven infantry divisions. The concentration of so large a force demanded a number of ingenious deceptive measures and precautions. It was especially necessary that enemy aircraft should be prevented from overlooking the [real] preparations. All this was attended by great success and the attack came as a complete surprise.

Churchill said he could not go into greater detail even in the years after the war. But we now know those details.

That was for postwar public consumption. What Roosevelt and Marshall learned from Churchill just a few weeks before the formation of America's own Ghost Army was that the deception played on Rommel was a tour de force. It included not only the dummy soldiers but black shadows *painted directly on the sand* to fool the constant reconnaissance flights by the Germans into thinking the main attack would come far to the south of El Alamein. In the harsh sunlight of the desert, often the only means an aerial observer had of seeing a building or vehicle painted desert tan was the dark shadow it cast.

The Germans saw hundreds of such "shadows" indicating tanks, buildings and a supply dump considerably south of El Alamein, the southernmost battlefront. What they didn't know was that the images represented nothing—not even real shadows—just black paint.

Artists were recruited and used to ensure realism in the depth and proportion of such shadows. The success of these artists led to the recruitment of artists such as Bob Tompkins and Bill Blass and Art Shilstone later on by the American Ghost Army. But the Germans took the bait, deciding this was where the big British counteroffensive would come. They massed their troops in the wrong place, south of El Alamein instead of to the north, where the attack actually came, hitting a thin spot in the German lines.

Meanwhile, Churchill said Montgomery had to carefully conceal the enormous buildup of tanks and supplies in the north near El Alamein where the real attack was to be made. Nazi reconnaissance pilots in the north saw no big supply dumps of the kind that always signaled a major attack. They saw plenty of them in the southern sector, however, so they concentrated their Panzer tanks there—just as Montgomery hoped they would.

In fact, Churchill gleefully confided to Roosevelt, British gasoline was stored along fence lines in the northern section and in the shade of olive trees, under pup tents, and spread out to avoid putting it all in one big supply dump, the usual practice before an attack. Tanks were skillfully covered with canvas and painted to appear to be mere trucks or even American-supplied jeeps. From the air, scale was not as important, so a tank could actually be disguised as a jeep. A pilot would merely assume that he was a few hundred feet closer than he was.

The Germans were constantly overflying the British position in a light aircraft they called "Storch," for stork. In fact, Gen. Erwin Rommel himself enjoyed the overview from his own Storch from time to time. Rommel, whom many called the most brilliant of all German generals, also was fooled.

All the while, Churchill informed Roosevelt, the fake buildup in the southern sector also included many tracks in the sand, most of them made during the night by half-track vehicles, *not tanks*. The tracks were going into and under camouflage netting. The camouflage netting in the southern sector was deliberately sloppy, and the supplies, including many empty boxes and empty gas cans, were stacked up somewhat ostentatiously. Then a probing attack by a contingent of Indian troops in the southern section convinced Rommel's forces that the British attack was indeed to come in the southern area.

When the real punch came in the north, Rommel's thinly spread troops were surprised and embarrassed. They also were routed and captured by the thousands. The Desert Fox had been outfoxed. German troops were soundly beaten in the first major British victory of the war. Many years later, when approaching death, Field Marshal Montgomery would request that his tombstone be marked "Montgomery of Alamein."

This decisive battle, made possible by deception, was the beginning of the end for the Germans in North Africa. Some even mark it as the point when the Allies began to slowly turn the tide against the entire Wehrmacht. Many thousands of crack German troops were captured in the battle. American troops helped later in North Africa, but learned of German battle prowess the hard way, particularly at the battle of Kasserine Pass, where Americans were badly mauled.

It was this battle that caused most Germans—not to mention many Russians and even British—to wonder aloud about the fighting ability of American troops. They were to revise this perception more positively by 1944. By pushing Germany out of North Africa, the southern flanks of the big Normandy invasion, "Overlord," could proceed as planned two years later. Overlord also included Operation Dragoon, a landing on the south coast of France, which would have been imperiled by a German presence in North Africa.

Erwin Rommel

Ironically, Montgomery borrowed many ideas for deception from Field Marshal Erwin Rommel, then 51, who headed German's famed Afrika Korps. He was an outstanding tactician who purposely turned down the chance to become a member of the German general staff in order to remain a front-line officer.

It all began, according to newly declassified military records, when Rommel and his Panzers invaded North Africa many months earlier, starting in Libya. Libya was filled with British and American spies. Rommel knew this because of German intelligence in the area. So when Rommel and his troops arrived in various towns, he would have trains carry long loads of what appeared to be tanks on train flatcars under canvas. Actually, along with the exposed real tanks, there were many wooden and cardboard props under the canvas to fool the Allies into thinking Rommel had many more tanks than he actually had.

In the early months, this had the desired effect of making the Allied armies timid, if not demoralized, and timid armies don't win battles. The Germans also had used deception in the invasion of Norway, flooding the country with German "tourists" just before the invasion, not to mention many fake newsmen, lecturers, diplomats, and refugees, all of whom rose up and greatly aided the invasion from within.

Rommel had become a master at having his armored columns repeatedly circle into towns to appear to the spies watching from buildings that there was far more heavy armor as they unwittingly counted the same tanks again and again. And before battles, Rommel had some small armored units drive back and forth in the desert, some dragging brush and debris, to stir up sandstorms and appear to be very numerous just before he attacked elsewhere. He also used fake radio traffic to simulate an impending attack in a certain sector.

The British finally caught onto these tricky tactics and adopted them, not only in North Africa but also later in "Operation Fortitude" in Britain, designed to induce Germans into thinking the main Allied European invasion would come at the French port city of Calais. The British deception was generally far more elaborate and detailed than that of Rommel's North African tricks. And Americans later even outdid the British with the intricacies of the Ghost Army.

While crude by comparison to later American efforts, the British Operation Fortitude worked well despite its lack of sophistication. All the world learned of Operation Fortitude just after World War II, but America's Ghost Army was ordered kept secret.

Operation Fortitude also used fake radio traffic and thousands of inflatable tanks (supplied by American rubber companies, particularly United Rubber and Firestone), phony Spitfire fighter planes, trucks, and even fake oil refineries made of obsolete sewer pipe, along with round wooden structures painted gray to simulate metal fuel tanks. Although Americans and American industries helped make much of this, and Americans, including the Ghost Army, helped the British, most of the American deception effort came *after* the Normandy invasion. It worked so well that it was classified top-secret until the mid-1990s.

War deception is as old as war itself. As recently as the Bosnian conflict, Americans learned that the Serbs had fooled American attack pilots with "tanks" that were made of hundreds of milk cartons wrapped in aluminum foil, with the whole shaped into the form of a tank. These dummies made a perfect profile for American aircraft equipped with target-acquiring radar. Many such phony tanks, costing just a few dollars, were hit by missiles costing several hundred thousand dollars.

Americans also took the British "Chinese soldier" trick one step further: It dropped half-sized but very authentic-looking paratroopers behind German lines. Some of these cast-iron paratrooper dummies had sound devices that sounded like machine guns firing. The GI dummies were crafted to explode upon hitting the ground in order to make Germans think the real GIs had tried to burn their parachutes before hiding nearby. Some drops contained a mix of real *and* fake paratroops. Some fake paratroop drops were followed by real paratroops. This was done to convince the Germans that they had nothing to fear, that it was a phony airborne attack. These fake drops often were accompanied by the dropping of thousands of ribbons of aluminum foil—"Operation Window"—to dupe German radar operators, who read the foil chaff as hundreds of aircraft.

Operation Fortitude duped the Germans into thinking there were 87 combat-ready divisions poised to attack the Pas de Calais on the French coast. The point marks the shortest distance between Great Britain and France. Actually, the entire Allied invasion strength at that time was just 42 divisions. Also, the initial Normandy invasion force for the first few days totaled just 150,000 American and British troops.

To put this into perspective, the British barely escaped the annihilation of its 300,000 men at Dunkirk earlier in the war. Without the success of the deception, the Wehrmacht could easily have thrown the Allied landing force into the sea by concentrating its Panzer divisions on the Normandy beaches, but it was afraid the Normandy attack was a diversion to draw away Panzer divisions from the Calais area.

In fact, Hitler was still convinced of this long after a strong beachhead had been established on the Normandy coast. He even overrode his generals, who by then had decided no diversion would be in such overwhelming strength. Hitler's paranoia had firmly convinced him that the Normandy invasion was a cover for the real Calais invasion, which he thought would be launched just as soon as German Panzers moved to Normandy.

To hurl the Allies back into the sea with a sudden concentration of highly mobile Panzer divisions, heavy with armor, was, in fact, Rommel's plan. He had been placed in charge of defending the French coast. Contrary to popular belief even today, the Germans had about the same number of divisions as the initial Allied invaders ready for defense of occupied France, despite its war with Russia on the Eastern Front. The Wehrmacht had 15 divisions in the vicinity of Calais alone.

Hitler realized too late that he had been tricked. Had it not been for Fortitude's deception, the results certainly would have been disastrous for the Allies. Some say this would have been such a serious setback that the war could have lasted until 1950 with the loss of many more British and American lives.

This was the view held not only by General Eisenhower but by Churchill and Gen. Omar N. Bradley as well. What lent credence to the deception was that the Allies let it be known that Gen. George Patton would head the Calais invasion force. The Germans had a lot of respect for Patton, particularly after his successful, hard-charging campaign in Sicily. To them, this seemed very logical and probable.

Such deception in warfare had its early roots as far back as the Trojan Horse that was used to get troops into the fortified city of Troy. And Confederate Gen. Stonewall Jackson often marched his troops back and forth and set hundreds of "campfires" at night to deceive Union troops while he made a forced march for a rear or flanking attack. But nowhere was deception carried out with such success and elan as during World War II by America's Ghost Army. *And it would all happen after D-Day.*

In the beginning, it was just an idea—an idea presented by General Marshall to the president. And Roosevelt became cheerful and animated as Marshall detailed the plans for America's own Ghost Army and its deception specialists.

The President loved the idea. In fact, he publicly told the Congress: "Today's threat to our national security is not a matter of military weapons alone. We know of new methods of attack, the Trojan horse, the fifth column that betrays a nation unprepared for treachery. Spies, saboteurs and traitors are all the actors in the new strategy. With all that, we must and will deal vigorously." He might have added that the United States planned to fight fire with fire, and the Ghost Army was to be part of that strategy.

Marshall had not seen Roosevelt so enthusiastic since earlier in the year, on April 18, when a handful of B-25s led by Gen. James

Doolittle took off from a carrier and bombed mainland Japan. Although this bombing run was merely a token effort, and the brave Doolittle pilots had to ditch in China or die in the South China Sea, Marshall and Roosevelt knew its psychological repercussions would be vast. They were, indeed.

For one thing, postwar interviews with the Japanese said it dealt a terrific blow to their national morale because they had been assured by their military leaders that they were immune from attack on the mainland. It also gave a huge lift to the morale of Americans; the news had been mostly bad in 1942. Historians also learned that the Doolittle raid was the impetus for the Japanese decision to attack Midway Island, leading to the decisive Japanese loss in that turning-point sea battle.

Roosevelt saw the Ghost Army as another bit of daring in the spirit of the Doolittle raid. Churchill also was an enthusiastic backer of the idea, and hinted at its success several times in postwar years. He was almost like a little boy with a secret, as we can now see when we read of his hints about the deception. But he, too, was bound by secrecy and would not live to see the American Ghost Army's feats declassified.

Meanwhile, with the exception of Midway, there was gloomy news for Marshall and Roosevelt. German U-boats were still sinking enormous tonnage in American shipping. British-held Singapore had fallen; Churchill called Singapore "the worst defeat in British history," and that included the momentous defeat at the Battle of Hastings in 1066. The war in the Pacific was still closely fought, despite Midway, and America had not recaptured the Philippines or avenged the heartbreak of Bataan. Germany still seemed invincible in Europe.

There were many who feared the Germans might easily conquer any invasion force that landed in France or Norway, then hurl their full might against Russia and win the war. The Allies also feared that Germany's rapid scientific advances, particularly in rocketry and later in jet engines, would lead to a victory.

Indeed, at this point, Russia seemed to be losing the war against Germany. These fears may be hard to fathom given the decades of perspective, but they were not groundless at the time. America's ambassador to Britain, Joseph Kennedy, was one public figure who thought Hitler's legions were virtually unstoppable.

This gloomy, unpopular view caused a rift between Joe Kennedy and Roosevelt that was never to mend. Roosevelt was an optimist and disliked negative, lugubrious people. Kennedy considered himself a pragmatist and a realist and wondered why Roosevelt could be so cheerfully optimistic about Allied chances.

A measure of the desperation of the early 1940s can be seen in the diaries of Harold Nicolson. This popular British broadcaster for the BBC, a friend of the royal family, wrote that even the Queen regularly practiced shooting a revolver, determined to go down fighting with her people when the Germans invaded Great Britain. The invasion was considered imminent and inevitable.

And in the underground headquarters of Winston Churchill and the British military leaders, now a tourist attraction in London, there is a Tommy gun on display in a case. It is the one that Churchill planned to use in street fighting in London against German paratroops when the Germans crossed the channel and invaded England. Churchill said he had planned to light a good cigar, take a sip or two of his favorite brandy, and go out in the streets and take as many German troops with him as he could, perhaps fighting alongside the Queen and the royal family when the end came.

"We tend to forget nowadays how serious a situation it was at this early stage in the war," said Col. Bill Enderlein, who was a member of the special Ghost Army. "We needed to play every card we had, and the Ghost Army was one of those cards."

In *Crusade in Europe*, Eisenhower commented on the British use of deception in a general way after the war:

> In the early days of the war, particularly when Britain stood alone in 1940 and 1941, the British had little with which to oppose the German except deception. They resorted to every type of subterfuge, including the establishment of a dummy headquarters and the sending of fake messages in order to confuse the German as to the amount of military strength available and, more important than this, its disposition.

Ironically, Eisenhower wrote these words shortly after the war, *knowing full well* that the United States had done exactly the same thing throughout Europe.

So Roosevelt and Marshall, as with most Americans, learned in those early days to take what solace they could, when and how they could. Marshall, with Roosevelt's enthusiastic approval, along with a directive from the Secretary of War (only recently declassified)

ordered creation and rapid implementation of the Ghost Army—
technically, the Twenty-third Headquarters Special Troops. Even
atomic secrets were not as closely held during the last fifty-plus years.
It is one of the supreme ironies of the war that Rommel started it all,
leading to British emulation and one-upmanship, then to America's
own Ghost Army, which was far more elaborate and sophisticated than
Operation Fortitude.

The directive by the secretary of war stated, in part:

> Subject: Organization of 23rd Headquarters and Headquarters
> Special Detachment, Special Troops. The 23rd . . . is constituted,
> assigned to the Second Army, and will be activated at Camp Forrest,
> Tennessee at the earliest practicable date. This unit will [have] an
> authorized strength of 13 officers, one warrant officer and 54 enlisted
> men. This unit is allotted an initial over strength in grade seven of
> three enlisted men. This allotment of over strength is not an increase
> in the authorized strength of the unit, but is an advance issue of loss
> replacements that will be absorbed as training progresses. Personnel
> for this unit will be furnished without requisition. By order of the
> Secretary of War.

This was the official nucleus designed to start a 1,300-man elite
unit, although its actual strength was 1,100.

As stated, one of its main goals was to make the Germans believe
that the U.S. had a greater fighting force in Europe than it actually
had. This small Army did, indeed, dupe the Germans successfully
in 21 separate operations during World War II. Some say this figure
should be 55 if each small operation by some of the Ghost troops,
detached and detailed to other troops in small units, were to be
included. *And it was never found out by the Germans despite operating
within a few hundred yards of the front lines throughout the European invasion all the way up until the German surrender.*

After the meeting with Roosevelt, Marshall and his subordinates
quickly put a plan into action to start the Ghost Army as ordered by
the Secretary of War Stimson. First, they had to find a man to head
it, a good organization man, and a handful of officers with enough
elan and imagination to make it work.

Lt. Col. Harry L. Reeder was picked to head the unit. He was a
no-nonsense World War I veteran and career soldier. He was more
like a small town cop or school principal than a soldier. But the thinking was that he was the kind of man who would be needed to counter-

Col. Harry Reeder, who headed the Ghost Army, shown eating GI rations somewhere in France. Photo courtesy William Enderlein.

balance his far-out officer corps because the officers chosen for the Twenty-third would have to be very unorthodox and willing to take chances.

For one thing, deceptive techniques went against the grain of most career soldiers—and Reeder was no exception. There was something less than straightforward about it. It was not slugging it out with the enemy toe-to-toe, letting the best man win. In some ways, it went against the basic American character. He constantly made no secret of the fact that he would far rather have been in charge of a front-line regiment than a bunch of actors, artists, fashion designers, radio operators, and writers. And yet, even he was to be very surprised at the success of the Twenty-third.

All of this came at a time when America was innocent, even naive. Only two years before, actor Clark Gable, playing Rhett Butler in the film *Gone With The Wind,* had said, "Frankly, my dear, I don't give a damn." America was shocked, and an intense national debate began about this mild public profanity. America was then a highly moral nation, with religion far more entertwined with daily life, schools, and even government than now. This had been part of the reason for its intense pacifism.

But Japan had awakened what Japanese Adm. Isoroku Yamamoto called "a sleeping giant," perhaps a more apt analogy than Churchill's "steam boiler." But before the giant could rouse its full war potential, it had to blink its eyes and rev up its metabolism. And it had to try chancy projects such as the Doolittle raid—and the Ghost Army. So that is how the American Ghost Army came to be.

Reeder and his staff had one rare privilege in putting the secret army unit together: They were allowed to bypass usual Army red tape—given special "without requisition orders"—to get the equipment, personnel, and supplies they needed. Marshall and his subordinates knew that without this special privilege, the war would be over by the time Reeder and his staff could wade through all the red tape and get off the mark. Regular army officers would have killed for such a privilege.

It was almost the same with personnel. If Reeder and staff learned of an electronics whiz working in Oregon or Florida, they got him. If they found some clever writers and artists in New England—where indeed they found most of them—then they got them.

Much of the Pentagon brass, as well as the Pentagon bureaucracy, stepped aside, said one of Reeder's top officers, Col. Clifford Simenson, because the new Army unit had "holy water sprinkled on it." Its approval had come from the highest echelons.

If the Ghost Army needed 5,000 feet of copper wire or 100 of the largest electronic speakers available, then they got them. If they needed a few hundred real tanks to spread among the rubber models, they got them. If they wanted to let contracts without time-consuming bids, then they were allowed to do so.

They also got the latest in radio and recording equipment, better than in any commercial studio. They got wire recording equipment, then a brand new, state-of-the-art technology. Not only that, but it was installed in large mobile studios.

But the personnel they got was the real key. Although it was nominally attached to the mammoth Twelfth Army, headed by Gen. Omar Bradley, the top brass of the Twelfth also stood aside and let the Ghost Army do its thing. In fact, the great bulk of the officers and men never knew the Ghost Army even existed. That was the way the top brass wanted it. Without utmost secrecy, the Army would not only be useless, but would certainly suffer great loss of life.

But there is still one major mystery about the Ghost Army. None of the survivors is sure who chose the officer corps for the Ghost Army. The men, who proved to be superb choices, were plucked from units all over the United States and abroad. Some feel it may have been one of Marshall's top aides. Others think it might even have been Marshall himself. But to this day, that mystery remains, even among those men who were at the very top of the chain of command in the Ghost Army. But one thing is certain: it was a championship team.

Chapter Two

A Mosaic of Experts

The Army searched its records and found experts in radio and electronics, meteorology, writing, acting, and camouflage. Many candidates came from the Army Special Training Program, a program designed to find bright soldiers and fit them to special training in a variety of fields, including electronics, camouflage techniques, special ordnance, and other areas.

Meteorologists were necessary because sound behaves differently in various kinds of weather conditions—and a major part of the deception would be broadcasting sounds of armored vehicles on the move in all kinds of weather conditions. Some soldiers had only recently been drafted and were being under utilized as average soldiers when their talents were discovered.

The Army also put out the word that it needed actors, artists, and designers, meteorologists, set designers, photographers—artistic people who could help create the phony army but make the illusion realistic. That is how it wound up with Bill Blass, among many others of artistic bent. One of its favorite raiding grounds was the Pratt Institute in Brooklyn, a well-regarded art school. Camouflage would be carried to extremes of high art. Its realism would be crucial—life-and-death crucial. And yet sometimes it was designed to be deliberately sloppy so the Germans could spot it and make wrong assumptions.

Col. Clifford Simenson—one of the prime molders of the Ghost Army—described the early days of the Ghost Army this way:

> In early January 1944, Gen. Riley Ennis informed me that I was being ordered to Twenty-third Headquarters Special Troops and that

he could not discuss it because of security. My hopes had been for assignment as an infantry battalion commander or a division G-3. Did my background and contacts with our mobilized units make me eligible to be operations officer of a tactical deception organization?

For training and preparation for deception operations, there were no manuals, no instructions, no guidance and no orders from higher headquarters except to prepare for overseas movement. The men were perplexed and wondered what they were supposed to do.

The training problem was highlighted in the official records of the Twenty-third Headquarters, newly declassified, this way:

> Since no one knew how a deception unit was supposed to oper-ate, the training program was not easy to write. There was very little literature on the subject. . . . Colonel Simenson . . . recently from AGF-G3, probably contributed more than anyone else to the forma-tion of the simulated appearance under various tactical conditions of units ranging from divisions to corps.

The components of the Ghost Army were formed this way:

• The 603rd Engineer Camouflage Battalion was placed under Lt. Col. Otis R. Fitz, whose men had been training and experimenting with deceptive camouflage in Louisiana for two years. Army records state, "It was composed mainly of artists from New York and Philadelphia with an average IQ of 119." (Many of the men were graduates of Pratt Institute.) It had 28 officers, 2 warrant officers, and 349 enlisted men.

• 244th Signal Operations Company, headed by Capt. Irwin C. Vander Heide. This year-old unit had just come off desert maneu-vers. It was radically modified in Camp Forrest, Mississippi, for use as a counter-radio intelligence company. Five new officers and 100 radio operators were added and an almost equal number of wire, teletype, and message center personnel were released. It then became Signal Company, Special. After the war, Vander Heide said he was most proud of the fact that postwar interviews and records showed the Ghost Army was never found out by the enemy, which he said was a remarkable testament to their stealth and ability to keep a secret. It had 11 officers and 285 enlisted men.

• Company A, 293rd Engineer Combat Battalion, headed by Capt. George A Rebh, a native of Detroit, Michigan, and a 1943 graduate of West Point. This company was chosen from a battalion that had

Lt. Dick Syracuse's Fourth Platoon assembled for review during training at Pine Camp in 1944. Photo courtesy Dick Syracuse.

been activated a year before and had gone through Tennessee and desert maneuvers. It was a hardy, disciplined group of combat engineers which the Twenty-third needed for security and rough jobs. It was probably Reeder's favorite part of the Ghost Army because it was not as deeply engaged in deception as other units. Because of this, Rebh is one of the few officers who can say that Reeder showed a genuine liking for him and his men. It became the 406th Engineer Combat Company, Special. It had 5 officers and 163 enlisted men.

Among the combat and perimeter safety personnel was colorful and feisty Lt. Dick Syracuse, who was a legend in the Ghost Army (as the reader will find out later in this narrative) and still leads an active life as an attorney in New Rochelle, New York.

• The 3132nd Signal Service Company was headed by Maj. Charles R. Williams of Warsaw, Indiana. It was the only unit within the Twenty-third that was formed solely for the purpose of deception, and not adapted for it later. It was activated separately at the Army Experimental Station at Pine Camp, New York, in March 1944. It did not join the rest of the Twenty-third until August 1944 after

D-Day in France. It had 8 officers and 137 enlisted men. Williams, who died in 1987, was one of the most popular officers. He was a graduate of St. John's Military Academy and Washington & Lee University.

After the war he became publisher of the Warsaw *Times-Union*, a daily newspaper in north central Indiana. He came by his military prowess naturally: his grandfather was Gen. (brevet) Reuben Williams, who commanded the Indiana Twelfth Infantry Regiment during the Civil War.

The Army also allowed the men forming the Ghost Army extraordinary powers to bring certain talented individuals into the service in order to use their special skills. Actors were recruited, and some of these actors later drove around in jeeps pretending to be generals to lend credence to phony battle divisions. Some of the phony generals were young men in their twenties skillfully made up and driven in cars with the appropriate number of stars in territory near the front lines.

Simenson still leads an active life in Boulder, Colorado, at the age of 90. A West Pointer, Simenson was quarterback of his Valley City, North Dakota, high school. He had been accepted to West Point from North Dakota, but was able to get in a year earlier, in 1930, through a political appointment by an Indiana congressman.

Simenson planned several field problems based upon the simulated appearance, under various tactical conditions, of units ranging from division to corps. These problems were not particularly satisfying because it was hard to make the mental transition from real soldier to dummy troops, or "Nazi bait," as some of the troops later called themselves. The results looked like so much window dressing with no place to go. Officers who had once commanded 32-ton tanks felt frustrated and helpless with a battalion of rubber M-4s weighing just 93 pounds fully inflated.

The adjustment from man-of-action to man-of-wile was most difficult at first. Few realized in those early days that one could spend just as much energy pretending to fight as actually fighting.

But formation of the Twenty-third also was facilitated by the fact that no one knew much about how it was to approach its mission, outside the limited experience in North Africa. For example, here is one officer's take on how it first got through to General Marshall:

Lt. Col. Merrick H. Truly, executive officer, Maj. Charles H. Yocum, signal officer, and David H. Bridges flew to Washington to present the modified plan after urging by General Devers and the British. American Maj. Ralph Ingersoll also was an ardent promoter of the idea. The plan worked its way up the chain of command. After Marshall's okay and the approval of Secretary of War Stimson, it was eased through the War Department with practically no opposition because no one knew any more about deception there than in Camp Forrest, Tennessee.

The units at first trained at various military bases around the nation in their specialties. Most of them had the minimum in basic training and even that was notable because of how they used their superior intelligence to avoid much of the hardships. For example, many of them stuffed their packs with toilet paper instead of the heavy equipment so that the long hikes would be more bearable. They drove their drill sergeants mad with such tricks.

Special engineers and the experts in using camouflage and inflatable tanks and trucks trained at Fort Meade, Maryland. Blass found himself painting camouflage scenes on burlap cloth at Fort Meade. The coarse burlap was a far cry from the fine silks and brocades he would use in his later career as a clothing designer.

"I remember one night when Bill was on the top bunk," recalled Tompkins. "He was always doodling or sketching something. He handed down to me, on the bottom bunk, a sketch he had made, and said, 'What do you think of this?' It was the mirror image of the two B's, back to back. 'That's going to be my trademark,' Blass told him, 'for my fashion design company.'"

Not long before, Tompkins, his beautiful young wife, Bunny, who had turned down a job as a Powers model to be with Bob, and Blass had taken a trip while Blass and Tompkins were stationed in Tennessee. They had driven to a hotel in a car Bunny owned. It was a beige 1940 Chevrolet. You could not drive far in those days because gas was rationed. And it was not beyond possibility that an OPA (Office of Price Administration) official would stop you and ask if the trip were really necessary.

At night, sitting around at the hotel, they all chain-smoked cigarettes and talked about what they would do after the war was over.

Here is the way Bunny described it:

> That Saturday evening I sat on the stairs at the McMinnville Hotel with some of the Fourth Platoon. Everyone was telling what they wanted to do after the war. I remember Bill saying he wanted to be one of the leading fashion designers in the world. By golly, he did it.

The three of them became such good friends that Blass wrote Bunny a letter each month when they were shipped overseas to reassure her that Bob was okay, and to tell her about life during the war. Bunny said those letters meant a lot to her and were a good illustration of how fine and decent a man Blass was and is.

Tompkins and Blass were in the camouflage section, but others in the Ghost Army had other specialties. Some radio experts trained at Camp Forrest, Mississippi. And at Fort Meade, men learned the art of camouflage was far more intricate than they thought because of the life-and-death necessity of realism, the kinds of foliage that the terrain might feature, and the kinds of colors that would best blend in with the environment. They spent hours painting green and brown branches and leaves onto large canvas, burlap, old vehicles, walls, and other practice objects.

They also learned, recalled Ed Biow, now living in Lake Oswego, Oregon, to make assault boats from the canvas covers of a 2½-ton truck. Luckily, the rest of the war effort went better than this one. Biow said the men were told to stuff tree branches and underbrush into the canvas truck cover, then test the impromptu boats—similar to the hide bull boats used by early pioneers—in the Severn River, near Fort Meade. He said the crude boats sank immediately, leaving men wearing heavy boots and carrying full ammo and equipment to try to swim despite the cumbersome weight.

"I had to throw away my rifle and swim for my life," Biow says. "My rifle was a 1903 Springfield—a very good rifle—and as far as I know it's still in the Severn River."

The other men did the same, and Biow insisted it was a miracle that no one drowned. Other Ghost Army trainees were spread out all over the nation for special training. Then, in 1943, most—with the exception of Capt. Rebh's men, who went directly to England—were brought to Pine Camp Experimental Station in Upstate New York, near the Canadian border. It is now called Fort Drum, the home base of the famed Tenth Mountain Division.

Pine Camp was then one of the nation's largest military reservations. It is on the Great Lakes Plain in northern New York about 20 miles from the eastern end of Lake Ontario. Midway between Watertown and Carthage, Pine Camp is at the gateway to the Adirondack State Park on the Black River. Each man who arrived at Pine Camp soon learned that he was a cog in a big wheel of deception. The big picture began to coalesce.

After training there, the next stop would be Great Britain, although the men were not told this for reasons of secrecy. Neither were they allowed even routine leaves for the same reason. From Britain, the Ghost Army would be among the very first units hitting the beaches on D-Day. But getting it ready in such a short time would be daunting—and scary. The men were told they would be going to a tropical destination and were even issued tropical clothing and equipment. This was for the benefit of any domestic spies residing around Pine Camp. The Army also knew some men would probably talk to civilians in the area or get word to loved ones, despite promises of dire consequences for any breech of security.

Colonel Simenson and Col. Hilton Howell Railey, the former magazine writer and newspaperman who had written the book *Touch'd With Madness,* drew up "problems" and asked the men to "solve" them at Pine Camp. The problems included scenarios in which a division of combat troops was called upon to quietly slip out of the front lines and make a flanking attack.

The men were to call each of their missions during the war "problems" based on their training nomenclature. The Ghost Army had to

Ghost Army troops with some of their real equipment—half-tracks—at Pine Camp shortly before shipping out to Great Britain in 1944. They are lined up for review. U.S. Army photo.

replace the "real" troops. The thorny problem was convincing the enemy that they were still facing a combat division and not a bunch of actors, designers, artists, "camoufleurs," and radio operators. That is where the finely honed deceptive techniques came in.

The idea was to create a camp that included big guns where the real big guns had been. Only this time the guns were inflatable. Tanks, half-track vehicles, artillery, and big 2½-ton trucks had to be replaced with rubber inflatables, filled with air from portable gasoline-powered compressors. Because the Germans feared the British Spitfire aircraft more than any other, even a few inflatable Spitfires were later made, along with rubber recon planes. These rubber aircraft were exceptionally realistic in appearance and were modeled after the Piper Cubs actually used.

The aircraft were so real that at least one American P-47 pilot would try to land at a fake airfield constructed by the Ghost Army after D-Day. Huge speakers had to make the sounds of a vast army. Up to 1,000 inflatable artillery guns, tanks, and even airplanes had to be placed where they would appear real, under or partly hidden by camouflage netting or in woodsy settings.

The Ghost Army personnel found that the biggest speakers available were those four-feet-by-four-feet kinds used on battleships and carriers, so they ordered scores of them for training and combat use. The speakers were then modified for the special use of the Ghost troops. Some were used singly, and others were put in banks, honeycomb fashion. They were so big and heavy that they had to be cranked up on special jacks, which in turn were bolted to the beds of trucks and half-tracks.

And things could get ridiculous in those early days at Pine Camp (Fort Drum). The long barrels on the rubber tanks and rubber artillery pieces would sometimes droop. Many techniques were used to stiffen them before they went into real combat areas, but the sight of a tank with a drooping gun was then a bit demoralizing to the troops.

They wondered what would happen when and if the Germans or the Japanese were to see this, or see the wind blowing the tanks willy nilly around the fields. The air was pumped into the dummy tanks through the big gun on the turret, causing plenty of crude phallic jokes. But mostly many of the troops wondered aloud if they would really be able to fool crack German or Japanese troops with such malfunctioning dummy equipment.

But things would get better as the men learned their strange new craft. They also figured out how to stiffen the gun barrels of the tanks with inserts.

Radio operators had to take over radio duties from real combat units and carry on with radio traffic so realistic that Germans listening in could not tell that it was all make believe. Tanks ordered into position by the radiomen didn't exist, but it had to sound perfect. Radiomen even had to sound frustrated and irritated on occasion as if facing a logistical impasse, just as real radio operators in combat areas would sound. The operators used the word "POL" constantly, which stood for petroleum, oil, and lubricants.

Big guns ordered by radio to be moved here and there were not really there, but they had to sound as if they were, even occasionally becoming stuck and requiring a tank to help pull them out of the mud. The radio operators had to use the correct jargon of the unit they were replacing, and every division's radiomen had their own idiosyncracies and peculiarities. Some had deep-South accents; others had the clipped and nasal accent of a Maine fisherman. Some were irritable and some were funny. All of this had to be duplicated when the time came.

Maj. Charles Williams, an unidentified two-star general, and Col. Howell Railey walk across the parade ground at Pine Camp in 1943 after reviewing Ghost Army troops.

Maj. Charles Williams, who led the 3132nd Sonics section of the Ghost Army. He was one of its most popular of officers. Photo courtesy Michael Williams.

And at night, the men of the Ghost Army had to fire small canisters—similar to pipe bombs but set off remotely by electricity—that flashed brightly to appear and sound like real artillery. It had to be so real that it would draw "counter-battery fire" from the Germans, usually just a few hundred yards away. Because of this, the men learned to avoid being anywhere near the exploding canisters when they finally got in combat situations.

The big question pondered over and over by Reeder, Simenson, Railey, Williams, Truly, and their staff officers—not to mention the ordinary GI—was would it work against the best military force in the world? There were some cynics among the enlisted men, as there always are, who said the whole thing was ludicrous and would just serve to get them all killed a bit faster than regular combat troops. There was a lot of tension because all of this was new and untried by Americans. It also went against the American character of a straightforward, fair fight in the open, no holds barred.

Some—including Colonel Reeder himself—often said there was just something "sneaky and weird" about the whole thing. But the British success was always the strongest justification, along with the American lives the project might save.

The Ghost Army, as well as the entire Allied effort, would find an ally in the German underestimation of and contempt for the West. Indeed, Albert T. Speer, Hitler's architect, adviser, and a top member of his inner circle, wrote in his diary that this attitude was epitomized by Adolf Hitler himself:

> He [Hitler] stuck unswervingly to his opinion that the West was too feeble, too worn out, and too decadent to begin the war seriously. Probably it was also embarrassing for him to admit to his entourage and above all to himself that he had made so crucial a mistake. I still remember his consternation when the news came that Churchill was going to enter the British War Cabinet as First Lord of the Admiralty. . . . His illusions and wish-dreams were a direct outgrowth of his unrealistic mode of working and thinking. Hitler actually knew nothing about his enemies and even refused to use the information that was available to him.

Meanwhile, Bill Blass and the other artists and designers learned to raise camouflage to a high art, making the crucial electronic equipment all but invisible in foliage. He helped make all of this realistic looking. If there were gun emplacements, then he and the others made sure there were a few empty but real artillery shells strewn about. Camouflage was of several varieties, including netting or actual foliage woven together in the netting. Yet some of it was later done poorly so the Germans could see it and assume it concealed deadly weapons of war.

The men were supplied with plenty of army-issue paint for this big palette. The twelve colors supplied in thousands of cans were: Number one light green; Number two dark green; Number three sand; Number four field drab; Number five earth brown; Number six earth yellow; Number seven loam; Number eight earth red; Number nine OD (Olive Drab); Number ten black; Number eleven forest green, and Number twelve desert sand.

Not listed in the army camouflage manual of 1942, but available, was white, used during the snowy months during the Battle of the Bulge. In years to come, there would be little in the fashion designs of Bill Blass in those colors, and perhaps now we know why.

The skillful camouflage had to make the things it concealed, like the speaker-carrying half-tracks, virtually invisible. After all, one direct hit would blow up everything because of the plastique explosive under the seats. The men had to drive half-track vehicles around and around to make the kind of tracks that the Germans would spot from the air and assume were made by tanks. This was particularly effective in the snow, which caused the tracks to stand out in bas-relief. Fortunately, the tracks made in the snow or mud by half-track vehicles were indistinguishable from the tracks of tanks.

Troop trucks had to be driven in and out of villages, over and again for hours, to make it seem an entire 17,000-man division had arrived. The men used to joke that this was the only rotation they ever got—and it was.

The penalty for being found out was death, not just for the Ghost Army troops but for those for whom they were acting. If the German divisions had known that they were opposed by just a few hundred men—many of them actors and stage designers, at that—a quick and brutal slaughter would have resulted.

Most of the men in the Ghost Army had only rudimentary combat training. It was hoped that their combat would be random and sparse. As it was, they were to encounter far more combat than anticipated, and many were wounded. Also, the set designs in this big play had to be perfect and imposing. The night sounds and radio traffic, always monitored by the Germans, also had to be right.

"We had to feel our way along," Simenson said. "Since we had never done this before, we had to hope we were doing it right. We wouldn't know for sure, of course, until after the Normandy invasion. And that could be too late."

At that time, of course, neither Simenson nor anyone else in the Twenty-third knew exactly where the invasion of the European mainland would take place. And the average trooper in the Ghost Army wasn't sure where he would end up.

Some of the officers would go into what was assumed to be "enemy" territory during the New York training period. They would listen to the big speakers from a vantage point in the pine and spruce woods. They would watch the canisters explode at night and, most of all, wonder if all of this would be realistic enough to fool the toughest fighting troops the world had yet seen, the fighting men of the Third Reich.

"We had nothing to measure ourselves against—this was all new to the American Army," Simenson explained. "Yes, we were apprehensive. But we were also gung ho."

The technical guys worked on stiffening the barrels and a using better system of weights with sand bags and tie-downs to keep the rubber dummies absolutely still in the wind. And one false note on radio traffic could blow the cover irretrievably. It was enough to keep Simenson and his fellow officers awake nights with worry. They knew it wouldn't be long before they would be in a real combat area.

Colonel Railey had another training device. Most new recruits to the Ghost Army—some of them men he went after and recruited himself—were kept well away from the sound trucks and the other equipment when they first arrived at Pine Camp. Then the devices would be tested on them at night. They would be questioned intensely later to determine the realism of the effort, and what they thought they had heard.

One of those new recruits was Robert E. Wendig, now of Huntingdon Valley, Pennsylvania. He was an electronics expert, but when he was sent to the Ghost Army, he had no idea what he would be doing there or what his mission would be. He described it this way:

> We arrived by train well after dark at Pine Camp, where we received a cold welcome, with the temperature and blowing snow creating a night to remember. Many of the new arrivals came from the ASTP— Army Specialized Training Program. These units were from the various colleges throughout the country. There used to be a saying, "Take down the service flag in your window, mother, your son is in ASTP". This was because many thought these specialized troops would never make it to Europe or the Pacific.
>
> Being quartered beyond fencing in the Army Experimental Station area, we questioned our fate. Were we to be guinea pigs for some kind of experiment? Guinea pigs for what? Medical experiments or new weapons? For about three weeks, we were kept in limbo, subject only

to physical training and several personal interviews, which we later understood was time for the government to investigate our backgrounds for possible security risks.

Finally, we were briefed one day by Colonel Railey, who advised us to take it easy inasmuch as we would be up most of the night.

By this time, we were wearing heavy winter clothing. After evening chow, we climbed aboard six-by-sixes and were taken out into the boonies of Pine Camp and dropped off in units of three, being spaced apart perhaps one-fourth mile with instructions to observe and note any happenings. After almost an hour, we heard tanks advancing toward us and then finally the sound receded. Then we heard a vocalist singing "I Dream of Jeannie with the Light Brown Hair" coming across the fields. Finally, the trucks returned and picked us up for a debriefing by Colonel Railey at the AES Airport.

There, to our surprise, was a half-track with a gigantic loud speaker mounted on its chassis. This was the source of the tank sounds and "Jeannie With the Light Brown Hair" musical refrain. A return to the mess hall found Pappy Beaver, a mess sergeant from Brooklyn, with his crew, passing out hot cocoa and doughnuts.

During the ensuing weeks we were trained in the night hours to operate the wire recording equipment and maneuver the half-tracks into various positions. Under proper, ideal weather conditions, these unique weapons were effective up to five miles. The three-man half-track was loaded to the gills with a large gas generator, two wire recording machines, and a huge Navy loudspeaker which was cranked up and down out of sight with a winch to avoid visual detection during the day. With a .50-caliber machine gun on the turret, a carbine apiece, a .30-caliber machine gun, known as a grease gun, and a bazooka, we had more firepower than our crew could handle. We also had several grenades on each half-track.

Some of the men assigned to the Ghost Army were not overjoyed; they wanted to be in a combat unit. Others were happy *not* to be in a front-line outfit. It was at a time when Americans were collectively angry. "You have to remember," said Colonel Enderlein, who served in the sonics section of the Twenty-third, "Americans were now angry and ready to fight. Pacifism had been replaced with an angry resolve."

Americans echoed Churchill's outraged sentiment delivered in an inspiring speech to the American Congress shortly after the attack on Pearl Harbor: "What kind of people do they think we are?" he asked to rousing applause. Churchill also said the British—and this could apply equally to Americans—had not journeyed over so many thousands of years and advanced so far and achieved so much "because we are made of sugar candy."

Americans wanted to fight the Japanese, whom they always referred to derisively as "Japs," or "Nips," and the Germans, usually called either "Krauts" or "Nazis." These words, now considered politically incorrect if not offensive, also were commonly used in newspaper headlines throughout the war. The enemy was demonized in the daily press, although the truth was bad enough—as Americans learned after the Bataan Death March and later the German massacre of American POWs at Malmedy. The Japanese were invariably depicted as goons with big teeth and evil slit-eyes. It was all part of the tenor of the war years, the drumbeat of domestic propaganda of a nation at war.

Therefore men assigned to the Ghost Army could understand, in an abstract sense, the value of the deception being planned, but some feared it would not be as satisfying as real combat. By the time their tour of duty was up, however, most of the men had come to appreciate the Twenty-third and its genuine value.

They also had seen more than enough combat to satisfy themselves. They liberated one French town all by themselves to a tumultuous welcome—quite by accident—and even captured many German troops, including some crack paratroopers. And all of this was just a few months following the bucolic tranquility of Pine Camp. Maj. Charles Williams' only crisis during this time came when his small son was cut by a nail and had to get a tetanus shot.

And the men griped about being trained in a northern army camp for duty in a tropical climate. They packed their light khakis and bug repellent and wondered if the Japanese would be fooled by their bag of tricks.

By far the most popular and interesting of the officers who helped form and shape the Ghost Army at Pine Camp, and later in Great Britain and all through the war, was Colonel Railey. Surviving members of the Twenty-third Special Headquarters Special Troops still speak reverently of him.

Colonel Railey

Colonel Simenson and most who knew Col. Hilton Howell Railey described him as a charismatic, very interesting man with an even more interesting background. He was a man with friends in very high places, including President Roosevelt. He led with authority, yet he had a great sense of humor. Some even wondered if he had a hand in picking the top men in the Ghost Army.

"I think he was hand-picked for the job," said Simenson, "by somebody high up. I always thought he had connections."

Many said the Ghost Army bore the imprimatur of Railey perhaps more than any other person, because it was he who implemented the ideas and plans of Simenson and dealt directly with the men. He got to know them and they got to know him, and they liked him, vying with one another for his attention and his favor. He also had an infectious enthusiasm for the job, and was confident he and his men could deceive and dupe the enemy.

Railey's background was as fascinating as he was, and it was interesting to see how and why he was the ideal man for the Ghost Army.

He was a native of New Orleans, the son of an aristocratic father and lovely mother, both of whom were cultured, well read, and moved easily in the top level of Southern society. His father had memorized long passages of Shakespeare and often recited them around the family home. He was equally interested in Dickens, Thackeray, Stevenson, and Kipling, and often read to young Hilton. The family also insisted that Hilton learn to play the piano, write well, and become a cultured young Southern gentleman. Railey's paternal grandfather had been a colonel in the cavalry of the Army of Tennessee.

Railey, who called his father "the Duke," once wrote:

> On Sunday afternoons we'd stroll down balconied Rue Royale in the French Quarter and through the Vieux Carre, where the Duke delivered his best monologues; or along the Stuyvesant Docks where, pretending to pay attention to his appalling statistics on the position of New Orleans as the second port of the United States, I would watch the gulls and with an ache that took my breath see myself outward bound on ships from far-off lands, anchored in the muddy waters of the Mississippi. It was an ominous urge. For, with uncertain legs and a touch of panic, even at fourteen, I felt the heave of uncharted seas.

Railey's father had decided his son would go to Tulane University in New Orleans, then Harvard law school. But young Railey decided he had rather sign on with the *SS Stenas,* owned by the United Fruit Company, when the regular crew went on strike. His father reluctantly granted permission, thinking that his son would return as scheduled in three weeks.

But Railey got a job in Panama City, Panama, instead. He lied about his age, being a big teenager with a mature look, and got a job working for the Panama Canal Company. His father had to write to the company and explain that his son was underage in order to get him back to New Orleans. His first adventure was soon over, and his father paid for his return passage.

Young Railey's next enterprise was as an actor in New York City. His father staked him with $100 per month, and Railey had modest success. But modest success was not enough, so he returned to New Orleans and studied journalism and English at Tulane. A short time later he landed a job with the *New Orleans American,* a short-lived political newspaper founded to contest the *Times-Picayune*'s dominance in the city. He covered politics and, because of his obviously partisan coverage, was beaten up one night by several hired thugs as he walked home.

Shortly afterward, he began carrying a pistol to prevent a recurrence of the beating. Politicians he had angered found out he was carrying a concealed weapon and succeeded in getting a warrant for his arrest. He fled to Philadelphia—this time with his father's anxious blessing—where he got a job as a reporter on the *Evening Ledger.* He enjoyed reporting and soon made a name for himself.

Then came World War I. He enlisted, again misrepresenting himself as being a few years older. He was sent to Little Rock, Arkansas, where he was placed in charge of a program to rid the troops of veneral disease and increase personal hygiene. Along with his new responsibilities, he was promoted to 1st lieutenant. In Arkansas he met a beautiful young woman named Julie Houston, whose family owned a large plantation north of the city.

After an intense and brief courtship, they were married. But he lost his commission when it was later discovered that he was not 27 as he had said but rather 22. Twenty-five was the minimum age for officers heading a group such as the Sanitary Corps, he later wrote. He later regained the commission as an infantry officer. He missed overseas service because the war ended before he could be shipped over. However, he rose to the rank of captain before he was mustered out of service.

By 1920, he had landed a job as a war correspondent to cover fighting in Poland for the New York *Evening Mail.* He also began writing for magazines, including *The Saturday Evening Post,* and later lectured on his experiences in Poland. At one point during fighting between the Bolsheviks and the nationalistic Poles, he joined the Polish army in order to get to the front lines.

After the hostilities ended in Poland, he returned to the U.S. and founded an enterprise devoted to fund-raising for various causes. Among them were Adm. Richard Byrd's polar expeditions. It was also during this time that he was asked to find a daring young woman pilot for a group of financial backers who had the money and the aircraft ready to make her—whoever she might be—a star. The plan was to use her fame in a commercial way.

Railey made inquiries and learned that Amelia Earhart was a young woman who had flown more than 500 hours and had even owned a few airplanes.

At their first face-to-face meeting, he noted:

> With intense interest, I observed and appraised her as she talked. Her resemblance to Colonel [Charles] Lindbergh was so extraordinary that I couldn't resist the impulse to ask her to remove her hat. She complied, brushing back her naturally tousled, wind-swept hair, and her laugh was infectious. "Lady Lindy." Somehow I felt that she would like being so dubbed even less than would her celebrated duplicate—but not the newspapers! Most of all I was impressed by the poise of the boyish figure at my desk. There was warmth and dignity in her manner, her speech.

It was the beginning of a successful collaboration. One officer, Lt. Richard Syracuse, has speculated that Earhart may have been on a spying mission for the U.S. under Railey's direction when she later disappeared in the Pacific. "Knowing Railey as I did," said Syracuse, "I wouldn't doubt this. But we'll never know."

Later, Railey raised hundreds of thousands of dollars for Admiral Byrd's polar expeditions, and soon became known as the man to talk to for dramatic and adventurous expeditions. He set up an office in New York and soon became familiar with many of the great figures of the era, including a young man with political ambitions named Franklin Delano Roosevelt. One of Railey's fund-raising projects was an effort to explore the sunken wreck of the *Lusitania.*

Later he was chosen to head the League of Nations Association, and during this time he traveled frequently to Europe on association business. He was very often the subject of news articles himself. The

British, it was made plain, thought that he might have a dual function as a spy for the United States. Although this was never proved, he was ideally positioned for espionage. If he were a spy, it would certainly explain why the higher-ups decided about a decade later that he would be the ideal man to help form and train the Ghost Army.

It was during the late 1930s, when Railey's reputation as an internationalist and a man with wide connections was at its apex, that he received a strange offer. As he later described it:

> The day before I was to sail for New York an old friend (British, and not without influence in the city) advanced a proposal so startling that at first I couldn't believe he was serious. Over the telephone he inquired, "How would you like to look after Germany's public relations in the United States and the United Kingdom?" I laughed. "And this, I suppose, is Herr Hitler?"
>
> "I'm not joking," he said. "It's quite a serious matter. Without mentioning your name, I have developed a very favorable atmosphere on your professional qualifications. An agent of the Nazis here [London], a certain Dr. Thost, will receive you in his flat in Chelsea this evening, if you care to go into it. Let me tell you a bit about him. He's the correspondent in London of the Volkishce Beobachter, the official Nazi journal. He organizes lectures and directs other Nazi propaganda in this country. He's apparently prepared to pay English lecturers well, provided they say the right thing, and to send them to Germany to get the right viewpoint. Of course, he's terribly anti-Semitic—a Jew baiter. Perhaps you can do something with him. If you can get together, I understand he would like to have you fly to Berlin . . ."
>
> "And talk to Hitler?"
>
> "It's quite possible. It's a rather biggish scheme."
>
> "Good God!"

Railey said the job paid a very large amount of money, and that at that moment he was unemployed, and that the money, during the height of the Depression, was enticing. But he said that the job involved perpetuating anti-Semitic viewpoints then current in 1930s Germany, so he turned it down. He later commented: "In London, I found my pot of gold—filled with Nazi Reichsmarks—and left it where it lay."

It was shortly after this that he was elected national director of the League of Nations Association by the trustees, some of the most distinguished people in America. This also was the time during which he met and befriended everyone from FDR to various high-ranking British government officials. He became especially close to Brendan Bracken, one of Winston Churchill's top advisors, even before the outbreak of the war. Although no one knows for sure how Railey later became such a key part of the Ghost Army, it is known that the British successes with deception was one of Churchill's pet projects.

Railey's being a good friend of Bracken might have led indirectly through British-American joint efforts after El Alamein to the choice of Railey, although no one is sure, including Simenson. It seems that Railey was simply thrust into the job from on high.

To get an idea of Railey's status at the time World War II erupted, he was the subject of several articles about the League of Nations and its role in the Roosevelt Administration. Some even speculated that Railey was the administration's probable appointee to the post of High Commissioner to the League of Nations.

After leaving the League Association, Railey became an international correspondent for *Fortune* magazine. His first assignment was to investigate the big arms manufacturers and their role in the political unrest in Europe during the 1930s. It was during this assignment that Railey worked closely with Brendan Bracken and traveled throughout Europe. Many governments supposed that he was merely a spy for the United States using the cover of the magazine to try to assess the military strength of Germany, France, and even Great Britain.

Railey was given large sums of money by *Fortune* to travel and set up shop in Europe. He had to meet the right people socially—people who were close to the Krupps and other large arms makers. He also had to be sure that he was not arrested on charges of espionage, one of his constant fears during this time.

Not only was this James Bond kind of duty especially dangerous in Germany and France, but even in England he had his nervous moments. For example, here is Railey's description of one situation in London, when he was asked by Dame Adelaide Livingstone to meet with him to discuss something important:

> Suddenly and seriously, Dame Adelaide explained why she had sent for me. "Yesterday," she began, "a friend I hadn't heard from for many months telephoned and asked me to give him a cup of tea. While we are actually old friends, it isn't often that we meet. For that reason I

was curious to learn what was on his mind—and for another, it happens he's the head of a Government unit which is generally supposed to have gone out of existence immediately after the World War. At no time since the war has it ceased to function. It is so secret that its address, its telephone, its personnel are unknown. I myself would not know how to locate it.

"When my friend arrived, we talked about Geneva for awhile. Then the conversation turned to Americans we both know. Soon he asked, by the way, speaking of Americans, do you know Captain Railey? Because I knew that he knew, I answered instantly, 'Yes, of course. He was here for tea a day or so ago.' And I was perfectly certain that he knew that too. He then said, 'My office is interested in Captain Railey. Do you happen to know what he's doing?' I replied that I thought I did. I said that I had known you here and at Geneva; that you had been the national director of the League of Nations Association, an office you had resigned, and that you were now in England gathering material for a book, and to write articles for various magazines and newspapers."

I was now studying Dame Adelaide with frank speculation—and a new comprehension; she must have seen that, while I believed her implicitly, I was puzzled by her omissions. She had said all these things assuredly. Had she not added in the confidence of this old and significant friendship that these were mere alibis cloaking my investigation of the traffic in arms? Had she not added that at least? In all truth, had the subject been dropped abruptly after her explanation. I put my first question: "Was your friend a person of high rank?"

"Very."

"Military?" She nodded. "Then I take it I'm under observation—suspected of espionage?" Again she nodded.

Railey wondered if Anthony Eden, whom he had met at Geneva, had put him onto the British list of espionage suspects. Or had it been Sir Arthur Willert, then head of the news department for the British Foreign Office?

This made the rest of his work more edgy as he looked into the activities of Vickers, the British arms manufacturer, Schneider-Creusot, and Krupp of Germany. He was afraid he might even come to a sudden and mysterious end.

It is not clear even now whether the *Fortune* assignment was indeed a cover for American espionage work or not. It is known that no series on arms was published by *Fortune* based on Railey's work. It also is known that *Fortune* had published a similar piece shortly before Railey went to Europe. Why then, one might ask, was he assigned to do a story on something *Fortune* had just written about? Why was no story ever done under his byline despite more than a year's effort and painstaking work?

It is the opinion of this author that Railey perhaps *was* engaged in soft intelligence gathering for the United States. This would certainly explain his return to the Army ranks and especially his unique assignment to the Ghost Army.

The only thing truly known is that Captain Railey—later Colonel Railey—had friends in high places in the United States, and later on, in much of Europe. When the search began for a man to be the very heart of the Ghost Army, it led straight to Railey. And by all accounts, it was a good choice. He proved an excellent righthand man for Colonel Simenson. And Reeder generally let the two of them do things their way.

Shortly after hostilities broke out in Europe and not long before the United States was drawn into World War II, Railey joined the Army again and quickly was promoted to colonel. Although he was very quiet about this part of his life because of postwar security orders, there is every reason to believe that his special knowledge of arms and European arms merchants and his unusual background resulted in an action in which he was all but recruited for the Army.

When the junior officers reported to Pine Camp, they found that although Railey reported to Simenson and Reeder, he seemed to be running everything outside of the office. Some of the men found it expedient to buy a copy of his book, which had been published in 1938.

Chapter Three

Eye of the Storm

After training variously at Pine Camp, Fort Meade, and Camp Forrest, most of the men were sent by train to Camp Kilmer, New Jersey, on April 21, 1944. They had eight-hour passes to visit New York City.

On the night of May 2, they boarded the Liberty ship *USS Henry Gibbons.* The top echelon officers had flown to England earlier by air. The men were asked to turn in their tropical gear at the last moment and were given regular summer and winter gear designed for Europe. The ruse was so successful that most all of the families and loved ones of the men had no idea where they had gone, or incorrectly assumed they were headed for the Pacific.

Some had telephoned Pine Camp, only to be told that the men had shipped out and only that. No matter the pleading from parents or spouses, the destination was kept secret. Husbands and wives having no secrets in the boudoir, as the saying goes, led many of the wives to assume the men were indeed headed to the Pacific Theater. The Ghost Army's top brass wanted it that way.

The voyages were at high speed in a zig-zag fashion to avoid German submarines. Some convoys dipped far down toward Africa before going north, and some convoys simply took a direct line to Great Britain. Ghost troops landed at Glasgow in Scotland and other ports, such as Avonmouth in Great Britain. Lt. Col. Frederick E. Day assumed command of all troops aboard the *Gibbons,* and Maj. David Haviland was named adjutant.

Tompkins said he and Blass "heard depth charges at night and we wondered what was going on. You have something to think about when you know your bunk is below the water line."

First Sgt. Jerry Gluckin, a natural comic, conducted a nightly deck show, and Army records state, "The chaplain objected to Gluckin's language and sulked in his cabin during the performances."

The *Gibbons* sailed up the Bristol Channel on May 15 without incident, completing the crossing in thirteen days. But during the night before debarkation, enemy planes bombed Bristol, and many people in the Twenty-third thought they were the target. It was their first taste of war. It was on this night that the men learned the truth of Gen. Omar N. Bradley's view that war is "a wretched debasement of all the thin pretensions of civilization."

Colonel Reeder and other members of the advance party that had flown over earlier met the ship at the dock. They brought word that the bivouac area was to be near Stratford-on-Avon in the green midlands of England. It took seven hours to get the Twenty-third to its destination as it rode the LM&SR (London, Midland, and Southern Railroad) to Stratford's pastoral meadows and lanes.

The slow train took them to a station near a large British mansion and estate called Walton Hall, quickly nicknamed "Moldy Manor" by the troops. It was owned by elderly Lady Mordaunt, who lived alone in a small section of one wing. The men rarely saw or talked to her. She was one of many among the British aristocracy who offered their large estates to the American armed services for training. This was an advantage because German pilots and aerial intelligence had difficulty deciding whether an estate actually hid military units or was merely a country home.

Dispersion was so complete that some of these big estates also had a few Spitfire aircraft concealed near impromptu runways as a means of hiding out during the air Battle of Britain. It was the air Battle of Britain that prompted Churchill's famous line: "Never in the field of human conflict was so much owed by so many to so few."

The enlisted men camped on the spacious lawns in Nisson huts (pyramidal tents with wood sides and floors) or inside the stables, with the officers living inside the old mansion, which was near Stratford-on-Avon, the birthplace and home of William Shakespeare during his early life. A lake on the grounds had a number of graceful black and white swans. It was hard to believe that the bloodiest and biggest conflict in the history of mankind was then under way around the globe—and soon to be just across the channel—because this bucolic scene was so tranquil.

Col. Clifford Simenson, center, during a 1999 reunion of Ghost Army survivors in New York. Simenson, who now lives in Boulder, Colorado, was one of the men who formed and trained the Ghost Army.

"We had the best of it. We stayed in the barns," said then-Cpl. William Enderlein of his stay at Walton Hall. "It was warm and dry there and the officers were always complaining that it was cold and damp in the mansion itself."

The men went to see a number of Shakespearean plays, including *Henry V,* in which Henry proclaims to his troops shortly before the Battle of Agincourt: "We few, we happy few. We band of brothers."

This was more than ironic because some of the Ghost Army would wind up—at one point—close to the site of the historic battle, and the war made many of them, too, seem as brothers. Another parallel: the British were heavily outnumbered at Agincourt, but their archers defeated a large and better equipped French army. The Ghost Army, too, was ridiculously small.

And many close relationships were formed, like that of Tompkins and Blass, or Richard Morton and Walter Arnett, or Bill Enderlein and Roy Oxenrider, or Dick Syracuse and Hypolite Briard. These friendships would endure for decades, bonded and annealed in the crucible of war. But more about these men later.

Simenson, Reeder and other officers did not use troopships to get to Great Britain, but flew directly to London. Simenson recalled:

> In April 1944, seven officers of the Twenty-third flew to England with Maj. Ralph Ingersoll as a guide. We billeted the first night in the Governor's Hotel in London. I telephoned my brother, Ed, who was the weather officer for the Eighth Army Air Force. He asked where I was and then exclaimed, "Holy smokes! I'll walk across the street and come over."

The brothers had a joyful reunion, a good meal, then took a flight over London.

"From about 6,000 feet we could see a few bombers take off from a small airfield, then from another field, and another," Simenson said.

> Finally there were several hundred bombers in the air at 20,000 feet all turning toward Germany like a swarm of bees. When I had the controls of the airplane, I asked "Ed, do you want me to fly between those two balloons?" He jumped a foot and then saw me grinning. [Barrage balloons tethered on steel cables were used to keep the German pilots from flying low and thereby being more precise in bombing London.]

The priority job now was supply, and the men immediately set about procuring the unit's technical equipment, which had been shipped separately to various other British ports. It was scattered in huge storehouses or seaport warehouses throughout southern England. As soon as half-tracks and 2½-ton trucks were obtained, the radiomen began installing its specially mounted radios and big ship's speakers.

At the same time, the camouflage troops were checking and repairing their dummy equipment, netting, and other gear. The engineer and artillery sections perfected a practical artillery flash, and various liaison officers were detached to London to gather information. The men were trying to become as proficient as possible before the invasion of Europe, which they knew would not be long in coming. Few, however, thought it would be as soon as it actually was, June 6, 1944.

One party of five Ghost troops was invited by the British to inspect their dummy equipment at Ramsgate and the equipment used in Operation Fortitude. The Americans were appalled at its crudity, but the English officers assured them that it all looked very realistic from the air. The men learned that these early examples of inflatable tanks and other vehicles were made by the B.F. Goodrich and Goodyear Tire and Rubber companies in America. Later examples, such as those used by the Ghost troops, were more realistic.

Training by all units was continued with much emphasis on athletics and recreation to make up for a lack of leave policy back home. Leave in England was also liberalized. Many men began hanging out at Leamington Spa, where there were plenty of attractive British women around. Some of the men went as far as London or Coventry, where they got their first glimpse of the war-devastated cities. Two big parties were held at the manor house. At one of them, Capt. Gerald N. Wagner, a dental surgeon, dozed off, to put it politely. When he awoke, all of the brass buttons on his Class A jacket had been snipped off.

"In the Twenty-third Headquarters we were very busy during April and May preparing for deception operations," Simenson said, but for the ordinary GI in the Twenty-third, things were far more pleasant. This brief sojourn in England before D-Day also was surreal in some ways, like the calm eye of a hurricane. Men played softball, sketched, played violins or other musical instruments, saw plays at Stratford-on-Avon. They had many smaller parties. Soon many had English girlfriends. It seemed far removed from war, although they saw an occasional German aircraft overhead.

But most of the aircraft they saw at this point in the war were Allied planes, especially the B-17, B-24, P-47, P-51, and British bombers such as the Wellington. To get an idea of how warmly the British regarded the Americans at this point, one need only chat with men who went to parties and social events.

One American pilot, Leroy Gover of Belmont, California, said the British women often showed their gratitude in unforgettable ways. Gover recalled, as one of many examples, a lovely socialite and sometimes actress who, upon learning that he was an American pilot, had a few drinks with him and then invited him to her room, where she expressed her gratitude more romantically. He said she made it clear she was giving herself to him as a bit of thanks from England to America. He had flown Spitfires for the Eagle Squadron, then became part of the American Army Air Corps when America entered the war and began flying P-47 Thunderbolts.

Generally, most of the men in the Ghost Army recall this time as dreamily pleasant. The impending danger and excitement led many to live as if there were no tomorrow, and for many of the young GIs, including a handful of Ghost troops, that was to be the case in just a few weeks during the Normandy invasion.

Those who lived in the stables on the estate said it may have been the most comfortable place they stayed during the war. The stables were very commodious, dry, and comfortable, although there was only one water spigot, which had served the fine thoroughbred horses.

"In fact, after actually going inside the manor house itself, which was cold and damp, I much preferred the stables," recalled one of the men.

Gradually, the social lines between the artists and the radio experts and even the combat troops disappeared in good fellowship. They all trained together, drank together, and brawled together. But the differences never did vanish altogether. One young soldier kept a Stradivari violin in his barracks. A young dress designer, rumored to be spoiled and rich, lounged on his bunk eating chocolate candy and endlessly writing letters.

One night, long after taps, the stillness of a 603rd barracks was broken by the sound of men speaking quietly and earnestly: "And there we were at Toots Shor's," one said, "when mother came in wearing this blue sequined dress. . . ." It was not always your usual GI palaver.

"While in England near Tidworth, some of us purchased second-, third-, and fourth-hand bicycles from other departing troops," recalled Robert Wendig.

> As units left the area, the bikes became a fire sale item. At that time, there were probably more military in the area than civilians. I recall that one night we biked to Birmingham, England and rode through the pitch-black streets from 11 P.M. to 2 A.M. We also attended the Shakespearean Theatre at Stratford-on-Avon, which was in summer operation despite the war.

Punting on the Avon, he recalls, or rowing small boats were other diversions.

The men also enjoyed seeing the half-timbered house where William Shakespeare was born in 1564 in Stratford. It was and still is one of the most visited places for tourists in Great Britain. A short walk away was New Place—Nash House, where Shakespeare lived from 1597 until his death in 1616. Only the foundation remained, but an original garden still grew on the grounds.

To round out a tour there was Anne Hathaway's cottage, the second-most-visited Shakespearean property. Part of the building dates from the mid-fifteenth century. The war seemed very distant during this time before the Normandy invasion. Some did a bit of light training near Weymouth, but even this lacked the desperation of real war.

"At Portland, near Weymouth, England, we learned that the terrain was all limestone as we dug frantically to make slit trenches, just in case," remembers Grant Hess. "Sometime in November 1944 we fought the battle of rain and mud with all vehicles bogged down together—along with our spirits. Our amenities included what we called 'a whore's bath'—bathing out of our helmets."

Training was continued at Walton Hall, and some of the men were peripherally involved in Operation Fortitude, mostly as observers, as the British hoped to convince the Germans that the main invasion was to come at the Pas de Calais, a French port. Few thought this early effort at deception would work. For one thing, the rubber dummies used by the British in this effort were far cruder than those later used by the Ghost Army.

The British argued that from the air detail was not that important. As it turned out, the British were right. The lack of detail was not visible from the air and the ruse worked beautifully, helping convince the Germans the British were massing for an attack on Pas de Calais instead of the Normandy beaches.

The Ghost troops learned that the British also had other ruses that worked well on the Germans. When night bombing raids occurred, they set big oil and tar fires near the intended targets. Waves of German bombers, seeing the fires and assuming a direct hit by previous bombers, would drop their bombs in the vicinity of the fires. The fires were in open fields away from the vital targets.

The British also put flare paths like those of a real airport on lonely country fields at night, causing German pilots to believe they were airport runways. Many bombs were dropped in the empty fields at night to the delight of the British. A few farmers had to be reimbursed, however, for bomb craters in their fields.

Some of the men wondered whether the British deception plan, Operation Fortitude, would really work, which in turn led them to wonder about their own plans after the invasion was launched. Gradually, many of the Ghost troops learned of the breathtaking plan that the British had worked out, one that involved a massive deception designed to make the Germans think that the long-awaited invasion would occur at the closest point to Britain, Calais.

If this operation failed, the Ghost officers knew, it would probably mean the dissolution of the Twenty-third Headquarters Special Troops or—at the very least—the radical diminution of its role in the months to come. Allied intelligence knew that no matter how large a landing force was sent to France, it could be hurled back into the sea with staggering losses if the Germans were ready for it. This could mean either a year or more delay in establishing a western front, as Roosevelt and Churchill had promised Stalin, or even lenient peace terms for Hitler.

It was therefore crucial that the British-planned deception known as "Fortitude" succeed.

At first, the British suggested that one division actually be sent to Pas de Calais. This was ruled out on the grounds that such a small force would obviously be seen as a diversion. In addition, because of German strength in the area, it would be a huge sacrifice of troops and bad for morale. Casualties would certainly be near 100 percent for such a small force. Some said it would be a Dieppe on a grand scale, referring to the disastrous raid at that coastal site by British and Canadian commandos two years earlier.

The British decided to disseminate the story that Calais would be the main landing site via a variety of subterfuges, not the least of which was the false information passed to double agents. This was risky, Colonel Simenson said, because double agents sometimes had a bad habit of becoming triple agents or simply reverting in loyalty. But the British said they would use only those agents in whom they had confidence based on past performance.

Eisenhower and his staff were most afraid that German intelligence would see the movement of landing craft southward and logically decide that the best place for an amphibious assault on such a grand scale would be between Brest and Ostend. From this conclusion, it would not be a stretch to pick out the best beaches for a landing and have Panzers and large numbers of infantry poised and ready. Eisenhower's staff had nightmares of a Dunkirk multiplied by ten.

The task for the Allies was to play down this possibility while playing up, without being too obvious about it, the probability of a landing at Calais. The main effort, therefore, was to simulate preparation for a large invasion force in southeast England. This plan would not work without the utmost security in the real invasion staging areas and along the south coast.

To avoid discovery in the fake staging area, it was made a highly restricted zone. Only trips in or out for compassionate or emergency purposes were allowed. The reason was that even a casual trip through the area by a spy or informer would readily reveal that it was a large-scale but phony operation. Anthony Eden, the British foreign secretary, objected to strictures placed on diplomats, arguing that they could be used to spread the false information. But he was over-ridden and after April, no diplomat was allowed to leave or send or receive any uncensored mail.

Eden, who was a pain in the side of the Fortitude planners, then asked that such restrictions on diplomats be lifted after D-Day. It was explained to him repeatedly that the deception would have to be followed through for weeks afterward in order to freeze Hitler's Panzers at Calais. Looking back, it is hard to believe how ardently many British people and bureaucrats fought the tight security restrictions in the sections of the country in which the invasion was planned or being faked.

Even Eisenhower almost made a mistake when he informed Churchill that he would call in a group of newsmen six days before the invasion and confide in them. Churchill strongly urged that he not do this, pointing out that the mere assembling of the newsmen might signal the impending invasion to an astute German spy or German sympathizer. Churchill also strongly doubted that all of the newsmen could be trusted not to talk about it to someone, who in turn would leak it to someone else. Eisenhower, who tended to be too open with everyone, agreed. He called it off.

One of the hardest tasks, the Ghost Army officers learned, was to conceal the vast preparations in the genuine area while making the fake preparations believable. The fully informed Ghost officers were particularly worried after they took a tour of the area where fake preparations for invasion were being made. Maximum concealment of preparations was carried out west of a point near Portsmouth.

The most sophisticated camouflage was made in this area, including using farmhouses and barns to conceal men and equipment. The concealment in this rustic farm country even extended to the banning of white towels by troops, the use of smokeless stoves for cooking, and intense camouflage of vehicles in groves of trees and orchards.

The problem in the East—the phony invasion buildup site—was not quite as severe, because many of the invasion troops were sent there to further the illusion of preparations for a massive invasion. The plan was to transfer them secretly and speedily at the last moment for the trip to the Normandy beaches.

The Ghost Army officers are quick to tell you today that they were perhaps inordinately worried about these plans, which seemed too obvious and heavy-handed to fool German intelligence. It was in the phony area that the Ghost troops were able to help with advice on how to make phony camouflage look bad without being so terrible that it was obvious to reconnaissance flights.

The Twenty-first Army Group soon took over the cover plan and the command of the Ghost Army efforts. The Ghost officers and the few enlisted men in on the Fortitude deception knew that if it failed they would all probably wind up in a combat unit. Perhaps only Colonel Reeder and Capt. George Rebh would have been happy with this outcome.

To impart verisimilitude to Fortitude, units of the U.S. First Army Group, nicknamed FUSAG, were moved into the phony staging area. This huge outfit consisted of the Third Army with nine divisions and the First Canadian with a pair of divisions. The fake radio traffic expertise of the Ghost troops was used, mostly in a consulting fashion, to make the traffic with FUSAG appear to be in preparation for a Calais invasion. The real Ninth Army of the U.S. also was shown as part of FUSAG for a time to add credibility.

To lend further credibility, the planners decided to leak reports that General Patton was in command of this invasion force. They had first considered General Bradley, but realized that his presence in France shortly after D-Day would ruin this charade. Also, Allied intelligence knew that Patton was held in higher regard after the Sicily campaign by the Germans than he was by his own senior officers. Because of his blustering, blunt ways, he was resented by many, and even Eisenhower and Bradley often found him hard to take.

In fact, Eisenhower at one point considered relieving him of command altogether after the celebrated hospital incident in which Patton slapped a soldier that he incorrectly assumed to be a slacker feigning illness. Perhaps the fact that he and Eisenhower were old friends from their West Point days saved Patton.

The simulated signal traffic for Fortitude was handled by the U.S. 3103rd Signals Service Battalion. The Ghost radiomen learned a lot from this operation, sometimes sitting in as fake radio traffic was sent. The Ghost Army had learned to carefully monitor real radio traffic, mastering the mannerisms and idiosyncracies of the real units, and this was done in the Fortitude operation as well. It was known via Enigma, which broke the German code, and other means that this radio traffic was monitored carefully by Nazi radiomen in France. It was imperative that transmissions sound as realistic as possible, including joking, casualness at times, and the use of the current military argot and jargon. One slip could cost thousands of lives.

The Ghost liaison group also learned that the Fortitude operation included fake landing craft—almost three hundred of them. The British nicknamed them "Big Bobs." These were placed in coastal areas opposite Calais. One problem was that they were so much lighter than the real thing that they had to be weighted to prevent detection. To add to the realism on the dummy landing craft, laundry was hung out on lines to indicate men aboard, and oil was even spread on the water now and then to indicate a faulty diesel engine. Fires of oil rags or rope were lit to simulate cooking aboard ship.

Another aspect of the Fortitude operation was the bombing of the beaches and communications in the Calais area, always the harbinger of an attack. The Ghost troops learned that mixing real and phony equipment with actual attacks was an effective technique, one they were to use throughout the remainder of the war.

Fake lighting systems were set up to simulate docking areas at night, while the real docks were in total darkness. This was so effective in the Portsmouth and Plymouth areas that German air raids at night attacked the area illuminated by lights. Because of the effectiveness of this ruse, some of the Ghost troops were recruited to go in within hours of the D-Day landing to help set up phony lighting on deserted sections of the Normandy beaches.

German intelligence, including reports by Field Marshal Gerd von Runstedt himself, suggested that an invasion might be launched from the southeast of England. If one looks at England as bell-shaped, then the southeastern part of the bell is nearest to Calais. From a logistical point of view, this would make the most sense, with a far shorter crossing time across the channel. The Normandy beaches are the farthest point across the channel, almost midway under the bell shape. The logical and methodical German mind had trouble conceiving that sometimes the shortest distance between two points is not the most effective.

Young George Rebh, now a retired general. Rebh became a captain in a combat unit charged with protecting the Ghost Army during World War II.

One positive factor for the Allies was their dominance in the air, which resulted in only 129 sorties flown by German aircraft in the six weeks before D-Day.

Field Marshall Rommel was in charge of defending the French coast. His basic plan was to rush Panzers and troops to the main point of the invasion and hurl the Allies back into the sea with horrible losses. But the Allies had one great secret weapon in its war of deception, and that was Adolf Hitler himself, who bought the Fortitude ruse completely.

Hitler was like the chess master beaten by a child because he over-thought and over-interpreted everything to the point that his head was filled, in paranoid fashion, with complex strategies and tricks planned by the Allies that did not exist. A straightforward amphibious Allied operation on the beaches of Normandy always seemed absurd to Hitler, *even after it happened.*

After all, he argued, the Allies needed deepwater port facilities like those found at Calais, Antwerp, La Havre, Cherbourg, and Brest. To land on beaches subject to high and low tides and filled with mines and navigation obstacles would be absurd. So he insisted in keeping most of the German strength concentrated around Calais. He stubbornly kept them there for many days after the invasion began.

The Ghost Army officers were not privy to all of these plans until they arrived in England. They constantly wondered how it would ever be possible to conceal such a vast invasion force. The strategy, the camouflage, the radio traffic, the double agents, and all the rest seemed amateurish and imperfect to some.

They were haunted, as were many others, by the memory of Dieppe. It is quite obvious that Churchill and the British military leaders also were haunted by it, causing Churchill to fret and worry more than most, and to later oppose a second landing in the south of France. The raid on Dieppe was a British trial run that ended in disaster. Launched August 19, 1942, brave British and Canadian commandos were slaughtered almost too easily.

The German 571st Regiment and some Luftwaffe anti-aircraft emplacements opened up on the landing craft at Dieppe as soon they came into range. Very few men got through the murderous fire. By 8:30 A.M. of the dawn raid, every man on the beach was either dead or a prisoner. The numbers told the story: of 554 Royal Canadians who had hit the beaches, 227 of them were killed. When the survivors of the morning got home and were counted, only 2,110 of almost 5,000 were present.

Although the Dieppe raid had inadequate support from naval bombardment and air cover, and was far too straightforward and well telegraphed, it caused many in the Ghost Army to wonder whether the British Fortitude deception might be prelude to another Dieppe. But Ghost officers kept those doubts to themselves.

Despite the doubts, a tour of British facilities, particularly in the fake buildup area, taught the Ghost troops a lot that they had not learned back in Pine Camp. For example, they discovered that two real artillery pieces could be arranged facing each other, with the wheels showing, then covered with a light framework and canvas to look like a jeep, a small truck, or an automobile. They found that the British routinely stored fuel and other supplies under canvas in the shape of a small vehicle, one that would seem almost too small a target for German strafing, yet actually hid tons of food or gasoline.

The dummy Big Bob landing craft, 160 feet long, seemed crude on close inspection, but Ghost troops who flew over them as low as a few hundred feet could not tell that they were fake. Although some of the inflatable British vehicles were crude by American standards—using old exposed inner tubes as tires—the Ghost troops found that from as little as 150 yards away they appeared real, particularly if slightly camouflaged. Flat, dummy Spitfire aircraft made of painted plywood appeared three-dimensional from the air.

Runways painted on flat fields often drew German bombs and attacks, yet up close the Ghost troops wondered how anyone could be fooled. The British often disguised a very large hangar filled with real Spitfires and Hurricanes as a country cottage, complete with chimneys and gables and half-frame timbers painted on metal. Although easily identified as hangars from a few hundred yards away on the ground, they looked like the real thing from the air, despite being far over scale. It was hard for a pilot to judge scale without something to which these cottage hangars could be compared.

The British repeated this all over the countryside to avoid having too many fighter planes in any one location and thus vulnerable to bombing. And, ominously, the Ghost troops bicycling in the countryside often found that haystacks and small farm sheds or even old cars were actually machine gun emplacements, leftovers from when the English thought that a German invasion and paratroop drop were imminent.

But the British were delighted that America had at last seemed to embrace the idea of a deceptive army unit. For a long time, the British High Command had been worried about the Americans' seeming rejection of deception. Some Americans discounted it as merely something the British had done out of sheer desperation.

Sir Archibald Nye, vice-chief of the Imperial General Staff, said the Combined Chiefs of Staff had instructed Eisenhower to prepare deception plans, but added, "We have reason to believe Americans in general and General Eisenhower's staff in particular have virtually no experience [in] deception." He was right in those early days before the Ghost Army was formed.

But the Fortitude operation was such a resounding triumph, being without a doubt one of the main reasons for the success of the Normandy invasion, that the American high command suddenly discovered the value of its own Ghost Army. A vital interest was then taken in its actions all the way up through Eisenhower's and Bradley's staffs. The only flaw was that coordination and liaison, particularly at lower command levels, as we will see, was often poor.

Enthusiasm was so great after the success of Fortitude that it was decided that the Ghost troops would be used in several major operations, particularly in the crossings of several great rivers, including the Rhine. Capt. George Rebh said he thought the main purpose of the Ghost Army from the beginning was to help effect the crossing of the Rhine.

General Eisenhower and his staff at SHAEF (Supreme Headquarters, Allied Expeditionary Force) coordinated the use of the Twenty-third. Some key Ghost Army staffers had to report directly to SHAEF for their orders and duties.

Meanwhile, the Germans, under the immediate command of Rommel, kept their Fifteenth Army concentrated around the area of the port of Calais across the channel. The Germans were convinced that Gen. Lesley McNair and General Patton would lead the major army group in an assault across the channel at its closest point to France.

Military historians are quick to blame it all on Hitler, but many of the other German officers also reasoned that the beaches were not a good place to land the enormous tonnage in supplies the Allies would need. Furthermore, they felt that any other point would leave the Allied ships in the channel too long—so long that even the much-reduced Luftwaffe would find them sitting ducks. They also reasoned that beaches would provide too effective a field of fire, allowing the German troops to slaughter any Allied troops foolish enough to try such a straightforward approach.

The Allies also succeeded through understated disinformation in giving the German high command the idea that General Patton would be involved in the Calais operation by allowing Patton to be seen driving in and around the phony buildup area. Patton and General Bradley had been virtually ignored by German intelligence until after their their successful campaigns in Sicily. Patton especially was admired by the German high command, perhaps to a degree, according to postwar documents, because he and Eisenhower had

German names. The ethnocentric Germans naturally assumed that this was a major reason for their superior abilities.

As for docking, Churchill had dreamed up and implemented a plan for artificial concrete docks that were floated into position, then sunk into place. They were code-named "Mulberries." They worked well until a terrific channel storm knocked them out a few weeks after the landing. But by that time, a solid beachhead was assured.

Eisenhower and his staff wrote a deliberately simple and inclusive order for Overlord, the Normandy operation, one that the British also approved. This is the short document the Germans would loved to have seen in April or even May or early in June of 1944:

> Land on the Normandy coast. Build up the resources needed for a decisive battle in the Normandy-Brittany region and break out of the enemy's encircling positions. Land operations in the first two phases under the tactical direction of Montgomery.
>
> Pursue on a broad front with two army groups, emphasizing the left to gain necessary ports and reach the boundaries of Germany and threaten the Ruhr. On our right we would link up with the forces that were to invade France from the South. [In Operation Dragoon, vehemently opposed by Churchill, to no avail. Churchill thought it would needlessly dilute the troops and equipment needed for Overlord, the code name of the Normandy invasion.] Build up our new base along the western border of Germany, by security ports in Belgium and in Brittany as well as in the Mediterranean.
>
> While building up our forces for the final battles, keep up an unrelenting offensive to the extent of our means, both to wear down the enemy and to gain advantages for the final fighting. Complete the destruction of enemy forces west of the Rhine, in the meantime constantly seeking bridgeheads across the river.
>
> Launch the final attack as a double envelopment of the Ruhr, again emphasizing the left, and follow this up by an immediate thrust through Germany, with the specific direction to be determined at the time. Clean out the remainder of Germany.

It was from this ultra-simple overall objective plan—which developed almost exactly as Eisenhower and his staff had hoped and planned, a rarity in the annals of the military—that all of the hundreds of small battles were to grow. The Ghost troops played a role in 21 of them, including some of the biggest and most crucial of the war, including the siege of Brest, the Battle of the Bulge, Metz, and the elaborate efforts to cross the Moselle and Rhine rivers.

Chapter Four

Ghosts Land in Normandy

Early on the morning of June 6, an invasion fleet of some 7,000 ships landed American and British divisions on Normandy beaches. Airborne divisions in gliders and in parachutes dropped behind the German lines. In the air, the Allies had nearly complete command, although the Luftwaffe still raided from time to time.

This invasion was decisive and the outcome of the war in Europe depended upon its success. Even Eisenhower was to be surprised at the success of the initial beachheads and the logistical feats that followed. In fact, in the short span of seven weeks in a logistical tour de force, the Allies had 20 American divisions ashore in France, along with 12 British divisions, 3 Canadian divisions, 1 Free French division, and 1 Polish division. The Ghost Army was part of this vast landing force.

Most of these men and materiel came in via Churchill's concrete docks, or "Mulberries." Although they were badly damaged by a storm a few weeks later, they were in place long enough. Then the Allies began to use Cherbourg and other ports. And gasoline was pumped over in a pipeline laid on the channel floor, an idea from Louis Mountbatten. It proved to be one of the best logistical ideas of the war. But the gasoline had to be pumped from the beachhead into tanker trucks and even in thousands of five-gallon cans for hauling in the 2½-ton trucks.

The Ghost Army troops, for example, had to have several trucks devoted only to hauling gasoline just to keep even this relatively small group going, a headache for supply officer Lt. John Walker, who said he also carried a Browning Automatic Rifle to protect his supply vehicles. Walker, by the way, although a supply officer, was

Bill Blass and Robert Tompkins read newspapers in their tent somewhere on the Brittany Peninsula in Normandy in August 1944. One of the headlines states: "Allies Drive for Paris." Photo courtesy Robert Tompkins.

chosen for the Ghost Army after higher ups saw that he had a master's degree in chemistry and an IQ of 135.

In the first week, the Allies established beachheads between Cherbourg and the city of Caen along a 60-mile-wide strip, and already some units of the Ghost Army had arrived. Within a week, Allies had fought and scratched about 20 miles inland. Casualties for the landing were about 15,000 out of some 150,000 engaged. Most of the men of the Ghost Army, however, were held in England for a few weeks until the beachheads could be broadened farther inland.

The British captured Caen on July 9. The Americans broke out of their beachhead positions on July 25. Armored columns headed inland, and Paris was to fall to the Allies on August 25, about three months later.

Soon, the Germans began to use new weapons against England: flying bombs, called V-1s, launched from bases in France, and ballistic missiles, called V-2s, launched from the Netherlands. Many of the men in the Ghost Army said they watched as the buzz bombs flew over. Many of the bombs were later aimed at Antwerp and even Luxembourg. But the majority fell on London. One was aimed at

A cast-iron dummy paratrooper of the type used by the thousands to fake a mass parachute landing. Photo courtesy Michael Williams.

the Ghost Army itself in Luxembourg, the Germans incorrectly assuming the Ghost Army to be a special unit designed to destroy rocket-launching sites. The V-bombs injured and killed thousands of English civilians and caused great damage.

When the Normandy invasion did begin, some elements of the Twenty-third Ghost troops were ashore within one day of the first assault. The fighting was still perilously near the beaches. Two Ghost Army troops were wounded on the second day, and the other two a few days after that. Various elements of the Twenty-third came in at different places and times, with instructions to assemble later, awaiting further orders from Colonel Reeder and his staff.

Each man had a different story of his shipping out to France. Corporal Victor Dowd, for example, had visited an English girl on his bicycle on June 12, 1944. When he returned, he was told to get in the barracks quickly.

He said, "Let me put my bike away."

A sergeant responded, "You're not going to need it."

So the next day Dowd found himself on a cargo plane flying to a landing strip near Omaha Beach, just seven days after the D-Day landing. The beachhead was still small and the area very dangerous.

"There were dead animals in trees, dead Germans all around. I could hear machine gun fire. The front was only a mile away," recalled Dowd, an illustrator who now lives in Wesport, Connecticut. (He later did a sketch of one young GI, Bill Blass. It was a sketch he later came to treasure, among many.) He had been a camouflage expert with the Ghost Army's 603rd Battalion. He quickly found himself promoted to sergeant when another sergeant was wounded. But war-time promotions and demotions were often irrational.

Bob Tompkins recalled: "We landed on June 24. It was still a relatively small perimeter and I heard battle noise. We drove up on the beach for assembly and it was almost dark. Then, after we assembled, we began the convoy, driving with cat-eye lights. After awhile, all of a sudden I could smell the sickly sweet smell of death all around. Once you smell that, you won't forget it."

Ed Biow of Portland, Oregon, recalled that he was demoted to private from corporal in a battle area by an arrogant and mildly hysterical young lieutenant—not from the Twenty-third or Ghost Army— merely because his trousers had come out of his combat boots. Elements of the Ghost Army were borrowed in the early days of the invasion to help camouflage American artillery and to set up phony lighting that might indicate wharf lights at vacant beaches.

The reason, said Dowd, was that "there was more German air strength than the Allies had anticipated. The hope was that the lights might draw German bombs to a safe, vacant area." Dowd later formed up with the rest of the Ghost Army to begin its secret operations. But meanwhile, Colonel Reeder was nowhere to be found, absent as the result of an Army snafu.

It was during the first days of the Normandy invasion that one of the weirdest snafus of the Twenty-third's war experience happened. A landing craft carrying Lieutenant Colonel Reeder got its orders mixed up, and Reeder and the rest of the troops on the craft halted and dropped anchor off of the Isle of Wight for a full week. Finally someone wondered why they were just sitting at anchor, discovered the error, and ordered them ashore. They apparently were initially asked to wait there until further orders, then were forgotten because of the controlled pandemonium of the landings.

Meanwhile, most of Reeder's troops already were ashore and wondering where he was. Reeder had not complained because he thought the delay had been ordered by some higher up for some good reason. Some even thought Reeder might have been killed since he had been away so long. He was very angry and frustrated by the time he finally got ashore. Some of his men had to hide their pleasure at his anger. For him, it was an inauspicious start.

Simenson recalled those early days after D-Day:

> During June 1944, segments of the Twenty-third were gradually arriving in Normandy. I went in on Omaha Beach on June 16 and didn't even get my feet wet. We bivouacked in the hedgerows using foxholes and pup tents and were quite comfortable being just beyond enemy artillery range. Getting to know the area was the first priority. We were pretty much left alone. The First Army as our boss was very busy holding the line and receiving new units.
>
> One day my jeep driver, Bernie McKeon, and I went out to observe a planned British attack on the Germans in Caen in the British Sector. We experienced being caught in bombs for one hour by the 600 U.S. B-24s which were supposed to bomb Germans and unfortunately were dropping their loads too early, landing on British troops. The British attack was canceled.

Simenson said he still vividly recalls when a kind French lady offered him and his driver an egg.

> Then we activated the French word phrase book and said, "Merci. Avez vous des outs?" Another day I went fishing with Lt. Col. Bob Warren, the engineer officer of the Second Division and an old fishing buddy. With four hand grenades we bagged four trout and winged a goose, which became a pet around the chow line, keeping the ground clean for the soldiers.

It took until August 8 to get the entire command of the Ghost

Army into Normandy. The strength was then 82 officers and 1,023 enlisted men. It took two months, two planes, and nine ships to get all of the Twenty-third from England to France.

One afternoon, during a lull, a small contingent of Ghost troops piled in a few jeeps and decided to visit St. Lo. One of them had said that he read in *Stars and Stripes* that it had just been liberated. They wanted to see the bomb damage. The service newspaper was wrong, and the Ghost troops had to make some quick U-turns and do a rapid retreat to avoid capture or being killed.

An Army report on this error later stated: "One group nearly got themselves decorated by being the first in St. Lo after they had read in the *Stars and Stripes* that the town had been taken. The news was a little premature."

The Twenty-third was grateful that the *Stars and Stripes* did not identify them.

The first deception operation by the Twenty-third Ghost troops— "Operation Elephant"—was not as successful as later operations would be, but at least the men learned a few things. Also, only a small part of the radio deception unit was used. The mission was to cover the Second Armored Division as it deployed from its reserve position. It was learned that fake stories for leaking by the ground troops would help, and the full sonic unit was really very badly needed. It was the last to fully assemble in France.

One of the early missions was dubbed "Operation Troutfly." A group of radio experts in Troutfly simulated by radio alone the assembly of the Ninetieth Infantry Division in the rear of the Eighty-second Airborne Division in the middle of the Cherbourg Peninsula on the day after D-Day. This operation was aborted and the radiomen used in other capacities. Two of them were seriously wounded by German artillery.

Corporal Dowd of Brooklyn, New York, recalled the early days of the Ghost Army's time in Normandy, en route to the Brittany Peninsula: "There were dead animals and Germans all over the land-scape." There was still much tough fighting left, and he was in the middle of it, specializing in camouflaging big gun emplacements. He was on loan even before the rest of the Ghost Army arrived, as were a number of Ghost Army troops with special skills. Dowd was so cool under heavy enemy fire that he was awarded the Bronze Star for heroism. Shortly after this, however, a policy of withholding medals would be enforced as a means of keeping the secrecy lid on the exploits of the Ghost troops. Dowd slipped in under the wire.

"I always felt guilty that I got the Bronze Star and the other men didn't get their medals," said Dowd. "They didn't even get their Purple Hearts. It's not fair."

During "Operation Elephant," the name given one small project, the Second Armored Division moved secretly to the line between the First U.S. and the Second British armies. Only July 1, the Second Armored began moving out of the Forest of Cerisy. As each unit moved, the Twenty-third replaced the real equipment with dummies, tank for tank. The Twenty-third held this position for two days, bluffing the Germans, until elements of the U.S. Third Army came up to relieve them. The objective of preventing movement of Panzer units to the left where the Second had moved was successful. This enabled a successful attack by the combined American forces. Cherbourg was captured a short while later.

It was here that many of the Twenty-third first came under fire. Several of the men were hiding under a truck during an artillery attack one evening when one of them quipped, "We'll never get overseas." The others laughed uproariously. It was funny only in context of their experiences, because during their stateside training, the men actually thought the war would be over before they could be sent overseas. A frequent refrain that became the standing joke about any difficulty was, "We'll never get overseas."

Some, more specifically, had said, "The 603rd will never get overseas." This became even funnier as the war stretched on and the dangers grew. It became the Ghost Army's humorous battle refrain and was most often heard in conditions of extreme danger.

The Ghost Army was to play a key but tragic role in Brittany, the same peninsula on which Julius Caesar had trapped a large contingent of hostile tribesmen many centuries before during his conquest of the forebears of modern France. Because the Allies would need good ports to bring in the huge numbers of troops and supplies, the decision was made by General Eisenhower to sweep right and then west onto the Brittany Peninsula.

An attempt would then be made to capture some of the excellent seaports there, including Brest, Lorient, St. Nazaire, St. Malo, and the Quiberon Bay. It also was hoped that if this maneuver were done with enough force and speed, it could trap a sizable number of Germans on the peninsula before they could escape. Maj. Gen. Troy H. Middleton was given primary responsibility for this effort, and the Ghost Army also played a key role. A major goal was the capture of Brest, which had been home to a large number of German submarines.

Maj. Gen. John S. Wood made quick and solid success in his sweep toward Rennes, leaving a pocket of German resistance in Avranches. Wood, perhaps with dreams of glory, did not sweep westward on the peninsula as planned in the general Overlord (code name for the Normandy invasion) scheme, but told Middleton that the best way to win the war would be to continue east to the interior of France. The Allies had carefully hashed all of this out before the invasion and had decided that the capture of the peninsula—or at least cutting it off—would be vital. So Middleton had to pay Wood a visit and make it clear that his main objective lay west on the peninsula.

Wood no doubt thought he would be in a backwater part of the invasion while others were in the main thrust. Even after meeting with Middleton, Wood continued to try to push eastward until he got a very direct and blunt message from Gen. George Patton to continue toward the west, particularly the ports of Lorient and the Quiberon Bay. He still later managed to go east to attack Nantes with Middleton's blessing.

Middleton also ordered his subordinates, including Maj. Gen. Robert Grow, to take St. Malo and therefore pause in the westward sweep. This infuriated General Patton, who countermanded the order. A pocket of German troops was cut off at St. Malo.

Ghost trooper Grant Hess set up a giant loudspeaker at the edge of St. Malo's front lines to broadcast a request for German surrender. Later he toured St. Malo after the surrender and picked up a Mauser rifle and a Walther pistol, which he still has today in his retirement home in Scottsdale, Arizona.

As a consequence of these Brittany Peninsula actions, it is clear in hindsight, many of the German troops on the peninsula had a chance to retreat to Brest, further strengthening that already formidable garrison port under the command of von Ramcke. Because of the resulting weakening of the Allies forces on Brittany to free up General Patton's Third Army, the Ghost Army was called upon to dupe the Germans in Brest, convincing them that the Allies had far more strength surrounding the fortified port city. In fact, the garrison at one point might have even broken out had they known the truth about the light, theatrical forces in front of them.

But shortly before this, in "Operation Brittany," the mission was to simulate four armored columns moving West into the Brittany Peninsula to prevent withdrawal of German units. The plan was to freeze the German Seventh Army in place while the real American units secretly disengaged for a major push eastward in Normandy. The Germans took the bait. The Allies hoped that the Germans would interpret this move as weakening the central section of the front, which was growing stronger each day.

Officers involved in the Twenty-third's movements said "desperate bands of Nazis" still roamed the countryside and the Twenty-third was in great danger. Meanwhile, they were so successful at imitation that the troops of the real units, thinking that they were being left behind, joined the phony Twenty-third in its maneuvers. It was a wild scene in Brittany for several days, with some Germans retreating to Brest and some retreating east, with American troops chasing them in both directions.

Lt. Col. Frederick E. Day of the Ghost Army, traveling along in a very lightly armed convoy, nonetheless "was instrumental in the capture of about 300 Germans and a good store of Wehrmacht chocolate," according to official records. The German POWs later said they were embarrassed to find they had surrendered to part of a small high-tech outfit they themselves easily could have captured. The Ghost Army troops—most of whom were armed only with .30-caliber carbines, .45 pistols, and little else—immediately turned its POWs over to nearby combat units equipped to handle them.

German Enigma radio traffic also proved the effectiveness of the Ghost Army operation on the Brittany Peninsula. The Germans never learned that the Allies had an Enigma machine that had been captured in a Polish raid in the early days of the war, and had cracked their secret radio codes. Ironically, captured German radiomen near the Ghost troops nearly always thought the U.S. troops were just stupid in broadcasting so much information on battlefield radios. Somehow it never occurred to the Germans eavesdropping on American battlefield radio, which they always monitored, that there was anything duplicitous involved in the constant chatter of American radiomen. Postwar records show the Germans were thoroughly confused by the Twenty-third's trickery and could not decide what the Allies were planning.

By August 19, the German Seventh—far to the rear of the Twenty-third's activity—was bottled up and destroyed in the bloody closing of the Falaise-Argentan gap after an abortive attack on Mortain, where the Allies had turned the corner into the Brittany Peninsula. It was a good idea and would have worked had the Germans had enough strength there to carry it off. It could have trapped the

Americans, including the Ghost Army, on the peninsula. But the attenuated German forces did not have sufficient armor or manpower to pull it off. Hitler's top command said Hitler seemed to think that the divisions listed on paper were as strong and effective has they had been in the early blitzkrieg days.

As the Twenty-third moved closer to Brest, much of the movement nearest the fortified city was at night. Corporal Enderlein recalled that convoys of the Ghost Army had to be guided down roads at night near Brest by a soldier walking along with a white handkerchief. No lights were allowed—not even the small "cat-eye" lights used in less dangerous areas—a headlight blacked out except for a tiny hole. The roads also were heavily mined and it was a frightening task. Each truck had a guide with a white handkerchief in his pocket who would keep his hand on the fender of the truck as he walked while the truck rolled along very slowly.

As Bill Enderlein walked along in the pitch-black darkness, illuminated only by flares from Brest and artillery flashes, he heard "all of this vile swearing from the driver of one truck a few trucks back." He was cursing loudly. Enderlein was alarmed because feared the noise might tip off the Germans, who were very close at this point. He halted the convoy and walked back to see what was the matter.

"What's going on? What's all the cursing about?" Enderlein asked the driver.

"That stupid moron S.O.B. put an OD (Olive Drab) handkerchief in his pocket and I can't see it!" he said of the man walking in front of his truck. They quickly gave the trooper a white handkerchief and continued the convoy.

A short time later, after they set up for the night, Corporal Enderlein and Cpl. Roy Oxenrider, his best buddy throughout the war, were ordered to advance down a narrow lane thought to be heavily mined, a lane that advanced very near the German lines. It was one of their most nerve-wracking experiences of the war. Any step could set off a mine. And at any moment a German patrol could appear and start shooting. The two men walked along as quietly as possible, every nerve ending alert. They tried to see in the darkness any ground that looked as it if it had been disturbed for the concealment of a mine. "I thought they just wanted to get rid of us," said Enderlein. "I really thought we had little chance of avoiding a mine or a German patrol. Roy and I were scared to death."

Then at one point they froze as they heard someone struggling

Dummy gun used by the Ghost Army. The two "men" on the left are dummies; the two men on the right are real Ghost troops. U.S. Army photo.

to get through one of the big hedgerows in the area. It was a soldier! They could not tell whether he was German or friendly, but they thought he could not possibly be friendly this close to the German lines. The two men pounced on him and were within a second of killing him when they realized the man squirming beneath them was a lost American GI who had wandered away from his outfit. It was a harrowing experience for all three men. They pointed the GI in the right direction and completed their reconnaissance without further incident.

Later Enderlein, Oxenrider, and a few others, including a French translator, had a clandestine meeting for the first time with members of the FFI, Free French of the Interior, and the guerilla group Maquis.

"It was just like a movie," said Enderlein. "The FFI had every kind of weapon you could imagine, wearing berets and turtle-neck sweaters. They had Bren guns, American .45-caliber grease guns, German assault rifles, you name it. It seemed as if each man had a different kind of weapon. And they were a tough looking bunch of guys."

Sgt. Henry "Hank" Rapsis of the 3132nd part of the Ghost Army said they were so close "we could hear the Germans talking. We were probably at one point only about a hundred or so yards away from them."

Bob Tompkins recalled the routine that began with Brest:

> We would move into an area with our 2½-ton trucks and jeeps at night, like we did at Brest. We would look for real tank tracks so we could put our dummy tanks exactly where the real ones had been. Then we'd drop one of the deflated tank bags, which weighed about ninety pounds, from the trucks. Then jeeps with air compressors would come along after the trucks and we'd inflate the tanks. Our rubber Sherman had eight to twelve air valves. So when the Germans looked us over the next morning, they would see tanks exactly where Patton had positioned his tanks before he left. Because our sonic boys had been making tank noises all night, the Germans sure weren't surprised to see tanks where they had heard them.

Although the overall Operation Brest was carried out well by the Ghost Army troops, it backfired, causing great loss of life of American troops. This was not due to a failure of the Ghost Army, which had done its job exceptionally well. In actuality, it was the fault of the brass who did not coordinate its activities with other regular army units. The army had not detailed this major blunder in its official public records, perhaps because of embarrassment, but the men of the Twenty-third and others who were there, including Colonel Simenson, documented the disaster. It was also alluded to in classified documents.

The Twenty-third was to simulate the Fifteenth Tank Battalion, using phony artillery and phony tank fire, phony radio, insignia, and various other devices. The objective was to frighten the defenders of Brest into surrender. Unfortunately, the Allies had incorrectly estimated that the Brest Peninsula was occupied by only 16,000 ordinary German troops.

In actual fact, it was occupied by 38,000 troops, most of whom were highly trained, crack German paratroopers, with plenty of artillery and heavy machine guns, mortars, and ammo supplies. It was far more powerful and dangerous than American G-2 had discerned. However, it had few armored vehicles because of the relentless Allied air attacks. The Twenty-third, in conjunction with the real Sixty-ninth Tank Battalion, was to create such a show of force that the Germans would be demoralized and surrender, or at least be frozen in place.

Bill Blass, left, and Robert Tompkins take cover near Brest, France, on the Brittany Peninsula during the first weeks of the war. Photo courtesy Robert Tompkins.

Ghost Army troops look over a burned-out American Sherman tank. Photo courtesy Robert Tompkins.

As the war progressed, the Allies learned that it was not this easy, especially in a situation where there were SS troops intermingled with other troops.

A previously classified report paints the picture:

> The Twenty-third divided into three deceptive forces: X, Y and Z. The notional 15th Tank Battalion was played by X in the area of the 9th Regiment, Second Infantry Division. The notional 69th Tank Battalion was played by Z in the area of the 29th Infantry Division. Both X and Z had tank companies of the real 709th Tank Battalion to act as a nucleus for their notional tank battalions. The rest of the picture was filled in by dummies, spoof radio, special effects and sonic noises. The deception was superb, but unhappily X deceived the enemy into believing that the tanks were going to attack from exactly where they did. The the 9th Infantry Regiment later learned that the enemy, on orders from von Ramcke, installed from 20 to 50 *more* anti-tank guns after the X operation. When the VIII Corps finally attacked on 25 August, Company D, 709th Tank Battalion met very heavy resistance in front of the X area.

The VIII Corps suffered 9,831 casualties in this operation. The real attackers had not coordinated with the Twenty-third, perhaps because they did not even know it existed, and the VIII Corps rolled into what was, in effect, an American-induced ambush.

Basically, the Germans at Brest, seeing and hearing what they thought were Patton's armored divisions, concentrated a huge force in addition to the added anti-tank and artillery forces along one of the main roads on the German right, leading into the port city, where the Twenty-third was doing its play acting.

Later, without checking with the Twenty-third, the fresh group of American troops and armor—unaware of what the Ghost Army had been doing—blithely and naively decided to attack down the road where the Germans were expecting Patton's armor. It was an unmitigated disaster. This was the low point for the Ghost Army, although they could be comforted in knowing that they had not caused the casualties; a lack of communication among the brass was responsible.

"When I saw all the carnage, I said,`Did we cause this?'" Enderlein recalled. "It was horrible."

A classified Army report stated:

> The deception was superb but unhappily, [Ghost troops] deceived the enemy into believing that the tanks were going to attack from

exactly where they did. The G-2 of the 9th Infantry Regiment reported that the enemy installed from 20 to 50 more anti-tank guns after the [Ghost] operation. When VIII Corp finally attacked on 25 August, Co. D, 709th Tank Battalion met very heavy resistance from of the [Ghost demonstration] area prior to crossing the line of departure.

On the plus side, von Ramcke at least did not attempt to break out of Brest and perhaps the Twenty-third's Ghost Army had a lot to do with this.

The Army learned a major lesson from this tragedy: always keep in touch with and coordinate with the Twenty-third. This serious error—which has also been a secret for more than 50 years—was almost as bad as the bombing of American troops by American bombers near St. Lo about the same time, an error far more commonly known than the Brest fiasco. Deception experts later, in an ironic Army understatement, agreed that this was "poor use of deception."

"The biggest lesson learned," said Simenson, "was the lack of proper coordination with the Company D, 709th Tank Battalion. Unfortunately when the Company . . . attacked down the same corridor, it suffered severe losses. It should not have attacked in that place or otherwise the Twenty-third should have employed deception in another area."

But, Simenson added, "Deception troops replaced real troops used in the main effort. Operation Brest gave much confidence to the Twenty-third headquarters that we were on the right track for employment of tactical deception." But things would get better for the Ghost troops in each subsequent operation.

Eisenhower's report described Brest this way:

Middleton vigorously prosecuted the siege but the defenses were strong and the garrison was determined. Any attempt to capture the place in a single assault would be extremely costly to us. Fortunately, our prospects for securing better ports than Brest began to grow much brighter just after the middle of August, and in any event we had never counted on the use of that place so much as we had on Quiberon Bay. In these circumstances, Middleton was directed to avoid heavy losses in the Brest area but was also directed to continue the pressure until the garrison should surrender.

I visited him during the conduct of the siege and surveyed the defenses that we would have to overcome. He skillfully kept up a

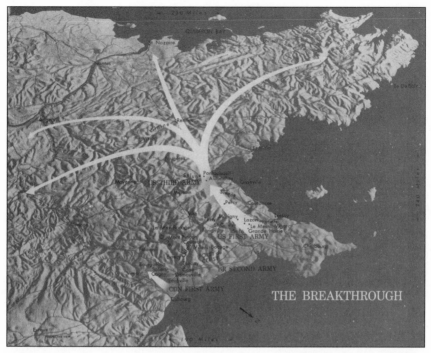

A U.S. Army map showing the overall operation of the Allied forces after the invasion of Normandy. This map shows the Brittany Peninsula and Brest operations, in which the Ghost Army was heavily involved.

series of attacks, each designed to minimize our losses but constantly to crowd the enemy back into a more restricted area, where he was intermittently subjected to bombing by our aircraft. In the garrison was a contingent of German SS troops. Instead of concentrating them as a unit, General Ramcke distributed them among all other German formations in the defenses. In this way, he used the fanaticism of the SS troopers to keep the entire garrison fighting desperately, because at any sign of weakening, an SS trooper would execute the offender on the spot.

Churchill had predicted to General Bradley that Brest "will die like flowers cut off at their stems." That may have been true had the Allies waited it out instead of continually attacking. It would have saved thousands of American lives.

A classified report about the Ghost Army stated after the Brest operation:

Operation Brest was notable for the Twenty-third's first employment of sonic and artillery flash deception. Five sonic half-tracks were
used by each of the two notional tank battalions. On the nights of
23, 24 and 25 August, within 500 yards of the enemy, they projected
the noises of tanks approaching, harboring, and withdrawing.
Friendly troops a mile away were firmly convinced that tanks were
assembling in their vicinity. The dummy flash batteries were located
600-800 yards in front of the 37th Field Artillery Battalion, 105
Howitzers. They were installed to draw off enemy counter-battery fire.
The phantom artillery operated for three nights (23-25 August) and
received some 20-25 rounds of enemy fire. The real battalion received
none up to the time the Twenty-third force was withdrawn.

Since World War II, military historians and military critics, officers, and many others have strongly criticized the entire Brest operation. They basically argue quite convincingly that the entire Brest
operation and its heavy casualties were unnecessary. Their argument
is that the Germans were pinned inside the peninsula city of Brest
and had no way out, neither by land nor sea, and could simply have
been held there for a few months until they were starved out.

This was a common procedure among Germans, whose military
term for this was "masking." Then again, masking could backfire, too,
as when the Germans decided to mask Bastogne and the Allies decided
to mask the Colmar Pocket, although the latter was more of a nui-
sance than a decisive factor in the war. Instead, the Allies continually
attacked this fortress with commensurate heavy loss of life. General
Bradley argued after the war that hindsight is wonderful, but at the
time he wanted Brest captured to prevent the fanatical Brest commander von Ramcke from breaking out and attacking the allied rear.

The role of the Ghost Army in the high casualties may fan the
controversy anew.

Bradley has argued that the siege of Brest has been "described by
some as a wasteful and unnecessary campaign, executed primarily
because of blind obedience to an outdated Overlord plan that called
for its capture." He said that it might be true that Overlord's need
for Brittany ports was made moot when the rapid Allied advance
uncovered the Channel ports and Antwerp. He said that the capture
of Antwerp, one of the largest and best ports in the world, caused the
cancellation of plans for the construction of a base on Quiberon Bay
and made Brest surplus. But no tonnage was to be delivered through
either port.

Why, Bradley wondered, did the Allies then spend three divisions on Brest at a cost of "almost 10,000 in American dead and wounded? Why not rope off Brest as we did Lorient and St. Nazaire—or as Montgomery did on the Channel ports?"

Bradley concluded that the difference was the kind of German resistance. The garrison at Brest was totally unlike those of the other ports. He noted that it had troops from from the crack Second Parachute Division, and was commanded by the fanatical von Ramcke, "too aggressive and fanatical a soldier to sit contentedly in that concrete pile." To have contained Ramcke, he felt, would have required more troops than the Allies could have spared.

But military critics responded to Bradley that he thought there were only 16,000 ordinary German troops in Brest when he made that decision, and that he did not learn about von Ramcke and the paratroops until much later. They also say that heavy allied bombing and a rapidly diminishing food supply in Brest—something learned from captured German troops on patrols outside of Brest— had left the place entirely too weak to break out. Perhaps the argument will never be resolved.

Military historians love "what ifs," such as what if Pickett had attacked earlier at Gettysburg, what if Stonewall Jackson had not been killed, what if the Confederates had continued on for 17 miles into Washington, D.C., after the victorious first Battle of Bull Run. The what ifs are endless and historians enjoy them even as seminary students enjoy discussing how many angels can dance on the head of a pin. The Brest operation is one of these what ifs. But historians must remember that Bradley and Eisenhower had decided even before the Normandy invasion that Brest must be taken, no matter how the course of the battles proceeded.

The Brest critics also argued that the resources devoted to Brest should have been used to strengthen an earlier breakout across France, using the Twelfth Army to better advantage. The argument was that this was a backwater of the war that did not deserve so many resources and so much effort.

To buttress this argument, it has been pointed out that the Army required 20,300 tons of ammunition for the final effort to conquer Brest. Eventually, Bradley found, many of the supplies destined for the eastward thrusts had to be ordered to make a U-turn and go to Brest. When Brest finally fell, General Middleton had 25,000 tons of ammunition ready to expend in the effort. Declassification of the Ghost Army's role puts the whole matter in a different light.

It is clear now that this was part of the thinking of the Allied leaders: to use the Twenty-third to help bottle up the Germans without using as much manpower. This was information that Bradley could not use in his arguments at the time he wrote his postwar memoir because of secrecy still in force.

Some say Bradley, smarting because of the heavy loss of American lives at Brest, may have indulged in a bit of revisionist military history to save face. Some may even conclude the tight lid of secrecy placed on the Ghost Army so many decades after the war may have even been due to the Army's embarrassment over the loss of life among the 709th Tank Battalion.

It was during this peninsula campaign that Colonel Simenson said he first heard the eerie sound of incoming artillery. "I dove for a foxhole. I got covered with debris and junk. Every time I moved, it hurt."

Simenson said he was sure that hundreds of points of pain he felt all over his body were places where shrapnel had entered. But "gradually I realized that I was in a foxhole with a rose bush. When I got up, I could see that the shells had blown off the tile roofs of the buildings, scattering everything all around. Luckily Bernie McKeon, my jeep driver, was also safe."

This operation also was notable for the Twenty-third's learning experience in its most thorough use of sonic and artillery flash deceptions since D-Day. Five sonic half-tracks were used by each of the two notional tank battalions. On the nights of August 23, 24, and 25, within 500 yards of the enemy, they projected the noises of tanks approaching, harboring, and withdrawing.

An Army report said of this operation: "Friendly troops a mile away were firmly convinced that tanks were assembling in their vicinity." But the best compliment of all came after the fall of Brest when Ramcke said he had held out pretty well against "three infantry divisions and one armored division." This proved he had fallen for the Twenty-third's elaborate act.

Fortunately for members of the Ghost Army, the Germans—at least in the beginning—had a very low opinion of American troops. By the end of the war, however, many German leaders had drastically revised this view. In fact, respected German Gen. August Wellm said after his strongly fortified defensive position was overrun at Falkenberg Stellung that the Americans advanced relentlessly through the heaviest fire "with their weapons at the ready and cigarettes dangling from their lips." He had high praise for their stubborn bravery.

But the Germans did not think Americans were very clever or imaginative enough to dupe them. In fact, after the war it was learned by interviewing POWs and examining German records that they thought Americans were too stupid to encode their battle radio traffic. In fact, much of the battle radio traffic they thought they heard was produced by the Ghost Army just to confuse or mislead the Germans. And even some of the coded messages were put in a childishly simple code called "Slidex" that American intelligence *knew* the Germans already had deciphered. In fact, the Ghost Army was counting on it.

The Brest operation also was recorded by Tompkins, who kept a small pocket diary. The full diary is reprinted in Chapter Eleven, and captures much of the flavor of the Brest operation.

Pvt. Lonnie Gault, an eighteen-year-old from Clinton, Iowa, also kept a memoir of his Ghost Army service. Most of his pocket diaries concerned his day-to-day life in the Army, but his observations got interesting when he arrived in Normandy within a couple of weeks after D-Day. His full memoir comprises Chapter Thirteen of this narrative.

The exploits and very existence of the Ghost Army were never mentioned in any public army records. The Ghost Army was not cited by General Eisenhower in his book *Crusade in Europe* or anywhere in official records. British Prime Minister Winston Churchill knew all about it, but he, too, kept it secret, even in postwar years.

Once in his writing, however, Churchill said, "It wouldn't do, even now," to detail the secret techniques of deception used by the Allies. Routine listings of battalions and regiments usually left out mention of the Twenty-third.

It was kept secret because America's military planners thought that the secret techniques might be used again in future wars. Even during the war, most all of its orders were verbal, with just one exception—the Rhine River crossing at Viersen—as a means of aiding secrecy. Medals were withheld because the Army feared that newsmen would question the recipients about what they did to earn the medals and disclose secrets of the Ghost Army.

Capt. George Rebh

George Rebh, a young captain just twenty-two years old and only two years out of West Point, was asked in 1944 to play the part of a regimental commander in one of the Ghost Army's many operations. Not only did all of the jeep and vehicle markings have to be realistic, the personnel had to be realistic as well. So a command post was set up and "Colonel" Rebh was supplied with the proper uniform complete with the requisite eagles.

It just so happened that several of Rebh's West Point classmates dropped by the fake command post, not knowing of the Twenty-third's special mission. When they walked in and found that their old pal from West Point had suddenly been elevated to regimental commander, they were flabbergasted. They showed him due deference and respect, as good West Pointers would, but some of them—when they left his office—asked how it had happened so quickly.

One of them, Rebh recalled, asked a sergeant outside the command post: "What the hell happened with Rebh? How did he become a regimental commander?" The sergeant smiled and said, "You know how it is: the fortunes of war—and being in the right place at the right time." But Rebh's former classmates walked away shaking their heads in wonder, and perhaps with more than a tinge of jealousy.

In many ways, George Rebh was a perfect choice for the Ghost Army. Until this day he does not know who chose him or how the various other choices were made for anyone in the Twenty-third. In fact, no survivor of the Ghost Army knows how the choices were made. Rebh and Colonel Simenson, who are good friends today and stay in constant touch, said all that they knew was that it was a mysterious process by someone far up the chain of command, and that in retrospect and with the advantage of time the choices turned out to be excellent ones.

Rebh, at just five feet seven inches tall, was a star athlete at his high school in Dearborn, Michigan, near Detroit. He was such a good basketball player, shooting ambidextrously with equal skill, that he was offered a full athletic scholarship to the University of Michigan. A guard, Rebh was also noted for his quickness and incredible energy. The valedictorian of his high school graduating class and class president, Rebh was about to accept this scholarship when one of the local political leaders in the Detroit area suggested that he could get Rebh an appointment to West Point.

The idea of a military career appealed to Rebh and the machinery was set in motion. He got the appointment, and entered the U.S.

Military Academy in 1939. He graduated twelfth in his class, and despite his rigorous academic schedule, he was captain of the Army basketball team and a member of the baseball team. He was commissioned in the Corps of Engineers upon graduation.

From 1943 to 1944 Rebh was platoon leader and company commander of the 293rd Engineer Combat Battalion at Camp Gordon, Georgia, and the Yuma Maneuver Area in California. One day while in California, he was taken aside and informed that he had been selected for an elite unit that would begin training in Camp Forrest, Tennessee.

It was so secret that his superiors did not know its purpose, but they assured him that he could view it as an honor to be chosen. Rebh would not learn the details about the mission of the Twenty-third until he arrived at Camp Forrest and was briefed. He was informed of the deceptive unit and told that his primary task would be as company commander of the 406th Engineer Combat Company, with a primary mission of providing combat protection for the Twenty-third as well as participating in various operations of deception.

His company differed from most in that it was given a number of extra .50-caliber machine guns and a number of extra half-tracks and trucks, which were to be used for making tracks in and out of camouflage nets for the benefit of German aerial reconnaissance.

Rebh's company, unlike many, did not go to Pine Camp, but shipped directly to England on the troopship *Gibbons*. His men did not join the entire Twenty-third until it arrived at Walton Hall, where Rebh camped on the grounds of the manor house along with his men. When they were not training, he visited Leamington Spa, and soon he began dating a few English women. But Rebh said he knew the Twenty-third would not be in England long when he began seeing huge numbers of bombers and, finally, hundreds of gliders with blue and red lights headed for Normandy on D-Day. Within the month, he and his men would be in Normandy as well.

En route to Brest, one of his most vivid memories involved a number of Sherman tanks knocked out by the Germans. Rebh said the American tanks had taken up positions in heavy fog unaware that they were near German anti-tank units, and when the fog lifted the American tanks were like sitting ducks. All were hit and burned out, the scorched and twisted steel carcasses giving Rebh an early taste of the battles ahead.

When he arrived with the company at Brest, he recalled the B-17s flying over during a relentless bombing campaign. "We could see the bomb bay doors open up and the bombs falling out. And at night the RAF bombers would come over and they also dropped flares."

It was here that he and his men ran into the famous hedgerows, which were more like groves of thick trees on mounds up to three feet higher than the surrounding terrain. The hedgerows were so thick that they could stop a tank or—worse—cause it to crawl up and expose its vulnerable belly to the fire of German 88mm artillery.

Although the 88 was designed as an anti-aircraft weapon, the Germans quickly learned that it could be a devastating anti-tank weapon when fired horizontally. It had a peculiar sound described as a loud "CHOK!" This soon became the most feared sound in Normandy, even more feared than the German machine guns, which were distinguishable because they had a much higher rate of fire than any American machine gun. The American machine guns, said veterans of the Twenty-third, sounded more like pop-pop-pop-pop-pop-pop-pop, while the German machine guns had such a high rate of fire that the individual pops blended into a loud Brrrrrrppppppppppp-Brrrrrrppppppp.

Because the West Pointers were an unofficial fraternity in many ways, Colonel Simenson took an immediate liking to Rebh and kept him informed on a daily basis as to plans for the Twenty-third. Rebh said one of the most dangerous aspects of this early fighting in Normandy, as stated by others, was the virtual rain of American shrapnel fired at German aircraft. "I found a piece of plywood and put it over my foxhole as protection," he recalled.

Rebh said he was startled by all of the destroyed American tanks, trucks, and other vehicles and all of the dead cattle, horses, and even the dead Germans still all over the landscape in the Normandy area.

He said a big part of the Brest operation was the erection of many camouflage nets to create the appearance of a large pool of American armor poised to attack the besieged city.

"I had real good officers and real good NCOs," said Rebh. The men became so close that after the war Rebh helped arrange a big party for the group in New York City. Many still stay in touch today.

After the Brest operation, Rebh and his men were ordered to Versailles. He said one of the most startling things there was the hair coloring of the beautiful women in the area. He said that was the first time in his life he had seen women dye their hair such colors as

A Ghost Army half-track laden with secret sound equipment. This photo was taken near the Maginot Line on Christmas Eve in 1944.

lavender, bright red, and other unnatural hues. But, he said, they were very pretty despite the exotic colors.

In the early weeks after the Normandy invasion, the Ghost Army often ran into opposition or received lukewarm cooperation from higher officers who were not well acquainted—by design—with its mission or even its existence. Some in the early days considered it a mere bother and perhaps an obstacle. But opinions changed quickly as the invasion progressed and the brass saw what it could accomplish. There is strong evidence that even General Patton did not know of it until several months into the war, as will be illustrated later in this narrative.

"We went to the division commander," said Simenson, "who remarked that he had never heard of such a thing. I explained that it would not hurt them and that it might help them, and that we would not interfere with any of their units. It was agreed to hold the information to four, namely the Division Commander, the Assistant Division Commander, the Chief of Staff and the G-3."

Simenson recalled that one of the valuable lessons learned in this first operation was that the area around all of the front-line operations was usually aswarm with enemy agents, requiring great care during daylight hours. It was also determined that liaison officers with the real units represented could smooth out things greatly.

A 1999 photo of Dick Syracuse, who now lives in New Rochelle, New York.

Chapter Five

A Ghost Named Syracuse

One of the men who became a legend in the Ghost Army was Lt. Dick Syracuse of the Bronx, New York. He came to the Ghost Army, one might say, uniquely and obliquely. Syracuse laughed as he recalled that he was playing cards with his buddies at Dugway Proving Ground, a military base in Utah, when a certain obnoxious major walked up to the card table and seated himself, uninvited. Syracuse, then 24, and the major had been dating the same nurse. The jealous major made no secret of the fact that he intensely disliked the tall and darkly handsome Syracuse. The major was spoiling for a fight and began insulting Syracuse.

Syracuse silently endured the baiting. A small group of soldiers watched as Syracuse—a big man over 6 feet and 200-plus pounds who, some said, looked and talked in a manner reminiscent of Rocky Marciano—smiled and continued to endure the major's vitriolic acrimony. The major was also a big, tough man.

Finally, the major went too far, but Syracuse knew he would be in for a court martial and maybe even a reduction in rank if he threw the first punch at a superior officer. So, when he was sure no one would notice, Syracuse sharply kicked the major in the shins under the table. The major lunged for him. To all present, it looked as if the major started the fight. Fists flew as Syracuse gave him a very sound beating—all apparently in self-defense.

The next day, Syracuse's executive officer, a lieutenant colonel, called him in and told him that had he not been attacked first, he would be in serious trouble. But he said he planned to take advantage of Syracuse's degree in chemistry and high IQ, and would send him to a special, top-secret unit at Pine Camp. He said he could not, under orders, tell him any more than that. Actually, it is doubtful if the lieutenant colonel himself knew any more than that. So he ordered Syracuse transferred to the Twenty-third at Pine Camp.

What Syracuse didn't know until later was that he was probably destined for this unit anyway because of his scholastic profile and high intelligence. The fight with the major perhaps accelerated the transfer.

En route to Pine Camp, Syracuse was ordered to escort a tanker train full of poisonous mustard gas to Edgewood Arsenal in Maryland. He was to stay in the caboose, where he was constantly coated with soot, during the long and slow journey. He said that may have been the low point in his military career. "I was filthy by the time we got there," he recalled. He then cleaned up well and took a train north to the upstate New York base.

He had no idea what he would be doing. His assignment could have been anything from a line combat unit to a backwater detail of boredom and unpleasantness. He was told to report to a Col. Hilton H. Railey, who would be expecting him. He was apprehensive when he walked into the colonel's office. He found a tall, handsome man with rimless glasses, a man who looked to be a combination of scholar and adventurer. Railey smiled warmly as Syracuse reported for duty.

As Syracuse reported to Railey, at Pine Camp, Railey looked him up and down and told him, "Son, the mission of this unit is to draw enemy fire. How do you feel about that?"

"Well, fine, sir, if we're allowed to give 'em hell in return."

Railey laughed at the young man's tough attitude, put his arm on his shoulder and said, "Lieutenant, I think I'm going to like you. Let's go have a drink and I'll tell you all about it."

Syracuse laughed as he recalled that about a year later in Belgium, military police guards, worried about Germans dressed as GIs, detained Colonel Railey in a battle area because he didn't know the password. They had never seen him before despite his protestations that he was a key part of the Twenty-third Special Troops. Germans dressed as American GIs were then causing havoc behind American lines.

At that moment, the group approached Lieutenant Syracuse, well known by the guards, and the guards asked him if he knew this self-proclaimed Colonel Railey. They explained that although he said he was with the Twenty-third, he did not know the password. They were very suspicious. After all, Railey did have a Germanic look, with his rimless glasses and light brown hair.

Without cracking a smile or blinking an eye, Syracuse said, "No. He looks like a Kraut to me." He quickly admitted he was joking. Railey enjoyed the joke—but only after the initial shock. Germans in American uniforms were routinely shot.

Shortly after the Brest campaign, Lieutenant Syracuse advanced ahead of his truck convoy into a small Belgian town. He saw a barber shop sign and decided to stop for a haircut, a luxury he had not had for many weeks. He went in, and to his amazement found that it was actually a brothel, with several gorgeous young French women inside and no customers. To his utter disbelief, the building also somehow still had power and running water, unlike most of the other shell-battered dwellings.

"I really think it was the only one in the area with running water and electricity," he said.

Syracuse decided to make his temporary camp there. It was almost a scene from a movie: Grimey, unshaven Syracuse decided to take a relaxing sudsy bath, along with several of the pliant demimondes, when a passing officer, Maj. Charles Williams of Warsaw, Indiana, saw Syracuse's Fourth Platoon convoy stopped outside. When Williams asked what was going on, the men told him Syracuse was inside getting a haircut, which is what they actually believed.

The major went in and found Syracuse in a Roman idyl, surrounded by caressing women, smoking a cigar. At first he was angry or pretended to be, but then the major threw back his head and laughed heartily. The scene was too much, even for him. "You rotten S.O.B., Syracuse," Williams told him. "Somehow you always get the cushy setups."

He then decided to set up his base camp in the same area and enjoy himself. Their war stopped—at least for a day or two. Syracuse and the major became good friends.

Syracuse, who was in charge of setting up machine guns and other perimeter security for the Ghost Army, was a tough and capable soldier. His men called him the "Hubba Hubba Jab" man because he always insisted that they show that they had heard his orders by responding with a jab gesture. And "Hubba Hubba" was a popular refrain of the time, as popular as the graffiti: "Kilroy was here."

They respected Syracuse and liked him, by all accounts, and one episode will help explain why. One of the Ghost Army troopers, Sgt. Hypolite Briard, had been sent back to Britain on emergency leave, but when he returned to the war zone to rejoin the Ghost troops, he found to his dismay that he had to go to a redeployment staging camp. Because there were so many casualties, Briard learned that Eisenhower had ordered a new policy of replacing the dead and wounded soldiers with the first men to show up, regardless of what outfit they belonged to. Combat units in need would get the men right away.

Surely, Briard thought, this would not mean specially trained units would also have to sacrifice their men to front-line units. But the officers at the redeployment center just laughed when he tried to explain his special duties. They told him they had heard every kind of excuse imaginable.

Briard was given a Garand rifle and told he would soon be in a front-line rifle platoon. He managed to get word to the Twenty-third, Syracuse in particular, but he felt his chances of getting out of the front-line meat-grinder were slim to none. It was a time when casualties were so high that Eisenhower also allowed any soldier serving time in the brig to have the time eliminated in return for serving in a front-line combat unit. Briard was like part of the Ghost Army family, very popular with the rest of the men.

The Twenty-third, after all, was about the size of a high school, not huge and impersonal as such outfits as the Third Army or the Twelfth Army. Everyone knew each other. When word got back to the Twenty-third that one of their favorite sergeants would wind up in a front-line unit, it swept through the whole outfit. They learned that, unfortunately, the new policy did not take into account unique skills required for special units like the Ghost Army. Briard had tried repeatedly to explain that he had special skills that were needed by the Twenty-third Headquarters Special Troops, and finally even played the top-secret unit card, against orders.

"Yeah, sure," they said. They laughed at him. For one thing, they had never heard of his unit.

Until this writing, most World War II vets have never heard of the Twenty-third, whose troops referred to themselves as the Ghost Army. So the redeployment officers thought Briard was just trying to avoid combat, possibly even fabricating the entire story. There were no written records of any such Twenty-third Headquarters Special Troops.

Although the redeployment depots like the one that almost reassigned Briard were bad for morale, in *Crusade in Europe* Eisenhower explained their necessity this way:

Replacements, whether newly arrived from the homeland or recently discharged from hospitals, are normally processed to the front through replacement depots. Thus there is a great intermingling of veterans from numerous divisions and of others who have not seen action. When the need for replacements is acute, efficiency demands that all men available in depots be dispatched promptly to the place where most needed. Individual assignment according to personal preference is well-nigh impossible.

When Lieutenant Syracuse learned of the problem, he and a sergeant hopped in a jeep and drove almost 200 miles to the recycling bivouac to try to get the young soldier back in the Twenty-third.

"I just bluffed 'em," said Syracuse.

I told them that I had orders to pick him up and bring him back, that he had special skills we couldn't do without. A colonel asked me for the orders and I pretended to have forgotten them. I offered to drive 200 miles back and get them. Then I explained about the Ghost Army and its secret mission. The bluff worked. He said never mind all that—go get him, and we picked up our buddy and brought him back. Boy was he glad to be home with us. And we were glad to get him back. He was a great kid.

Despite this, it is now clear because of studies of fighting ability of troops that men fight best when with others they know and consider a kind of surrogate family. It is doubtful that the efficiency could make up for the demoralized lack of fighting ability such impersonal redeployment depots would cause.

It was shortly after the Brest campaign, when the outfit moved to Luxembourg near the French border, that the Ghost Army was almost found out by two French bicyclists, recalled Bob Tompkins. It happened on a cold September morning in 1944, when two cyclists in a small French town near the Luxembourg border decided to ride out into the countryside.

The nighttime rumble of tanks had stopped. Americans were in control, and sometimes gave chocolate to local civilians. So they cycled on the road that passed the bivouac. They saw the usual scattering of mud-stained vehicles, partly hidden under camouflage nets, a couple of trucks, some trailers, and a few Sherman tanks with their big guns protruding from the trees and camoflage nets.

Then a young Ghost Army sentry stopped the pair. He was friendly but firm: they must explain why and where they were going. The Frenchmen suddenly stopped talking, their eyes bulging with astonishment. Over the sentry's shoulder they saw four GIs in muddy uniforms and the usual olive drab steel helmets walk over to a monstrous tank and pick it up, turn it around, and set it down again. Thus the cover of the Ghost Army was almost blown. But no damage was done, although the cyclists were held for a time to be sure they were not German spies, as were many of the Vichy French.

During one strafing run by a German ME-109, men of the Twenty-third Ghost Army dived under their rubber, inflated vehicles, recalled Art Shilstone. Afterward, they all had a good laugh as they realized this afforded no protection whatsoever. Some of the vehicles had, in fact, been riddled with bullets, the air hissing out as they slowly deflated. Fortunately, the German pilots had left. The rubber dummies were quickly patched up and reinflated during the night. But the Ghost troops comforted themselves with the knowledge that their actions may have lent authenticity to the setup for the German pilot. Some of the men also mocked General Eisenhower's message to them that if they saw any aircraft, they would probably be Allied planes.

Shilstone said one lieutenant in the Twenty-third was petrified of the razor-sharp shrapnel from American guns that would rain down after anti-aircraft fire at overflying German aircraft. He was so scared of this stuff, said Shilstone, that he would not only dig a deep foxhole, but make an L-shaped underground extension to make it even safer.

The shrapnel was indeed dangerous, and one major almost had an arm and shoulder lopped off when he was hit with a piece of it. But the lieutenant's fear of it seemed excessive to the rest of the men. Pvt. Ed Briow said most of it was razor sharp and sometimes weighed up to half a pound or more and could easily kill a man if it hit him right. But the lieutenant's fear seemed all out of proportion.

Because of this, the men decided to play a joke on him. They had been gathering the shrapnel for days, putting it in a bucket, without the lieutenant's knowledge. Soon they had a full bucket. Then one night when a German recon plane flew over and the lieutenant, as usual, burrowed into his elaborate foxhole during the loud and thunderous anti-aircraft response, the men spread the shrapnel all around the edges and in the foxhole.

Later, after the shooting had subsided, the lieutenant crawled out. He saw all the shrapnel surrounding his foxhole and became nearly hysterical.

"See! See all of this shrapnel! You guys are always kidding me—well, just look at all of this. It's everywhere. Just look at it."

The men just laughed. Soon it became apparent to him that it was all a joke and the men all laughed even more. His behavior was even more disgusting, said Shilstone, because back in the States during training this lieutenant was a swaggering, tough-guy type.

Enderlein recalled an evening when he and a buddy, Roy Oxenrider, set up a string of small bombs that could be detonated one at a time by remote wire. They were designed to simulate artillery from an American 155mm howitzer. The two had placed them along a roadside near the front near Metz, France, near the Moselle River. This was a standard part of the Ghost Army operations. Enderlein and Oxenrider had paused for a smoke, well hidden from the nearby German lines, when they saw an American platoon newly arrived at the front. The men were walking smartly in cadence down the road in uniforms with creases still in their pants.

They were obviously green troops and looked as if they were fresh from back home. One tell-tale sign: Not one of them had a beard, unlike most all of the grizzled combat vets with the Twenty-third. Also, they were squeaky clean and looked well fed. Oxenrider and Enderlein couldn't resist. They remotely detonated a couple of the small bombs—not near the green troops but about 50 yards away. The men hit the dirt and began wildly firing in all directions, cursing, yelling, and generally panicking.

"I've often wondered why we did such a thing," mused Enderlein, "but then again, I also have wondered what these men said when they related the first time they were under fire by German 88s. Our canister bombs *did* sound more like German 88s than our own artillery."

On one occasion, the Twenty-third had gone for days living off K- and C-rations. Finally, a rare treat arrived: a couple of mess trucks. In order to help morale, the Army tried to occasionally give the men an exceptionally delicious hot meal, especially those near or at the front. The men were served pork chops or steak, mashed potatoes, green beans, and a fruit cocktail dessert. They were just sitting down to this marvelous repast when some GIs showed up with a few captured German soldiers, recalls Art Shilstone, now living in Connecticut, and Ed Biow, now living in Lake Oswego, Oregon.

The Germans hadn't eaten in two days and stared, mesmerized, at the delicious food They seemed most interested in the pork chops on some plates. So the GIs—not yet as embittered toward the

Germans as they would soon become—reluctantly decided to give them each a plate. As the German troops ate, they looked at each other in disbelief at the quality of the food and shook their heads.

One said, in broken English, "We'll never win this war. Not when your front-line troops eat like this." Everyone laughed—but no one told them the truth.

Ed Biow said that three times during the war his 2½-ton truck—the men called it a "deuce and a half"—was almost hit by the dreaded German 88 artillery fire. In each instance, he said, it just seemed to be a strange quirk of fate that he survived. Once a lieutenant warned him that he had just driven into an area zeroed in by Germans artillery. Biow said he should have noticed that the village he had just driven into seemed eerily quiet, with dead livestock scattered about on the streets and the smell of cordite hanging in the air. He quickly did a U-turn after profane urging by the lieutenant, and seconds later German artillery exploded, digging a huge hole where his truck had been.

"I jammed the accelerator pedal down trying to get the hell out of there, but the damned truck had a governor that kept the top speed at forty miles an hour. I felt like I was crawling."

On another occasion, the Germans had zeroed in on an intersection and were waiting for an American vehicle to pass through it. Biow said he slammed on the brakes seconds before reaching the intersection to take a photograph of a French road sign as a souvenir. It saved his life. The Germans poured artillery fire into the intersection, not dreaming he would suddenly stop. Another time, Biow and other Ghost troops had just left a bivouac when the Germans destroyed the area with artillery.

One of the saddest occasions, said Biow, came when he tried in vain to flag down a jeep but the troops in the jeep ignored him and plunged into a zeroed-in intersection and were killed by artillery fire. Even today, he said, he often thinks back on that incident and wonders what he could have done differently to stop the jeep. Perhaps, he says, he should have sideswiped it with his truck.

With each operation, the men of the Twenty-third became more proficient and effective. They were so good within a few months that many of their fellow troops—not in the Ghost Army—were fooled. The Army deliberately made no effort to inform adjacent troops about the Twenty-third. It was all part of the "need to know" practice of security in effect during the war.

Syracuse recalled that a major from another unit once drove up in a jeep, stopping dramatically in a cloud of dust. He was the kind of guy, recalled Syracuse, "who apparently had a Rambo self-image—of course, that was long before Rambo, but you know what I mean." His field jacket was festooned with grenades in the style made famous by Gen. Matthew Ridgeway. He carried a Thompson sub-machine gun. He affected a dramatic persona. He and his driver walked into the Twenty-third encampment, and he approached Syracuse with a theatrical flourish.

"Lieutenant, where are your tanks?"

"We don't have any, sir."

He uttered a few choice curses and added, "I heard them last night, lieutenant. I think I know what a tank sounds like. The sound was coming from right over there."

At that point, given his lower rank, Syracuse explained the mission of the Twenty-third and told him a bit about how it functioned.

"Well, you certainly fooled me, lieutenant."

"That was not our intention, sir," said Syracuse with a big grin.

Syracuse was an expert poker player. He was so good, he tried to play with men in other units during calm times in the war because he did not want to take money from people in the Ghost Army—his surrogate family. Before the war ended in Europe, he was to amass $30,000 in poker winnings. Men who thought there was a good chance of not coming home were reckless with their money, but not Syracuse. Others may have treated it like Monopoly money, but he kept adding to his nest egg steadily.

Army regulations required that such substantial sums not be kept in combat areas, so he placed it on deposit with a finance unit, a field office that stayed far behind the front lines. Some of the men in this unit kept eying Syracuse's growing bankroll and conspired to fig-ure a way to keep it. It was a rather unofficial bank. They hoped he would either be abruptly transferred or fall to some mishap. This was to cause a dramatic confrontation later. But the men in the finance section did not fully understand the nature of the man with whom they were dealing and the toughness of his character. But more on this later in proper chronology.

A Ghost trooper with fond memories of the Ghost Army and Lieutenant Syracuse is Grant Hess, who often tries to explain to his children and grandchildren what he did during the war. He was a communications expert, yet he sometimes finds it difficult to fully convey to his children the nature of the work he did with the Ghost Army.

Hess said, with very frank honesty, that he joined the Army not only because of his patriotism but because his father was on the Buffalo, New York, draft board and it would have been unseemly not to join. He was sent to Camp Croft in Spartanburg, South Carolina, and then to the Army Special Training Program, where his high scores brought him to the attention of his superiors. Recalls Hess:

> They sent me to Statesboro, Georgia. And from there they sent me to the Signal Corps Camp in Monmouth, New Jersey. I missed my buddies from Spartanburg. They were a regular combat infantry unit. Then I applied for OCS in the Signal Corps. Because I had radio knowledge, they sent me to Pine Camp. We were fenced in there and secrecy was strictly enforced. I served under Colonel Railey, a very affable, likeable fellow. We trained up there that winter near Watertown, and then we finally got overseas.
>
> Maj. Charles Williams, who was head of our outfit, was a really good guy. So was Dick Syracuse, the Fourth platoon leader. And Lieutenant Davis, who was my platoon leader. In Watertown, they told us to go into the local Army-Navy store and buy a whole lot of different patches not long before we shipped out. I remember I was wearing a Fourth Armored patch. We never did wear anything but patches of other units.

Hess, now 79 and living with his wife in Scottsdale, Arizona, did well in electronics, and was chosen for the 3132nd Signal Service Company, a key segment of the Ghost Army. He says:

> I remember stringing wire through a field full of dead cows in plain sight of the Germans. I was in such a hurry that instead of the usual good connection and splice, I just stripped the wire a little and tied a square knot in it. You didn't want to linger in plain view of the Germans very long.
>
> We were in the New York City area, before we shipped out, and had got there at night. The ship left during the night and it was the first time I was ever on the ocean. I'm originally from Buffalo, New York, the "City of Good Neighbors." We landed in Glasgow, Scotland, about two weeks later. Good thing we had candy bars because we missed a regular meal or so after we first got there and had to have them to live on. Those things happened now and then in the Army.
>
> When we went over, each of us got a free carton of Mint Julep

cigarettes—a terrible, nasty cigarette—they really were awful—and this guy bought all of them from the rest of us for 25 cents a carton. Then he sold the Mint Juleps through the fence to the Scots, who were hungry for American cigarettes. But they were so terrible that the Scots came back mad as hell but couldn't get in past the fence. They wanted their money back. I didn't blame them.

I was at Walton Hall last year with my wife. I showed her where we stayed before we went to Normandy. We used to ride bikes from Walton Hall to town. Now it's a time-share vacation place. We did more of our training there, and then from there we got down on the channel and went over in a landing craft.

If I had shipped with the guys in my first training camp I would have been making amphibious beach landings in the Pacific. Because I learned telephone and radio mechanics, I set up communications for our company with my platoon sergeant, Clifford O'Brien. We used telephone wiring instead of radio to control the operation of half-tracks for security reasons. O'Brien and I ran the wire to the observation post, command post, and the half-track broadcast deployment places during the day so when the units were deployed at night under cover of darkness the communications for each were already in place for a quick hook up.

Telephone communications worked well whenever we operated. The half-tracks had radios but we only used the half-tracks to play the wire-recorded sound of tanks and other sound effects.

Hess recalled that the Ghost Army parked all of its special equipment behind the former girls' school in Luxembourg, where they were billeted in Luxembourg City under heavy 24-hour guard. He said the people in the town were very curious about what kind of equipment it was and somehow the rumor began that it was perhaps special equipment designed to stop German V-1 rockets at Penemunde.

When our company was housed in a school in Luxembourg City, we got to know the owner and two or three of the regular Luxembourg customers in a tavern not far away. One of them was a large, fat and friendly butcher. We of course never talked about our outfit and the secret work we did. But one day when I had my half-track out for a test drive, the butcher spotted us and came running to jump on the running board. I'm sure he was trying to get a look inside. Our half-tracks were always kept closed up and covered to conceal the wire player, speakers, and generators. I gunned it when I saw him to keep him from getting a look inside.

I am pretty sure that those men in the tavern were informers for the Germans because one night the school building was shelled by long-range German artillery. The shells did not hit our school building or the vehicles parked in the area behind, but they pretty much did circle the school building area. It was too accurate to be an accident.

About a week later on an overcast afternoon while I was outside working in the school yard on some equipment, a V-1 buzz bomb flew directly over the building. It kept going for a few minutes and then paused and came down, making a huge explosion. It hit somewhere out in a field and did no damage in the city. After those two incidents, we figured that the Luxembourgians were more sympathetic to the Germans so we stopped hanging out in that tavern. It looked like the people of Luxembourg had three flags—theirs, Germany's, and ours, and they were ready to fly each at the appropriate time.

I also recall another incident when four of us were broadcasting to the German positions on the Siegried Line. Our technical guys installed a speaker, amplifier, microphone and generator in the back of a three-quarter-ton truck. It was good for voice transmission over a distance. Because I was familiar with that type of equipment, we—the four of us—would drive up to the lines and park it on a hilltop facing the German line. We had a man—some loud military type who spoke German—and we would crank it up.

He would try to talk to the German troops, telling them if they deserted to the American lines they would be treated well, and would be safe and well fed. Each time he would say we would be back tomorrow to talk some more. The first time, nothing happened. The next day the Eighty-third troops captured a German bazooka team in the woods of the edge of the place where we usually went. They were sent there to knock out our truck. Were lucky that they had been spotted and captured.

On the third day, after we had the truck in position on the hill, the Germans fired two artillery shells at it. One hit behind, one hit in front, bracketing it. The third shell never came because one of our L-4 artillery spotter planes came over and I guess the Germans didn't want to expose their gun location. I have to tell you, however, that, in a strange way, I would liked to have seen that third shell just to see if they could hit our truck. We were some distance away, using a long cord.

I can't tell you if we talked any Germans into surrendering. We were told that the Germans had men in uniform who weren't too keen about fighting for them. At any rate, just one man in the Eighty-third Division caught some shrapnel from the first shell, which we felt bad about because that area had been very quiet until we showed up with our loud speaker.

One time they sent us up to St. Malo where the Germans were on an island—a fortress island. They sent us there to try to talk the Germans into surrendering, using our big broadcast equipment. I later saw a whole line of [British] Lancaster bombers hit the place. Later on, when they finally surrendered the island, I went out to the place. It was elaborately tunneled and had big guns on it. I went out to look for souvenirs. I found two Mauser rifles. I kept one and gave one to a friend. I also found a Walther P-38 pistol with the Nazi markings on it. I guess it's worth about $750 today. I finally found a regulation holster for it. It's still in beautiful condition.

Hess said one of his most pleasant memories during the time was near Paris, when he was staying in a former French barracks. He said the women were beautiful. He recalled when the cooks were boycotted and forced to leave because the rumor was that one or two of them had contracted a venereal disease from some of the French prostitutes.

"We complained to Major Williams and he made the cooks get medically checked out or leave," he said.

Chapter Six

A Ghost Named Arnett

Walter Arnett and his wife, Leila, had attended church on Sunday, December 7, 1941, then had lunch. They were about to have a nap on this sleepy afternoon when the orchestral music they were listening to on the radio was interrupted by a special bulletin. The announcer said Pearl Harbor in Hawaii had been bombed by wave after wave of Japanese airplanes and that several ships had been hit, resulting in many casualties.

On the following Monday, they sat near the radio and listened as President Roosevelt addressed the Congress, reading the famous words:

> Yesterday, December seventh, nineteen forty-one—a date which will live in infamy—the United States of America was suddenly and deliberately attacked by naval and air forces of the Empire of Japan. No matter how long it may take us to overcome this premeditated invasion, the American people—in their righteous might—will win through to absolute victory.

Overnight, a nation of pacifists had become an angry nation of warriors, a hornet's nest of fierce patriotism. Arnett was no exception. The sleeping giant America was at last awake. Churchill's description of America as a boiler slow to start but powerful and unstoppable once it got going was now fired up. The boiler was lit and cooking. And Walter Arnett was ready to serve his country.

Arnett, despite being happily and contentedly married, was so righteously indignant that—like many Americans—he decided to enlist. Because he was a good artist, cartoonist, and sign painter, he hoped somehow he could use his talents in the war effort, perhaps in camouflage. Luckily, he read in a newspaper an article about the 603rd Camouflage Battalion, which was to become an integral part of the Ghost Army. After assurances from recruiters that he could join the 603rd, he walked to the Custom House in Nashville and joined in October 1942. On the bus, one guy said, "Hey, some guy back here joined up in camouflage."

"What kind of outfit is that?" another fellow asked.

"Well, I think he is going to herd camels over in the Sahara Desert."

The recruits got a good laugh, along with Arnett, but he did wonder where he would wind up.

Arnett's luck in being able to select a special unit to join was different from the experience of fellow cartoonist and war buddy Richard Morton. Morton, eight years younger than Arnett, was from Dallas, Texas, and had grown up in Oklahoma City, where he attended Classen High School. Like Arnett, Morton had always wanted to be an artist. After graduation, Morton headed for the Pratt Institute in Brooklyn. He spent the next three years there honing his craft, never dreaming he would use his talents in the Army.

When the war began, the Pratt Institute added a course in camouflage. Morton, after completing his work at Pratt in 1942, returned to Oklahoma and enlisted. He was sent to Fort Sill to await assignment. At first, the Army did what it is famous for: it assigned him to a job that did not use his talents. He was assigned to a map unit because someone decided an artist could draw maps. But a few weeks later, someone finally decided this was not the best use of his skills and he was reassigned to the 603rd, in the Twenty-third Special Troops. Soon he was sent to Fort Meade, Maryland, where he met Arnett. The two men became good friends right away.

Morton and Arnett each were given a Springfield model 1903 rifle, and later an M-1 carbine, when they arrived at Fort Meade. Arnett soon began basic training, drilling and marching. He climbed telephone poles and marched "on nearly every road and by-path in the state of Maryland," and bivouacked on the Severn and Potomac rivers and other spots, learning to live on the land. He and Morton learned some of the art of camouflage, using barbed wire, chicken wire, and painted burlap. They were told that color-blind people could easily detect camouflage.

"We tried to enforce camouflage discipline in our training and everyday life,"Morton remembers. "For instance, we were never allowed to hang our mess kits on the pup tent ridge poles for they could serve as reflectors and give away our position."

The 603rd Engineer Camouflage Battalion was one of four groups in the Twenty-third Headquarters Special Troops. There were 400 men in the battalion divided into five companies of about 80 men each: Headquarters and Service Company, known by the men as H&S, and companies A, B, and C. Arnett was first assigned to C Company and then H&S Company. Morton was also in H&S.

Although most of the troops they served with were brand new recruits, the Army made sure there were many career soldiers to help maintain military order and discipline. There was a First Sergeant Teaney who reported to Captain Spiegel, who was subordinate to Colonel Reeder. Arnett learned that Teaney had been a salesman for the International Shoe Company before the war. Arnett mentioned that his merchant father had bought most of his shoes from that company. He and the sergeant became pals.

One of Arnett's first jobs was to break down the rations for the company. He used a slide rule to be more precise, but this angered many of the mess cooks, who were not able to inflate their estimates of food supplies because of Arnett's precise measurements.

Morton was given the responsibility of coordinating activities of the mail room and delivery for the battalion.

To keep the men sharp, Capt. Charles Spiegel began asking each of them a question about the Army and the mission just before a sergeant handed them their paychecks. One day, when Arnett stepped up, he said, "Corporal Arnett, how big is a two-man foxhole?" Arnett replied immediately, "Big enough to hold two men, sir!"

All the troops waiting in line burst into laughter, including the captain.

"Great! Sergeant, pay that man."

As he reached for his check, Arnett said that he actually knew the real dimensions if Spiegel wanted to hear them.

"Forget it," said Spiegel. "That is the best description I have heard. You are excused."

Arnett soon learned that he was in good company. He found among fellow his troops Bill Blass, the fashion designer; Ellsworth Kelly, originator of hard-edge painting; George Diestel, who was to become a renowned Hollywood set designer; Art Kane, a famous photographer who later worked with *Life* and other major magazines; and

Col. Howell Railey, author and editor, world traveler, and probably a former American espionage agent.

After sixteen months of training at Fort Meade, Arnett learned the outfit was shipping out. As usual in wartime America, the Army was very secretive about the destination. But the men, who had repeatedly quipped that they would never get overseas as the months dragged by, were jubilant. They assumed they were headed for Europe.

But the train they boarded rumbled on to Baltimore, then turned northwest toward Harrisburg, Pennsylvania, then continued on through Altoona, Pennsylvania, to Columbus, Ohio, and then to Louisville, Kentucky.

The men were confused and apprehensive. Some thought they were headed to Fort Knox, and rumors swirled. Their greatest fear in that time of super patriotism was that they would never make it overseas at all. But the train continued on to Nashville and then to Camp Forrest in Tennessee. The men trained for two months at Camp Forrest, then were sent to Camp Kilmer, New York.

Meanwhile, Arnett's wife, Leila, had moved to Maryland and gotten a job in Baltimore to be near her husband. So next she moved to Nashville, not realizing he would only be there for two months. When he shipped out, she was several months pregnant, so she moved to Richmond, Virginia, to stay with her parents. He father was an editor there.

After she found she could no longer reach Arnett by phone at Camp Kilmer, she sadly realized he had probably been shipped overseas. Many wives and girlfriends learned their loved ones were gone in similar fashion. Secrecy was necessary to conceal troop movements.

Shortly before being shipped overseas, Arnett and other members of the 603rd had a brief pass to visit New York City. He had never been there before, and went to the top of the Empire State Building and then to Chinatown. When they got to the dock to board a Liberty ship, they found an army band on the dock to send them off.

Despite the darkness and the high security, Morton said he was moved when the band played "Over There," the famous words to which included "Over there, over there—the Yanks are coming, the Yanks are coming . . ." It was 2 A.M. when Arnett and Morton trudged up the gangplank with full battle packs, carrying their M-1 rifles.

The trip across the Atlantic, then swarming with German submarines, took thirteen days and was the largest troop convoy ever to cross, before or since. There were about 150 ships in the convoy with the cruiser *USS Cincinnati* in the center. Arnett was on the *USS Gibbons* on the extreme right front. He learned that this spot was dubbed "Coffin Corner," because it was usually the first ship torpedoed. Making him even more apprehensive was the fact that his berth was very low in the ship.

"If the Germans had fired a torpedo at us, it would have gone 100 feet over our heads," he figures. Although they were lucky, traveling fast in a zig-zag pattern with some aircraft cover provided by PBY seaplanes for part of the voyage, "It was hard to sleep because the destroyer escorts were dropping depth charges continuously."

Arnett and Morton continued their cartoons of various members of their outfit, and there were skits performed at night to take their minds off of the danger. Arnett recalled doing imitations of Roosevelt, Churchill, and Hitler in one skit.

"A day or two out of New York the men were the deck gazing at the endless stretches of dark green waves and water on the ominous Atlantic," Arnett recalled, "when a large ship appeared on the horizon. It came fairly close to our convoy and soon left us behind. It was the *Queen Mary* traveling alone at high speed to England. The Queens never traveled in a convoy. They were so fast and zigzagged across the ocean so that a German sub could never sink them."

Because of the threat of German U-boats in the channel, the convoy swung north of Ireland and approached England from the north, eventually entering the Bristol Channel to disembark at Avonmouth near Bristol, England. Other ships with Twenty-third troops landed in Scotland.

Standing on the Avon River, Arnett recalled the poem he learned in school years earlier concerning John Wyckliffe, the fourteenth century English theologian who had been burned at the stake for his religious beliefs: *"The Avon to the Severn runs, the Severn to the sea, John Wyckliffe's dust shall spread abroad, wide as these waters be."*

Arnett recalled that on arrival at Walton Hall, a "castle-like mansion of more than 100 rooms," most of the men camped in pyramid-style tents on the grounds. More pleasant was the free time, during which they enjoyed visiting the White Swan Inn, seeing the cottage of Shakespeare's wife, Ann Hathaway, and taking in some plays at the Sheakespeare Memorial Theater. Arnett visited Coventry after it was heavily bombed by German planes.

(Churchill and British intelligence had learned Coventry would be a target because they had cracked the German secret code. But had they warned Coventry, the Germans would have realized the code was broken. Churchill and his staff had to make the agonizing decision not to warn the city because in the long run they decided many more lives would be saved by silence. It was one of most difficult decisions of the war.)

While visiting Coventry, Arnett found some pieces of stained glass from the famous Coventry Cathedral, which he later crafted into a lead-and-glass cross. It is still in his family.

Three days before D-Day (June 6), Arnett and a driver were sent to Portsmouth and Lands End to pick up a shipment of pyramid tents for the upcoming invasion. He passed through Cheltenham, Bath, Tauton, Exeter, Clouchester, where he saw the cathedral, Torquay, and Dartmouth. Plymouth was just ninety miles across the channel from Brest on the Brittany Peninsula, then occupied by 40,000 German troops.

He learned that German planes flew over from Brest and methodically machine-gunned people on the streets and destroyed many of the buildings. He had no idea that he and others in the Ghost Army would play a key role in hemming in and conquering the German troops on the Brittany Peninsula, particularly those such a short distance away in Brest.

After completing his business, and unaware of how soon he and others would be shipped across the channel, Arnett visited the spot in Plymouth Harbor where the Pilgrims set sail for the new land America in 1620 aboard the *Mayflower*. Nearby there was a plaque commemorating the flight of the U.S. Navy plane NC-4, which made the first crossing of the Atlantic, in 1919.

"We returned to our base at Stratford-on-Avon the next day and the place was in a real stir and fury," Arnett recalled.

D-Day was imminent. The afternoon and night before the June 6 invasion I have never seen so many planes in the air at one time. There must have been thousands of B-17 Flying Fortresses and B-24 Liberator bombers. It was a steady drone and looked like a bright sheet of aluminum as the evening sun shone on their surfaces. The Allies were in control of the skies all the way to Berlin, and we knew by all this show of air power that we were getting ready for something.

Arnett wondered if he would soon use his artistic skills in camouflage or his M-1 carbine. It was a tense time, and he recalled: "A platoon from our battalion was going on D-Day. I volunteered but was turned down. I didn't know if it was because I was married and my wife was expecting, but shortly after that I was called to the tent of 1st Lt. Sterling and given special secret orders for a mission in Swansea, Wales, on the coast."

As a platoon from the 603rd crossed the channel from Plymouth to Utah and Omaha beaches on D-Day, Arnett traveled via Cardiff to Swansea, where he supervised the off-loading of equipment from the U.S. to be transported to France later. He spent nearly a month in Swansea and Stratford-on-Avon coordinating the transport of special inflatable dummy tanks, dummy howitzers, dummy aircraft, and other equipment for the Ghost Army's deception plans. His job was to check every box of special equipment and make sure it was routed to Stratford-on-Avon.

This may sound simple, but it was very easy during the war for equipment to go to the wrong place—even the wrong theater of operation. Getting the equipment to the Ghost Army was a vital job. His officers knew his sense of responsibility and precise nature would be right for the job. Arnett said that in "cloak-and-dagger fashion," every night he had to call from a pay phone in Swansea and talk to a Colonel Rapwatt—"probably a fake name"—whom he'd never met but who he learned was at General Eisenhower's headquarters in London. Using various code numbers, Rapwatt would tell Arnett what was in the boxes and where they should go.

For example, Arnett recalled that a box labeled "GLUE 6676" was actually an inflatable rubber replica of a Sherman tank. Among the contents in addition to the tanks were inflatable 155 and 250mm field artillery pieces, anti-aircraft guns, jeeps, trucks, and even dummy Piper Cub reconnaissance planes. These particular items were finely crafted by the United States Rubber Company in Rhode Island.

In checking this equipment, Arnett learned what the Twenty-third was going to do on the mainland. The big picture was suddenly evident to him as probably to few other men below the rank of captain. The special orders Arnett had for his top-secret assignment entitled him to travel on any ship to any port, no questions asked.

One day, when stopped by an MP, the questioning MP exclaimed, "If I had orders like that I'd be on my way back to the States." But Arnett was eager to get into action with his outfit in France.

While in Wales, Arnett had devised a method to let his wife, Leila, know where he was. It happened when he attended a Baptist church, where he heard the organist play one of his favorite pieces, "Melody in F" by Anton Rubenstein. In letters to Leila, of course, he was strictly forbidden by censors to say where he was or describe anything about his miliary mission or even the scenery or landmarks in the vicinity. She only had an APO numbered address and, although she was reasonably sure he was in Britain, for all she knew he could have been in Saipan or North Africa. So he mentioned the name of the pastor, Dr. Gordon Hamlin, and the censors let it go through. Then Leila's father was able to look him up in a directory of British Baptist ministers and thereby learn that Arnett was in Wales.

There also were various other codes Arnett and Leila and his mother and others used—remember, these troops had very high IQs—to show where he was. They had set up a number code for place names. For example, he would say "I received your 13-page letter . . ." and they would look up 13 on a code list and know that he was in Paris. When he was in Luxembourg, however, one letter slipped through the censors with the location clearly named, "Luxembourg, Luxembourg."

After a month in Wales, Arnett completed his work and returned to Stratford-on-Avon, riding in the caboose of one of the equipment-laden trains. There he joined the 3132nd Signal Service Company, known in Army code as "Heater." This unit had arrived in Glasgow June 11 aboard the *USS Exceller,* from Fort Monmouth, New Jersey. The 3132nd, he learned, was "a highly trained technical outfit which possessed two 250-watt radio stations, olive-drab-painted vans and phonograph records of every sound imaginable, including tanks on the move, planes dive bombing, soldiers laughing, and even a single soldier walking along with his canteen cover jangling."

Arnett stayed with Heater for two or three weeks in July. He could only listen as the invasion was meeting stiff resistance, being pinned down in some places on the Normandy coast. It was not all a sure thing in those days. Americans and British held their collective breaths, hoping the beachheads would be established and a break-out would be made.

Finally, less than a month after D-Day, they were loaded aboard LST No. 1195 and made an uneventful night-time crossing of the channel, driving ashore up in half-tracks on the flatter, eastern part of Utah Beach at dawn. As it crossed, the LST, like many other ships, floated its own barrage balloon high above by a steel cable as a means of warding off low-flying German aircraft that might attempt to strafe the vessel.

Arnett and the rest of Heater then joined the rest of the Twenty-third near Isigny and Mandeville, France, just a few miles inland, near the front lines. Here Arnett was reunited with his buddies in the 603rd Battalion. The main body of the Ghost Army had crossed the channel aboard the *John W. Mosby* and had disembarked at Omaha Beach just two weeks after D-Day on June 6 when there was still plenty of fighting.

Some of the Twenty-third had been busy with deception in Operation Overlord—code name for the D-Day invasion. For example, some of the Twenty-third's electronics experts had rigged up lights to fake a landing wharf in an area where there were no troops. This was designed to mislead night-flying German reconnaissance aircraft about where the troop strength really was.

On August 3, the outfit moved by convoy 30 miles south to La Fremondre, France, just north of Coutance. During this time, deception operations near Brest were begun. For two weeks, Arnett lived out of his two-man tent set up over a foxhole. Many of the GIs were souvenir collectors. One day, to Arnett's horror, he found a GI had lined his foxhole with live German hand grenades he planned to bring home. Arnett and others convinced the GI of the stupidity and danger of the idea. One slight mistake and he would be blown to bits. This GI obviously had not been one of the high-IQ troops and was from another outfit.

Arnett said that during the early phase of operations, and from time to time during he coming year, one of the functions of the Twenty-third was reconnaissance. In order to be able to impersonate the other units in the Twelfth Army, it had to build an extensive library of that army's Standard Operation Procedures, radio peculiarities, and other idiosyncracies easily identifiable by the Germans, who constantly monitored battle area radio.

Soon, according to Army archives, "they had copies or specifications for every corps and divisional shoulder patch, bumper marking, and CP [command post] sign. They could duplicate the appearance of any U.S. unit in the Twelfth Army Group. By VE-Day, the Twenty-third probably contained the most widely traveled and best-informed officers in the European Theater of Operations. A majority of the Twenty-third's jeeps and trucks had driven over 16,000 miles." So secret was this Ghost Army, however, that very few other troops even knew of its existence. This led to some strange conflicts and even clashes among Allied troops that no one dared explain at the time. But more on this later.

The American breakout occurred in mid-August, and the Germans retreated with Patton and others in pursuit. Patton received favorable press because of his rapid pursuit, which was made possible in part because the Germans were trying to rapidly get behind the Siegfried Line. Other Germans retreated west on the Brittany/Brest Peninsula, taking refuge in Brest, an unusually strong and well-fortified bastion. It was so strong, Arnett recalled, that had the Germans known that the huge army in front of them was actually just the Ghost Army, they could have broken out and caused real trouble for the Allied invasion force.

Before Patton left the Brittany Peninsula, he was barreling along in his jeep headed to see General Middleton, mad as hell because the push west had stalled. Middleton has ordered subordinates to pause and occupy St. Malo, and Patton wanted to ignore it, leaving it for mop up later. As he drove along, he spotted a contingent of the Twenty-third.

Although he was supposed to be aware of the Ghost Army, perhaps at that point he had not been fully briefed or had forgotten about it. So when he saw the troops with so many different arm patches and so many different markings on their jeeps and trucks, he immediately assumed that they were stragglers or—worse—cowardly troops who had lagged behind. He was furious, and commented to his driver and staff officers about it, but did not stop and get himself into trouble, as he was prone to do.

It was about this time that Arnett found some rubber material in Torce that had been used to make barrage balloons. He used it to devise an inflatable rubber mattress. He was about 25 years ahead of the Army. This mattress may seem to be a small thing, but it loomed large in his life at the time. Trying to get a comfortable night's sleep was a constant challenge. Some men slept on the canvas between staves on $2\frac{1}{2}$-ton trucks. Others piled brush and leaves and put canvas mats over it. Some slept on the ground under trucks. Some slept on the inflatable vehicles.

But Arnett's rubber mattress proved to be one of his best contributions, giving him many comfortable nights for the duration. The Army supplied all troops after the war with a rubber mattress. In Vietnam, they called it "the rubber lady." But Arnett was ahead of his time and the envy of men trying to sleep on sticks and gravel or mud.

It was during this time of dodging in and out of thick hedgerows, planted to cut the high winds from the sea, that Americans ran into one of the cruelest of German devices. They had taken to stringing piano wire across various roads, lanes, and highways so that it would decapitate Americans riding along in jeeps. Although jeeps had a folding windshield, it was rarely placed upright because the mud and grime soon made it opaque.

But American troops countered this threat by welding a piece of angle iron onto the front bumpers of their jeeps. At one point on the angle iron, they cut a notch with a welding torch or hacksaw to catch the piano wire. This saved many lives.

The same American ingenuity devised a system of forks made from steel bars taken from German beach barriers. The forks were welded onto the front of the Sherman tanks, which had been turned back or over by the very strong, tall, thick hedgerows of Normandy. The forks allowed the tanks to bite into the roots and plough through with great speed, surprising the Germans.

Arnett said the Germans also had done a deadly and thorough job of mining the roads in Normandy. The Ninetieth and Twenty-ninth Divisions had mine specialists who painstakingly found and cleared the mines. Arnett recalls that they left signs saying, "This Road Cleared of Mines to the Edges Courtesy of the Ninetieth Division."

As they neared St. Lo, American tanks and other vehicles, including half-tracks, had to be marked on top with bright paints so that the roving P-51s, P-47s, P-38s, and other fighter-bombers would not mistakenly strafe them. This was far easier than one might think. For example, one P-47 pilot was returning from a mission and saw what he thought was a German tanker truck not far from the front lines. He dived toward it, unleashing a hail of .50-caliber bullets from his eight machine guns, four mounted in each wing. With satisfaction, he saw fluid pour from the holes.

Oddly, though, there was no explosion, so he made broad turn and came around for another pass. He thought perhaps his tracers were used up or missing. He raked the tanker truck again. Getting low on fuel, he headed for the landing field near the Normandy coast. No sooner had he landed than officers at the airfield received a scathing message from the Free French of the Interior. They were angry because the pilot had shot up a truck containing the juice from grapes in one of the finest wine-producing regions of the area.

Col. William "Bill" Enderlein, retired, in 1999. He was a corporal in the Ghost Army. Photo by Jack Kneece.

Chapter Seven

Corporal Enderlein

Bill Enderlein was a bright young farm boy living in Portage, Pennsylvania. At one point he thought he might have to stay on the farm the rest of his life, and he didn't like the idea. But he was soon to become a corporal and sonics expert, sometime machine gunner, and driver of half-tracks and trucks.

He did a little of everything, like Bob Tompkins and Bill Blass. He often detonated the canisters that sounded like American artillery fire and made a flash—a sound and a flash that often drew counter-battery fire from the feared German 88s and other artillery pieces. Enderlein was among those who were in Normandy early and wound up in many dangerous missions near Brest and later, during the Battle of the Bulge, came close to capture.

"I wanted to get off the farm," said Enderlein, who rose to the rank of colonel and now lives in Johnstown, Pennsylvania. "When I was in high school the war had just started. There were about five of us in our class who went to our homeroom teacher and said we wanted to enlist. But we were given the word from our families: Graduate first!"

We did, and then went through basic training in Camp Crowder, Missouri, near Joplin for 17 weeks. Then I went into the Army Specialized Training Program, just known back then as the ASTP. They took anybody with an IQ two points higher than a stone, and I was selected to go to electrical engineering school. I went to the University of Kentucky at Lexington.

I really had it made there. I was just one of a handful of men at a coed college. Most of the male students were off at war. I can't even tell

125

my wife half the things about my time there. Let me just say I had a wonderful time. I wound up with close to 70 credit hours and then they pulled us out and sent us to Pine Camp, New York. All of a sudden I was up there in the snow and cold. We went through the secret training there and then were shipped overseas. I didn't know what we would be doing until we got to Pine Camp. Were told we were going to be issued mosquito nets and shorts. I guess they knew that troops would talk so this was to fool any spies in area. It fooled me, too. This was just more deception—but it was also deceiving your own troops.

Then they put us on a train to New York City and in the back of the train station they loaded us onto trucks with sides pulled down. We got on ships in the wee hours of the morning. We were not allowed out of the ship while we sat in harbor, in the hold.

We found we were the only company on the ship. I was assigned to be an assistant gunner on 20mm guns for the duration of the voyage. I did get to see the Statue of Liberty as we left because I was on deck to familiarize myself with the guns.

We were green, so many of us got seasick. The heads were constantly filled with men throwing up. We headed to the Azores, and then abruptly turned back toward the north. We were, believe it or not, the only troop ship in this particular convoy and were put in the middle. We were just a company, 63 men or so. Some of the Twenty-third had gone over and some were yet to come. Our equipment had been sent over already.

We landed in Glasgow, Scotland. Then we went to Walton Hall at Stratford-on-Avon.

We used to call it Moldy Manor. They took the horses and cattle out and we lived inside the barns. It was warm and dry. Damned comfortable. Officers inside Walton said it was cold and drafty, damp. We were the lucky ones.

Enderlein smiles with a nostalgic, faraway look when he recalls his time with the Ghost Army in Europe.

It seems that we were all nineteen. We were homesick kids but we could receive two packages sent from back home each month. One guy used to get a bottle of Mennen's Shaving Lotion in every package, along with the usual cookies and a few cans of Vienna sausage. It was a big Mennen bottle. He would take the bottle out and share his cookies. He got two bottles of Mennen's each month.

I remember asking him, "When did the Mennen people create an amber-colored shaving location, and if you use that much shaving lotion, why do you always smell like the rear end of a goat?"

The guys laughed and the young soldier admitted that his mother sent whisky in the Mennen bottles.

"How the hell does she get the liquor in that tiny hole?" someone asked.

"I don't know how she does it, but she does it," the young soldier said, "maybe with an eyedropper."

Everyone agreed, recalled Enderlein, that this was maternal love of the highest order.

Enderlein recalls that a person could get busted in rank on the whim of the officers. He related that the driver was responsible for raising the tailgate of a truck, and on a brief trip he forgot to do it. When he returned, a lieutenant and a sergeant noticed he had not put the tailgate up and he was busted to private. The reason this was a serious matter, Enderlein explained, was that with the tailgate down the spies in the bivouac area might see into the trucks and determine that there were only two men sitting at the rear instead of a full contingent. Or they might see some of the specialized equipment.

Later the group was on an LST headed for Normandy. One of the Ghost Army cooks, a sergeant, ordered Enderlein to throw the garbage from the mess overboard.

"Throw out your own damned garbage," Enderlein said. "I'm a private. You can't have me busted any more."

One thing led to another, and soon he found himself in a tussle with the cook. Enderlein grabbed him and threatened to throw him overboard. What Enderlein didn't know was that the cook was deathly afraid of water, which was why he had asked him to throw the garbage overboard. Nothing came of it, but Enderlein did find that his food portions after that seemed very small.

Enderlein's best pal was a giant of a man named Roy Oxenrider from Nebraska, a friendly farm boy—a Li'l Abner-type fellow who was noted for his incredible strength. He was several inches over six feet and strong as a weightlifter. The two were assigned to the same half-track and found they had a lot in common. Oxenrider was the driver.

One day, Enderlein said, the men found a cache of cognac and other booze in the basement of a bombed-out house. The officers allowed the men to drink all they wanted.

"I had never really had much to drink before then," said Enderlein,

> and I don't think Roy Oxenrider had either. So we all began drinking it like water. I downed a bottle of cognac and date an entire D-ration, which was just a very large chocolate bar. That night it poured down rain.
>
> We were in tents on edge of a big woods somewhere in France. I went into the tent. The rain poured into the tent. I vomited all that chocolate and cognac all over the place. I was sick as a dog. It was all over my uniform. It was still raining and I just lay there and let the rain clean me off. I swallowed half a dozen aspirin and soon began to feel a little bit better.
>
> Then someone said they couldn't find Oxenrider. We looked all over the place and found him lying on his back in a creek, the water flowing over him, and he was passed out. He's lucky he didn't pass out face down.

Lt. John Walker of Watertown, New York, was a supply officer and platoon leader. He was in charge of keeping part of the Ghost Army supplied with ammo, electrical supplies, food, clothing, and fresh meat. One van was filled with parts for the broadcast and recording equipment. Four or five of the trucks were filled with five-gallon Jerry cans of gasoline to keep all the trucks and vehicles running. As the men would find a cache of wine and other liquor, Lieutenant Walker would see that one of the 2½-ton trucks was filled with the liquor.

"I used this liquor to swap for things like fresh beef and other supplies for my men," he said. And by night "I was a combat platoon leader." He said he kept a Browning Automatic Rifle handy and filled two roles, as a combat and supply officer.

"I didn't get much sleep. We just wanted to get the job done and come home," he said.

Walker said Brest and the Battle of the Bulge were the two most dangerous times for the Ghost Army, although there was danger in every operation.

Enderlein and the other men learned the hard way that if you woke Oxenrider suddenly, you had better not stand near him. He had a habit of coming up flailing in a semi-conscious state. "He could almost knock you out. We would wake him up with a rifle or move his foot and he would come up flailing."

One day when we were in Luxembourg staying in a girl's school, we told one of our guys, Manny Frockt, to wake Roy. Manny didn't know about the danger of this. Roy was on a bottom bunk asleep. Manny came in. "Everybody up," he said, trying to be a big shot. That's when we said, "How about waking Roy. Just whisper in his ear and shake his shoulder." Well, Roy came up with a jab that hit Manny in face and knocked him clean across the room. Almost knocked him out. Roy ran over, but Manny wanted to run away from him, yet all Roy wanted to do was help him. It was just reflexive. Roy was embarrassed. We all got a big laugh out of it.

When the Ghost Army got close to the Germans, I was terrified. I never told anybody. I didn't want people to think I was a coward, which I wasn't. I think we were all scared. I just took it. It was particularly bad when you had to go out on a patrol at night where there were German patrols and anti-personnel mines. But you become a fatalist after awhile. One day there was a story in *Stars and Stripes,* and this quickly became a big joke, about a guy who had carried a Bible in his breast pocket. He claimed that the Bible had stopped a German bullet and saved his life. Well, within a few days everybody carried a Bible in his breast pocket, including Buddhists, Jews, and men of every religion—it didn't matter.

The Bibles were passed out by the Red Cross. They did a big business in them after the *Stars and Stripes* story. Then one day we tested one and fired a pistol at one, and the bullet went right through it.

Enderlein said that only once were written orders for an operation given to the Ghost Army, and that was for Operation Viersen, when the unit faked a preparation for crossing the Rhine River. All other orders were verbal to help maintain secrecy.

Our unit was attached directly to Omar Bradley, commander of Twelfth Army Group. Bradley had liaison officers with the Twenty-third. But nothing was written. Some officers were reluctant to use the Twenty-third because there were no written orders. And we never knew where we would get food, ammo, or supplies. We were just told that the Twelfth Army Group would get us those things. But it was different with Viersen. Because it was such a tremendous operation they finally put down orders. These were the only orders in the entire war.

After the corps commanders, division commanders, and regimental commanders learned what our unit could do, we suddenly became very popular. It became a little hectic. Soon we were running all over the various battlefields. We were on the move constantly. We never had a rest or any leave to speak of. There is no record of a few weeks rest like was normal with other units. And we operated in complete secrecy. We never got any awards. During the Battle of the Bulge, we operated with the Twenty-eighth and the Seventy-fifth, but we never got any awards. Yet these people got awards and they didn't even know who we were. They thought we were some stray unit in their division. So when the commendations were handed out we were not mentioned.

Even today, it is hard to get recognition. Who would think that a signal company would have so much armor and firepower, for example? We were a unit they couldn't understand. When I talked to the people in the awards branch not long ago, I told them we are all old men now and that our time is short. They sat on this thing for about fifty years. We would like to get some recognition while we are still around. The [Army] personnel center in St. Louis just sends us a form letter every once and a while saying we're still checking, don't call us, we'll call you.

Even when we were disbanded, all the men were taken out of the unit, ordered to another place in the United States, and they handled all the paperwork. We were totally dispersed all over the place. There are no mentions in any war books about the Twenty-third. This is because of the secrecy. Even commanders often didn't know we were impersonating their troops. The old-line troops think of deception as holding up a helmet on a stick.

You know about the plastic explosives we had to carry under the seats of our vehicles, 10 pounds under each of the front seats. Well, we had a driver, [Sergeant] Alvin Link. He was a great guy. But he was a real low key guy. Didn't say too much to anybody. Major [Charles] Williams gathered us around one day and had everybody sit down around him. He stood in an opening in the center of the men. He had his great big satchel filled with plastic explosives.

He began explaining to us how to hook it up and how to detonate it. He went over everything thoroughly, one thing and another. Then he suddenly picked it up and tossed it right into the center of the men. Well, sir, men screamed, hollered, and ran off in all directions. I'll tell you the truth. If he hadn't been an officer we'd have killed him. I guess Major Williams was trying to demonstrate it was stable without a cap or primer explosion. I guess he was having a little fun. But that was a little much.

Now, Lt. Dick Syracuse was a piece of work. He was a kind of ladies' man, but he was a man's man, too, and we all liked him a lot. When we were going into the Battle of Verdun, he ran over a mine with his jeep. It smashed him into the windshield, him and his driver. They had shrapnel wounds, and it smashed his teeth. He never got his Purple Heart. No recognition whatsoever. He is one of hundreds of us who got no Purple Heart—no medals of any kind.

We kept quiet about it all until a few years ago. They just don't seem to be able to tie a signal company or a camouflage outfit into a combat company. They just don't understand what we did. Then Tom Winfield of Stratford, Connecticut, is the one who first found out that our records had been declassified.

Many of the men said Colonel Reeder was so unhappy about his not being placed in a line outfit that he really didn't look out for his men or care too much about their effectiveness. Fortunately, the men agree, this was more than balanced by the efforts of Major Truly, Major Williams, colonels Simenson and Railey, and others who *did* care. According to Enderlein:

> Reeder desperately wanted to be made brigadier general and wanted his officers to write a letter to Twelfth Army Group recommending this. None of them liked him. They refused. This made him mad as hell. After the war there was a hearing, and so many of his subordinates testified against him that they removed him from the Twenty-third. By the way, if you check the list of those who got medals, Reeder made sure his son, Boyd, got one. If Colonel Railey or Colonel Simenson had been our commander, or Colonel Truly, we'd have gotten our medals by now. Reeder didn't care about getting us recognition.

Oddly enough, the Legion of Merit was given to Simenson. "He still doesn't know how he got it," says Enderlein.

> He knew it wasn't Reeder. Reeder would have shot him first. The only one he signed medals for was his son [Boyd Reeder]. He was in the wrong position at the wrong time. We used to think that Reeder hated Major Williams because of the harassment he gave him. We wondered what Williams had done. Then we found out later he hated them all— particularly the West Pointers. He was not interested in any idea that was not his.
>
> Some said it was like Captain Bligh's envy of Fletcher Christian's aristocratic background in *Mutiny on the Bounty.*

Walker and Enderlein and many others in the Ghost Army recalled watching Patton drive by with his pearl-handled revolvers and his tough scowl, sitting in a jeep as his long line of tanks headed for Bastogne during the Battle of the Bulge.

"We saw the famous 90-degree turn." said Enderlein.

We saw a column of tanks going full speed with headlights on rolling up, the Fourth Armored Division, headed north of the city of Luxembourg. All they had north of the city was the phony Seventy-fifth Infantry Division and that was us! The real Seventy-fifth was back in England, still training and waiting for deployment. There was nothing there, but we halted the Germans because *they thought* the Seventy-fifth was there. We then pretended to be part of the Fourth Armored.

Then Gen. Creighton Abrams sneaked out and he and his men attacked at Bastogne. He never got enough credit. Everybody gave all the credit to Patton, but Abrams was a gutsy, tough guy who should have been given a lot of credit at the Bulge, too. The Ninety-ninth Infantry Division disrupted the German attack and really caused the failure of the Bulge breakout.

Sometimes, particularly during the Bulge period when we were getting the hell out of there, we didn't get food. We found C-rations much better than K-rations because you could heat them. K-rations we ate cold. And D-rations were just big thick chocolate bars. Everybody smoked then, and there were four packs of cigarettes in the rations, crazy brands like Mint Juleps, Wings, Twenty Grand. When you found some Camels or Lucky Strikes, you counted your-self lucky or you used them in trade.

American troops may have joked about K-and C-rations, but they practically lived off of them. Records show that 60 million of the three-meal K-ration packs were shipped to Normandy in the first three weeks of the invasion. Soldiers have groused about the food since the days when Roman legions were fed a handful of grain each day if there was no plunder. America's Confederate troops lived for months at a time on rock-hard biscuit—called hard tack—and a bit of dried "bully" beef. Coffee and vegetables were gleaned either from the countryside or from plunder from Yankee troops.

The Ghost Army became adept at gleaning, too. But the K-rations were like gold to German troops when they were captured. The thousands of displaced Europeans, with the exception of the French, were grateful for the K- and C-rations, which also contained jams and jellies and a few other condiments.

"When we first started a mission," said Enderlein,

we would remove the machine gun and tripod from the half-track. That was about 150 pounds to carry. Roy Oxenrider would carry two boxes of ammo, our rifles, and we would choose a site for good field of fire. Lots of times we would tear up the countryside with our half-tracks. We wanted the Germans to see all the tracks, which looked just like tank tracks, from their air recon flights. Then we would go in and out of net camouflage and try to come out in the same tracks and then go in to make different set.

We knew at 11 P.M. all American planes were taken out of the air, except for bombers, so that's when the Germans came over. Around 11 o'clock old Bed Check Charlie would fly over and take pictures of our rubber tanks in the moonlight. You'd find it impossible to see that they were rubber unless you were right up on them, even in the daylight.

You know, we had one guy who never bathed, even when we had a chance to clean up. He smelled terrible. So we stopped at a creek and the officers and a few men took him out in a field at rifle point and made him strip, even though it was cold as hell in Belgium right before the Bulge. They took everything he had on him and poured gasoline on it and burned it. Then they made him take soap and wash himself thoroughly. He got the hint and began washing often after that. That was shortly before the Battle of the Bulge, which surprised the hell out of everybody. Ironically, from December 15 well into February, none of us, during Bulge, had a chance to bathe as it turned out.

The Ghost Army troops were given orders never to try to start a firefight with the Germans.

"If they didn't see you, you didn't want to start anything," said Enderlein.

That was what we were ordered to do. Sometimes it was funny when they saw us and got out of there, seeing all those "tanks" and "armor." By the way, our half-tracks would go places a tank couldn't go. Also, they were a lot more comfortable than a tank. They had a bit of suspension. Roy found that half-track tires could have a hole in them from a bullet but would not deflate. I don't know how they did it, but they would stay up. [They were filled with rubber foam.]

"I believe that they had self-sealing tires," explains John Walker. "They were very heavy tires and made very well for rough terrain."
"Despite the best efforts of men like Walker," said Enderlein,

we had trouble getting gasoline because front-line combat units got first choice. So we would fill our tanks up, and we carried nine cans across the top of that half-track. I once asked, "Can't we carry it somewhere else?" I told them that one bullet and we're done—not to mention the explosives under the seat. We would take the gas cans off the top every chance we got.

Nobody else in the war had to have explosives under the seat like we did. We carried plenty of explosives anyway. Two half-tracks were hit one day and completely destroyed. Everybody scooted because of the explosives. A shell from a big German railway gun hit just twenty feet from a half-track and blew it to hell and it wasn't even a direct hit. They were shelling and everybody took off. But no one got hurt because we had gotten the hell out of there.

Axis Sally thought we were the Seventy-fifth when the Seventy-fifth was actually back in England. We enjoyed her music, and even more, enjoyed it when she got things wrong. Her broadcasts were a good litmus test for fooling Germans.

Axis Sally played a lot of Glenn Miller and songs such as "Sentimental Journey," "Don't Sit Under the Apple Tree With Anyone Else But Me," "Paper Dolly," and "You Call Everybody Darling." The men paid no attention to her propaganda but loved her music. And because the Twenty-third Ghost troops were electronics experts, there were plenty of radios and aerials around to pick up the German propagandist.

"Late in the war, we started capturing some of the German Jugend—teenaged troops. They were just basically suicide troops. Some were old men," said Enderlein. "There were so many civilian spies around that we used them," he continued.

We played to the Vichy French. You were an actor whether you liked it or not. If you were an introvert you would not be sent out into town with a cover story. We gave them cover stories to match the phony markings on our vehicles. We often saw people taking down the numbers and markings on pads.

Between missions, Ghost troops enjoyed collecting German memorabilia, at least until they learned that they would be shot on the spot by the Germans if they were captured and found to possess German guns or any German item. After hearing this, the men stored their souvenirs in compartments on the truck and in the smaller compartments on half-tracks.

"Lots of us had German weapons," said Enderlein, who acknowledged having Lugers and P-38s.

Our vehicles hit small personnel mines constantly. Once one of them damaged one of the bearings on our half-track. We went to supply ordnance depot at Verdun and the maintenance yard there. We had no facilities for repair so we had to take it down to those people. Everybody at Verdun were Garrison Troopers—that's in between front-line and rear-echelon troops. Well, the mechanics said they could fix it in a couple of days. "How about making it a week?" we asked, because we wanted the leave time just to hang around. "Okay," was the reply, "but it'll cost you."

So we gave them a few souvenirs, pistols, and that kind of thing. But our company commander called and wanted to know what in the hell was taking so long. So we only got three days to goof off.

We also used to swap C- and K-rations for items in Belgian shops, or for breakfasts, haircuts, or watered-down booze. We would never carry our rifles or helmets, but just walk around town wearing our soft caps. One day we went across a small bridge across a creek. Suddenly a squad of fierce-looking American soldiers jumped up from a creek and pointed their loaded weapons at us.

"Identify yourself or we'll shoot!" they shouted. Turns out the Seventeenth Airborne had made a practice jump on the city of Verdun. Soon we calmed them down and began chatting with them. They halfway apologized. They wanted souvenirs. I had a broken P-38, with the firing pin missing. I thought I'd get about ten bucks for it. One of those airborne guys gave me $98 for it—all that he had on him.

"Such souvenirs had become almost a medium of exchange," said Enderlein, who added:

And our soap and candy bars would buy anything you wanted from booze to food or a woman. But it was too good to last. Here's what happened: unfortunately, the damned Garrison Troops began upping the ante, giving them several bars of soap and candy. This ruined it for the rest of us. I have a theory, by the way, about the French attitude toward Americans today. I think the French hated us because we used to give them K-rations. Here are a people used to fine food and wine, and we made them eat K- and C-rations. Probably made them mad as hell. But they were hungry and had to eat it—just like we did.

When we were cut off during the Bulge, we were seconds away

from detonating our equipment to keep it out of the hands of the Germans. But we weren't too worried about ourselves. We figured we might get out of there. We had been in those hills around there so often and knew all the little roads that we thought we could slip out of the noose.

Once, when we were close to the Rhine River and were pretending to build a pontoon bridge—a "notional" pontoon bridge—the unit decided to go halfway down the slope to the river, where we had to stop to wait for it to get dark. Remember, we never operated in daytime. Everything was in the dark. Then we saw a company of tanks coming up. They got in under cover and hid. We saw several German patrols.

We had at that time a brand-new replacement, a young kid. He was trying to fit in by acting like a vet. We called him a kid—actually he was probably just a year younger than us. I remember he had clean pants on. So we could hear this random rifle fire. None of us were paying attention to it. We were used to it. A couple of bullets came whizzing over, hit branches, and knocked one down. We knew it was just random and not directed at us so we didn't worry about it. But the kid went crazy.

"Get down! Get down! They're shooting at us," he yelled. "What's wrong with you guys, get down!" We laughed at him and he was very embarrassed.

Then those tanks began shining spotlights across the river. They were using the spotlights to try to blind the Germans while we got a few boats with men across. Of course we had to move from that spot because we knew the tanks would soon draw fire from across the river, which they did, and once the artillery fire came the tanks got out of there in a hurry.

Enderlein said one of the interludes of the war stuck in his memory came after the Ghost Army's Viersen operation, detailed elsewhere in this narrative. He said his outfit camped in a small village en route to Wiesbaden in a village of about ten or twelve houses dominated by one medieval castle in a large field by itself.

We had to move two burned-out German half-tracks blocking the gate to the castle to get in. The woman who lived there said she was a baroness and she spoke fairly good English. The castle had a moat and the whole works. She said she would relinquish the castle to us while we were there and asked only that we feed her chickens. Of course, we ate all of her chickens. We also rummaged around the place and found a motorcycle and Roy Oxenrider and I got the motorcycle running. But we had chicken for breakfast every day. I felt kind of bad about it, but we left without seeing her. She also had all kind of canned goods that we helped ourselves to. We hadn't been eating that well ourselves.

I found a beautiful German music box and it played beautifully. It was a real treasure and later an officer saw me with it, threatened to have me court martialed for looting, and he took and it I found out later he kept it for himself.

Enderlein's fellow Ghost and friend Tom Winfield recalled that during that same period he had lived in a house with a peasant family, all of whom wore wooden shoes even though they were German, not Dutch. They were very neat and very nice to him and his men.

"They gave us the best room in the house; like the American equivalent of a living room," he said. "We had our sleeping bags. Never used their beds."

Winfield also recalled finding a half million German marks hidden away. He said he later learned that the cash trove was not worth much because of the war.

"I still have them. We also found a number of top hats, black formal hats. We wore them in kind a celebratory way. There I was with half a million marks and a top hat."

Enderlein recalled seeing a large, carved, wooden eagle with a six-foot wingspan in the lobby of the German castle. "They had done a beautiful job carving the thing. Years later when I was visiting West Point I saw the same eagle. I guess someone had taken it as part of the spoils of war."

Chapter Eight

Ghosts of Paris

No GI ever forgot his time in the fabled city of Paris. And although the Ghost Army was bivouacked to the east of the city, most of the men managed to get there frequently—at least for a short time.

Paris was a pleasant but enjoyable interlude before the really heavy fighting. The Germans were hoping the Rhine crossing would be such a bloody disaster for the Allies that they could at least hope for good peace terms.

Although San Franciscans may argue, Paris has been the city to which all others have been compared and found wanting. The Ghost troops could hardly wait to get passes to visit the famed "City of Light," left unharmed—at least physically—by the very recent German occupation. It was so recent, in fact, that the French were still chasing and beating *collaborateurs* on the streets when the first Ghost troops arrived.

They had read of Paris in Hemingway novels, and people had said that just living in Paris was an art form. Now they wanted to see its wonders close up. They drove all over the city in jeeps, scout cars, and even 2½-ton trucks, inspected its many monuments, peered up at the Eiffel Tower, flirted with Parisian women, ate French food, and tried to absorb as much of the city as possible in a short time. They knew they would soon move on toward Germany because the war was far from over.

The troops ate the day's *baguette*—a warm and marvelously crisp and skinny loaf of bread that would spoil them—somehow still available at Parisian bakeries. They sampled French cuisine and wines, sat at outdoor cafes, and enjoyed being heroes to the French people.

They visited the Tuileries Gardens and the Louvre. They sent home postcards, which still had to get by the censors. Men produced small Kodak cameras they had carried in their duffel bags, waiting for this moment. Some knew they probably never would have had the chance to visit the fabled city had it not been for the war.

Some explored the Ile de la Cite in the Seine River, where Caesar had encountered the first Gauls in 54 B.C. The men visited the venerable cathedral and religious structures of Notre Dame, Ste-Chapelle, and Sacre-Coeur; and the great public edifices of the Louvre, the Opera, and the Hotel des Invalides, once an army hospital and now the site of an army museum and Napoleon's tomb. They strolled up the fantastic Avenue des Champs-Elysees, which only a few weeks before had been occupied by Nazi troops. They took photos of the commanding vista of the Arc de Triomphe.

But most of all they were fascinated by the sophistication, despite the ravages of war, of the Parisians themselves, slender, elegantly dressed women and worldly and cynical men, many of them FFI walking about proudly with their weapons slung on their shoulders.

Because the Ghost troops were men of high IQs and well educated, they fully appreciated the city's cultural significance and its importance to generations of intellectuals, including Americans such as Ernest Hemingway, who was setting up shop in the Ritz Hotel while the men were there, and F. Scott Fitzgerald. But the city also had been home to philosopher and mathematician Blaise Pascal, such novelists as Honore de Balzac, Victor Hugo, Marcel Proust, and many others.

The Ghost troops fully appreciated the sheer joy of being in Paris and spent as much time there as possible, conniving passes however they could. Some used the time-honored "search for blue paint" trick. If they were stopped by an MP they said they had been sent to look for blue paint. There was no blue paint anywhere in the Army, so the search could take awhile. Somehow, recalled Enderlein, the MPs never caught on.

"Some of the guys were lucky," said Bob Tompkins.

They got to stay several days in Paris. I was only in Paris for eight hours. After leaving Brest we bivouacked briefly in Foantainebleau—right behind Patton. We had to go back all the way back to the beaches to get gasoline. I drove back with several other guys. When we got back with gasoline we went to St. Germain [to bivouac] just outside of Paris. We parked our trucks right in front of Notre Dame

Ghost Army troops relax at a Paris sidewalk café. Photo courtesy Robert Tompkins.

Cathedral. We sat at a café and watched the people walk by. All of this took place in just eight hours for me because of having to go back to get the gas. The single guys got to go to Paris, the lucky ones. From there we went to Luxembourg.

On the morning of August 24, Bierre Billotte's French armored force entered Paris from the South, and on August 25 Gen. Charles de Gaulle accepted the German surrender of the city. Patton's Third Army could have taken Paris easily, but SHAEF (Supreme Headquarters, Allied Expeditionary Force) and the governments of Britain and America thought it would be good for French morale for de Gaulle and French armor to first reoccupy the town. Paris was hysterical with joy, with the exception of the collaborators, many of whom were brutally dealt with by the FFI and others loyal to the original French government.

Walter Arnett was among the first American troops to roll down the Champs Elysees. "The French were all glad to see us, waving flags and throwing flowers," he remembers. The Twenty-third was billeted at St. Germain in Camp les Loges, a French military base that had been hastily deserted by the Germans. The Headquarters Company and 406th Engineers of the Twenty-third took over the nearby Maison d'Ecole de la legion d'Honneur, a palace Napoleon had built for his wife, Josephine.

De Gaulle had asked Eisenhower to make a big show of force in Paris to help give substance and credence to de Gaulle's authority in France. Eisenhower reluctantly agreed and told de Gaulle that he would divert two divisions that were headed to the front anyway through the city in parade formation.

Because the ceremonial march coincided exactly with the local battle plan, it became possibly the only instance in history of troops marching in parade through the capital of a great country, then engaging in pitched battle later that day.

Some of the British press commented snidely that "the Americans love a parade." They added that British troops had also been involved in the campaign to free France, said Eisenhower, writing in his *Crusade in Europe,* and that none of the Allies should seek to take the glory.

This did not sit well with Eisenhower, and he made sure the offending newspapers learned the truth and that retractions were printed. But the British pique was symptomatic of a feeling that went all the way up to Churchill that Gen. Bernard L. Montgomery and the British troops were sometimes given short shrift by the Americans.

Many of the Americans, including the brass and rank and file of the Ghost Army, thought Montgomery was a glory hound who wanted nothing less than to run the entire war. Later, when the Ghost Army played a key role in the successful crossing of the Rhine, Montgomery told his adoring entourage that the fighting was much tougher in the north than where the Americans were advancing. He also made many excuses about the Americans' rapid breakout, saying he was supposed to anchor a great pivot action, and that was the way he planned it all along. Americans from Eisenhower on down were disgusted after Montgomery's preening, self-serving remarks hit the press.

During these few weeks near Paris, Arnett, Morton, Enderlein, Syracuse, Oxenrider, Simenson, Blass, and the other troops were able to thoroughly enjoy themselves as never before since Normandy. But John Walker, a Ghost Army supply officer, said he did not go into Paris because he did not drink and was not interested in the women there because he was a happily married man, having been wed since 1942. Walker, now 80, lives in Cambridge Springs, Pennsylvania. Walker, known for his deep and resonant baritone voice, travels about the country pursuing his hobby, barber shop quartet singing.

A visit to the Louvre showed that most of the art had been removed to the countryside and hidden by the French before the German occupation. The Germans also had been prevented from dismantling the Eiffel Tower for scrap metal, and most of the city had been spared. Arnett recalled standing inside the Hotel des Invalides (from which the revolutionary citizens had set out the morning of July 14, 1789, to storm the Bastille) and looked down on the tomb of Napoleon.

Colonel Simenson described his own Paris adventure:

> We traveled to Paris, where we arrived about 11 A.M. We were billeted in a Parisian hotel, which was the first time any of us had seen a bed since landing in Normandy in June 1944. I checked the room where the two lieutenants were, and they both had been assigned to a single bed! I was angry, and with my helmet, pistol, and rough-looking appearance, demanded better accommodations from the night clerk, who told me he had nothing.
>
> I grabbed him by the collar and we went to the manager, who was already asleep. I told him to get out his bed and that I was going to sleep there (in his bed) that night. He quickly resolved the situation by supplying a new room for the lieutenants. Our whole group had six hours of sleep in real beds. What a luxury!

Manny Frockt of the Twenty-third didn't smoke, so he saved all of his cigarettes that came in K- and C rations or from the Red Cross or from buddies. When he got some leave time, he went to Paris to sell them on the street corners. Cigarettes were like pure gold to the tobacco-starved Parisians. Soon he was doing a land office business. Unfortunately, a general came along, saw him in uniform selling cigarettes, and had him put in an Army jail.

Officers from the Twenty-third had to come and cajole and plead and explain that Manny's skills were needed in the Twenty-third to secure his release. Years later, Manny's wife would chide him, saying, "No wonder you didn't get the Good Conduct Medal." But Manny *did* get the Good Conduct Medal; it was merely held up, like all of the Twenty-third's medals, because of the secrecy that lasted more than five decades after the war.

Fellow soldiers and twins Alan and Gilis Wood-Thomas from New York had been born in Paris and their grandmother still lived there. Their father was a landscape architect who had designed Lincoln Park in Chicago. Because they both spoke French fluently, it was easy to get around and see the sights of Paris while evading the American MPs, who were keeping the city off limits to many GIs. Arnett could claim some ancestry with the French through a line of his family named Gruelle, and a remote uncle, Antoinne Phillip Grouvelle, who as secretary of the National Convention had read Louis XVI his death sentence in January 1793.

One night in Paris when they had decided to stay late while Alan visited his grandmother, an MP stopped them. But Alan spoke such excellent French (Arnett kept quiet) that the Captain presumed them to be Free French of the Interior. He let them go, remarking, "Aw, go on, you damn Free French."

Arnett enjoyed his visits with the Wood-Thomas boys and their grandmother and shared several black market chicken and veg-etable dinners with them. He listened as she told of the hardships of living under German occupation for four years, though she was never harmed. She said she could have fled Paris in 1940, but pre-ferred to stay, hoping the Germans could not hold the city forever.

Richard Morton was gratified by the trust the Army showed in the troops by allowing them into Paris on their own, even though it was only for a short time, just 10 days after the city was liberated. When Morton got his chance, he looked for French girls who spoke English. He found one named Nicole Guerende, a pretty sixteen-year-old, who hailed a horse and carriage and driver to take them all around Paris in those four hours with her acting as his guide. Upon completion of the tour, she gave him an engraved card with her name and address on it and invited him to write her.

Morton said the 603rd quickly moved on across northern France to Luxembourg where he found time to write to Nicole. After exchanging several letters, Nicole wrote that her school was requir-ing each student to adopt an American or English soldier as a *filleul*, or "godson," for the balance of the war as a means of establishing friendships and perfecting their English. It was later learned this was a custom dating from World War I. Nicole invited Morton to be her godson, and of course he had no trouble accepting.

Morton and Nicole carried on a correspondence that lasted throughout the time he was in Europe and even continued when he returned from the war. While on a three-day pass to Paris in February 1945, Morton saw Nicole again and met her parents, her nineteen-year-old sister, Hugette, her fourteen-year-old brother, Michel, and little brother, Henri Claude "Rignet," age five. While going any place with Morton, Michel was required to accompany them as a chaperone. He did not stay right with them, but would follow about half a block away.

While in Paris, Morton stayed in the famous Grand Hotel, which was devoted solely to quartering American and British soldiers on leave from all over Europe. Ernest Hemingway spent much of his time not far away in the Ritz, where he was gradually abandoning one wife, Martha Gellhorn, and courting the woman who would become his fourth wife, Mary Welsh.

Morton wrote Nicole in English and she would reply in French. Both had to have translations done, but soon she began writing in English. The Woods-Thomas boys translated the letters for Morton.

While the Ghost Army was stationed near Paris, various entertainment groups began coming over from the States to entertain the troops. Arnett recalled one day when he was in a perfume shop and Dinah Shore and her entourage came in. He asked Dinah what would be a good perfume to send home. She suggested Scaparrali, which he bought for $11.

When his wife, Leila, received the perfume, she was thrilled but asked him why he didn't also get some Chanel No. 5. Arnett said he had seen that name all over Paris but thought it had something to with the Seine River, which flows through the city.

The troops found that vehicles in Paris had to be guarded carefully. The city was in such a state of need that tires and even the vehicles themselves would be stolen. And any truck carrying food was sure to be a target unless it was guarded. Troops began sleeping on and in their trucks. Once a truck carrying fresh meat for the troops was stripped in less than an hour while its naive driver did a bit of shopping, having left the truck unattended.

Some of the young men found a brothel in Paris where the women dressed as showgirls or can-can girls. The prices were more than reasonable because of the economic depression in all of France during the war, but many warned that these women had been just as available to their recent German captors. The men also were warned about venereal diseases. But like young soldiers throughout history, the lure of the flesh overcame reason, and many availed themselves of what was offered. At one point, some of the women were even brought back to camp for those who could not get passes.

Grant Hess said some of the prostitutes were beautiful and dressed like can-can or showgirls. Unfortunately, because of the promiscuity of the men, including some the cooks for the Twenty-third, venereal disease afflicted a few. Hess said this is what caused the men, as related earlier, to rise up and demand that the cooks be thoroughly checked or removed before they would eat any more food prepared and served by them. This was done, although it was never clear that it was necessary.

One Ghost Trooper reported in a secret journal about the Paris sojourn:

> Paris was put off limits and on limits so often that everyone in confusion visited it whenever possible. It was a great town. Architecturally it had not changed at all. The girls looked like delightful dolls, especially when they whizzed past on bicycles with billowing skirts. They were in considerable contrast to the red-faced Norman farm daughters. The Parisians were very happy to see us, but on the surface did not look particularly maltreated. The thin-legged children were the most obvious products of the war.
>
> Perfume and fineries were fairly easy to buy, and the prices did not become terrible until later. Cigarettes, D-ration chocolate, and K-ration cheese made welcome gifts. Many friends were made. While driving down the Champs Elysees with a jeep-load of fashionable civilians, one had a tendency to think the war was over.

One Ghost Army vignette about Paris occurred at the Ritz Hotel. Some of the Ghost troops went to the Ritz to have a drink and perhaps catch a glimpse of the great one, Ernest Hemingway. Hemingway, sure enough, was at the bar, holding forth, talking like an expert on everything. The handful of Ghost troops kept their distance and listened, according to Ghost trooper Grant Hess, while Hemingway talked and drank, and drank and talked.

They noticed that everything he said was with grand certitude, ex cathedra, as if it were the final and most sagacious observation on everything, the proverbial last word. Then he got around to how men behave in combat, and he began to talk of bravery and cowardice and resolve, what made some men heroic and what made some men run for their lives.

As he spoke, an American infantry officer fresh from heavy combat during which, it was later learned, many of his buddies had been killed, finally could stand it no longer. He suddenly stood up and slammed his drink down on the bar and faced Hemingway.

"Mr. Hemingway," he said with steely calm, "with all due respect, sir, you don't know what the hell you're talking about. Screw you, Mr. Hemingway. With all due respect, Mr. Hemingway, screw you."

Hemingway took one look at the man and correctly sensed that he was looking at the real thing, a product of brutal and recent combat. He also could sense that he'd better not respond. Hemingway just turned back to his drink, took a sip, and said nothing. The young officer then paid up and walked out.

Although no one said anything, and the men *did* respect Hemingway as a writer, they knew that the young officer was probably right. Soon the conversations began again, but Hemingway was subdued for the rest of the evening. The men wondered how Hemingway himself would act *in extremis,* in a heavy combat situation. They wondered if he were not—as Thomas Wolfe once said he was—"a man with phony hair on his chest."

Ironically, it was not long after this that Hemingway was in the Hurtgen Forest with the troops when the position where he bivouacked suddenly was overrun by Germans. According to several eyewitnesses, both officers and enlisted men, Hemingway, in a violation of the rules for war correspondents, grabbed a sub-machine gun and several clips of ammunition. He began fighting fiercely, mowing down Germans, ignoring the bullets buzzing all around him, showing every bit of the courage he so admired in others, courage he had once called "grace under pressure." He later got the Bronze Star for his conduct. Of course, the Ghost troops did not learn of this until after the war.

Many of the troops, including the Ghost Army, had the feeling that the war was just about over after they reached Paris. But Paris was not the Rhine River, and not the fortified city of Metz on the Moselle, and not the Ruhr, and not Berlin. The war was certainly nowhere near over.

Far from it. While Allied support was diverted to the First Airborne Army's unsuccessful attempt to slice into Germany, the First U.S. Army was impaled on the Siegfried Line and the Third U.S. Army halted on the Moselle before the historic fortress city of Metz.

On September 14, the Twenty-third headquarters returned to the war. This time it was to carry out Operation Bettembourg, a purely defensive role in southern Luxembourg for XX Corps.

Paris was therefore a strange interlude because there was much

Sketches of Parisian women drawn by Ghost trooper Vic Dowd during the Ghost Army's stay near Paris. Courtesy Vic Dowd.

Ghost Army soldier Vic Dowd drew this sketch of fellow Ghost trooper Bill Blass on April 18, 1945, near the end of the war in Europe. Blass, who later became a world-famous fashion designer, is shown making sketches of his own. Courtesy Vic Dowd.

heavy fighting yet to be done, and the best and most successful deceptions of the Ghost Army were yet to come. Then there was the little matter of the Battle of the Bulge, yet to occur, that would involve the Ghost troops. There was also Operation Metz. All of this seemed a harsh dose of reality compared to the dreamy pause in Paris.

About half of the Ghost Army soon found itself headed for the vicinity of Metz on the Moselle River, a cold shock after the enticements of Paris. They found Corps Headquarters was in a virtual sea of mud just west of Metz. It was attacking the fortress city with two divisions from a bridgehead to the south while the Ninetieth Infantry contained it from the west. This left only part of the Third Cavalry Group to fill the 50-mile gap to the north. Actually it was nearly 70 miles between the Ninetieth Command Post and the nearest V Corps Division.

Therefore the Twenty-third, in the guise of the Sixth Armored Division, was thrown into this muddy hole. Its mission was first to draw enemy pressure away from the Metz area and second, to reinforce the Forty-third Cavalry Squadron. Later, the second mission became more important than the first, however, after the Germans apparently reacted strongly to the ruse. Originally the operation was scheduled to last not more than 60 hours. But as a hollow checkmate to the newly arrived German Thirty-sixth Infantry Division, the Ghost troops were held in position for seven days, until relieved by the U.S. Eighty-third Infantry.

It was a nervous time, and stressful enough to erase all thoughts of Paris. The troops knew the Germans had the strength to walk through the Ghost troops at any given moment. During this period, the real Sixth Armored was moving east from Lorient.

Four means of deception were used: radio, dummies, sonic effects, and special effects. The radio picture was considered the most effective in this operation and the best executed to date. It involved ten radios in five nets, three of which were real. Only 23 decoy items were placed because enemy air reconnaissance was virtually absent and the danger of compromise by ground agents was considered high.

The sonic company played the tanks in various movements for four nights. On these black, moonless nights the roaring columns were extremely realistic. During the day, the sonic half-tracks were used in special effects. Other visual measures included shoulder patches, bumper markings, military police, busy vehicular activity—

a platoon of light tanks was borrowed from the Forty-third Cavalry Squadron—water points, and a phony major general who was sent into civilian areas.

A short history of the Sixth Armored was given all the men so they would know what they were talking about. They were then sent into nearby towns for church services, showers, and recreation, but primarily to spread the story as subtly as possible that they were the Sixth Armored troops. More than one shifty-eyed civilian was observed photographing bumpers, taking notes, and asking more than friendly questions. The area was brimming with would-be German spies, who probably thought the American soldiers quite naive.

Only half of the command was used in this operation. The rest of the unit stayed in St. Germain near Paris until September 20 and then moved up to Verdun. It was later felt that these personnel could have been used to better advantage at Bettembourg, and thereafter no major operation was performed at less than full strength. Despite this and the fact that XX Corps prolonged the operation longer than a ruse normally could be sustained, Bettembourg was considered a resounding success by Army intelligence analysts at the time.

This was when the Sixth Armored Division won the nickname from German intelligence, as was learned after the war, of the "Phantom Division." The Germans were mystified as to how it could pop up in several places so quickly.

On September 25, the entire Twenty-third reassembled in Luxembourg City. At that time, the worst pessimist could not predict that the headquarters would remain there for nearly seven months. It was not such a bad city. In fact, the quarters were considered excellent by the men and the officers, but the forward motion was missing, and the prospect of less activity was depressing after having been on the move.

The staff first seized the spacious German legation but was subsequently ranked out of and down to the slightly less sumptuous Italian legation quarters. This building was not as roomy but the china was gilt-edged and the wine glasses rang like bells. A "Mademoiselle Nestgen"—a splendid cook—was engaged together with a fireman and two upstairs maids. Headquarters Company and the 3132nd were billeted in the Hollerich School and the Engineers and Signal Company took over a big seminary full of atrocious Nazi murals, which they covered over. It began to look to some of the men as if the Twenty-third was bedding down for the winter.

About a week later, the Twenty-third was called on again. As the front was reshuffled and U.S. striking power moved north, the Twenty-third could be employed to advantage. In this case, the Fifth Armored Division, which liberated Luxembourg early in September, was being pulled 60 miles north to the area around Malmedy, Belgium. In Operation Wiltz, October 4-10, the Twenty-third was asked to "cover" the movement of this division.

The original plan was to cover the Fifth Armored completely; that is to say, permit the entire division to rumble 60 miles undetected and persuade the German G-2 that it had never moved at all. In order to have done this, it would have been necessary for the division to blackout thoroughly or remove all visual means of identification, then go north by infiltration at night. Unfortunately, it was impossible to secure such camouflage cooperation at this time. The division did remove its bumper markings, but Fifth Armored shoulder patches were still obvious, and the huge clanking columns blocked the roads in full daylight.

So the Twenty-third decided to ride with the punch and admit that the Fifth Armored had moved, but not as far as it actually had. The Twenty-third notional unit set up in the vicinity of Malscheid, Belgium, which was about 20 miles short of the real setup. The notional division headquarters established their command posts near Wiltz, Luxembourg, or about 35 miles to the south of their real counterparts.

In Operation Wiltz, deception relied mainly on spoof radio and special effects. No dummies and very little sonic were used. The signal picture employed 17 radios over an area of 1,000 square miles. This cover operation was notable for an advance in deceptive radio techniques. Since the Fifth Armored radios were active in the old area, the Twenty-third radios began "infiltrating" into the real nets two days before the actual operation began.

This meant that Ghost radios had enough time to be briefed thoroughly by the real Fifth Armored operators and gradually take over the operation of the nets. The transition from real to spoof was therefore smooth, and the enemy radio intelligence should have had a hard time detecting it. Naturally, the real Fifth Armored moved north under radio silence while the Ghost Twenty-third used its call signs, frequencies, cryptographic systems, and distinctive traits.

The big lesson re-learned in Wiltz was the absolute necessity for coordinating deceptive efforts with the actions of the covered unit.

Because of the unconcealed movement of the Fifth Armored Division, the chances for success of the operation were considered greatly reduced.

On October 10, when Operation Wiltz was terminated, most of the Twenty-third returned to Luxembourg. A sonic task force, however, headed north for what appeared to be the first operation inside Germany. This operation was called Vaseline, but it never materialized. Its mission was to indicate an armored division—the Fifth—concentrating for an attack across the border just south of Monschau. It would have been loud, short, and possibly furious because the play area was under intense enemy observed artillery fire.

The sonic unit was heavily supported by a company of medium tanks, a company of armored infantry, and a battery of armored artillery. The action would have jumped off the following morning from a concealed position farther south. Vaseline was postponed over a number of days and finally called off altogether when the Fifth Armored was deployed elsewhere.

For the next three weeks, the Twenty-third mostly enjoyed Luxembourg. Many soldiers and officers found friends among what they humorously termed "the Luxembourgeoise." It wasn't long before the native *moyen* replaced "hello," and the girls seemed to grow less plump and became more appealing, although never quite Parisian, the men said. General Bradley's Twelfth Army Group forward command post, called Eagle Tac, moved in and the social competition became more intense. Perhaps in deference to General Bradley, the Germans started pumping some large caliber railroad shells into the city.

Finally, on October 22, an assignment came down from V Corps of the First Army. It was another "cover job." The Ghosts were destined to play a distant hand in the grinding autumn operation to seize control of the Roer River east of Aachen. At least it was supposed to make it easier for the Fourth Infantry Division to participate in this operation.

Operation Elsenborn, November 3-12, revolved around a complicated series of divisional moves. First, the Twenty-eighth Infantry—known as the "bloody bucket" because of its heavy losses and high turnover—left Elsenborn barracks to replace the Ninth Infantry for the abortive push toward the Roer River dams. Eisenhower was afraid that the Germans would blow up the dams to block the Allied advance.

The Ninth Infantry then came to Elsenborn for a much-needed rest. After it had caught its breath, it planned to relieve the Fourth Infantry Division, which in turn was going up to the Hurtgen Forest to put its strong back behind the Twenty-eighth's drive. The Elsenborn sector was under V Corps. The Roer River came under VII Corps. The Twenty-third's objective was to cover the northward movement of the Fourth Infantry Division by simulating the division in the rest camp at Elsenborn barracks.

Since the Ghost troops were involved in two other simultaneous jobs, only one-third of the command took part in Elsenborn. No dummies or sonics were needed for this one, although plenty of radio and special effects were used. The Twenty-third radios began to infiltrate into the Fourth Infantry nets, just as in Operation Wiltz, while the Fourth was still holding part of the front. For over a week, the Twenty-third radios and operators handled all of the Fourth's transmissions. It was ample time for the Twenty-third radios to become identified as those of the Fourth.

When the Ninth Infantry was resting at Elsenborn, it was instructed by V Corps, prompted by a request from the Ghost Army, to take a three-day radio exercise, or testing procedure. Otherwise, its radios would naturally have been silent. This established a precedent and enabled the phony Fourth to take the same Corps-directed exercise. Every afternoon from November 8 to November 11, Ghost radios that had been spotted as the Fourth Infantry by the German Signal Intelligence blared forth from Elsenborn. One hundred operators and 22 transmitters were engaged in this massive radio deception. As usual, the Germans thought the Americans were just plain stupid for chattering away on their battlefield radios, giving away everything from troop strength to the approximate numbers of armor and artillery pieces.

The rest of the operation was filled out by the Special Effects section, whose road signs were especially effective. As far as the U.S. Army was concerned, everyone thought the Fourth was resting in Elsenborn barracks, even officers of the real division were sucked into the phony command post and stared blankly around at the unfamiliar faces.

It was like a Rod Serling or Alfred Hitchcock drama when they would walk in and find all the familiar markings, yet not one face they knew. It was like coming home and finding another family living in your house. It was a constant source of amusement for the

Ghost troops. The first snow of 1944 made vehicular movement difficult, but Fourth bumper markings and MPs were spread liberally around the neighborhood.

This operation was especially notable for the cooperation given by both V Corps and the Fourth Infantry. The old days of skepticism and doubt were finally erased among the leaders of the regular units. It was a model in respect to cooperation. The division signal section made the Twenty-third radio infiltration very easy, and originated sustaining traffic in order to keep the nets alive.

Before moving, the division blacked out thoroughly by erasing all visual evidences and then infiltrated north on secondary roads at night. V Corps also did everything that the Twenty-third told them was necessary to make Elsenborn a success. And when the Fourth finally jumped off into the terrible woods of Hurtgen, the Germans were shocked at their appearance. In fact, a captured German overlay showed that they were still in Elsenborn. This was typical of the proof of the success of the Ghost Army's deception time after time.

Meanwhile, General Patton's Third Army was also on the offensive and the Twenty-third was engaged down there also. In operation Casanova November 4 to 9, a detachment of the Twenty-third supported a river crossing in the vicinity of Ukange. The idea was to use the 3132nd sonic bridge-building program together with a diversionary crossing by a battalion of the Ninety-fifth Infantry Division dressed as soldiers of the Ninetieth. This would draw the enemy's attention away from the main XX Corps effort of the Ninetieth backed by the Tenth Armored Division 11 miles down the Moselle.

At the last moment, it was decided not to use sonic because Patton had decided not to build a real bridge at Ukange and did not want to call his shot in advance. Therefore Operation Casanova was limited to special effects alone. It splattered the Ukange area with Ninetieth Division "atmosphere."

But despite this, according to a Twelfth Army Group G-2 report, the enemy was surprised by the Ninetieth's crossing north of Thionville, and Metz soon fell to the Third Army.

Another part of the XX Corps' final action against Metz was the secret move of the Corps artillery to a support position behind the Ninetieth Infantry Division's main effort. The Twenty-third also had a big role in this. From November 2 to November 10, Operation Dallas maintained an extensive display of dummy guns and flash devices in the old XX Corps artillery area around Jarny, France.

Operation Dallas did not attempt to support the deception by myth alone. The phony artillery brigade was not completely phony. Every battalion was reinforced by at least one battery of real artillery guns. One battalion had a battery of captured German 88s, which they fired, giving the Germans a taste of their own most terrible artillery piece.

The Dallas battalions were built around the gun batteries and expanded to regular size by the addition of rubber dummies and flash devices. In all, XX Corps supplied over 500 men and 12 guns to replace 2,230 men and 48 real artillery pieces. The Ghost troops here consisted of just 195 men, 36 dummies, and artillery flashes. A couple of well-armed German patrols might have run through the entire operation had they known the truth. The same tempo of harassing fire was maintained.

The mock flashes were synchronized with the real fire orders to provide the effect of battalion concentrations. Patrolling and adjustment of fire by liaison planes was continued as before. Real Corps units departed secretly and in the dead of night. Operation Dallas did not use radio or sonic deception, however.

Nearly a month elapsed before the Twenty-third was given another "problem" to solve. Although this inactivity led to boredom, obesity, and internecine strife as with any Army group with time on its hands, the weather in Luxembourg was getting colder by the minute and operations lost their picnic attraction. The troops were kept busy, but unhappy, taking basic courses in military courtesy, interior guard, first aid, and even sanitation.

It was very difficult for men of far above average IQ to have to submit to this waste of time, so there were many practical jokes, a lot of reading and friendly debates, card games, and long philosophical discussions. Because the men had high IQs, the discussions were not what you would hear in most Army barracks.

The irrepressible Sergeant Berry helped save many nights with his "Blarney Theater." This was not the first or last location in which he set up his old faithful 16mm gun, or 16mm camera. He said he shot many hours of the entertainment. It may have been amateurish, but it was a welcome diversion during this lull in Ghost Army activity.

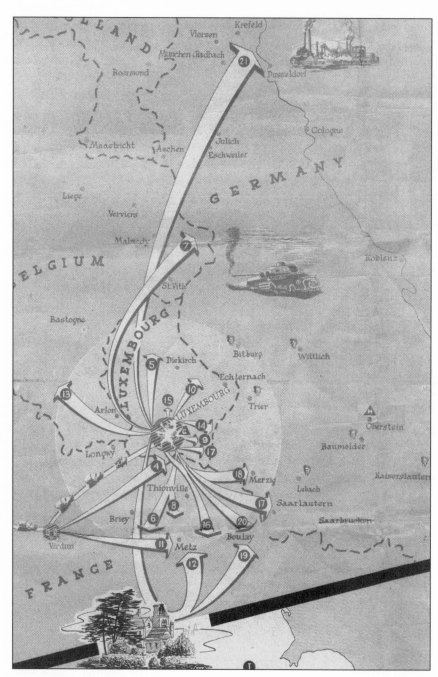

An overview of the Ghost Army operations, a map made as part of the unit's official history and not declassified for more than 50 years after the end of World War II. U.S. Army map.

Chapter Nine

Liberation of Torce

After leaving Paris, the Twenty-third's Ghost Army was directed to take a position at Bettenbourg, Luxembourg. But enroute to Bettenbourg, the Twenty-third was ordered to set up a temporary command post to await further details of the Bettenbourg operation. While camped, the men heard that a nearby French town, Torce, still had a few good restaurants that were functioning, along with running water, electric lights, and plenty of food. It was somehow virtually unscathed by the war that had swept around the town.

A convoy consisting of most of the Ghost Army, headed by Colonel Reeder, decided to visit the town for a bit of decent food and relax awhile. It would be a chance to clean up, shave, wash dirty uniforms and underwear, and recuperate a bit. What they did not know was that American front-line troops had virtually bypassed the town in hot pursuit of its German occupiers.

As a consequence, the Ghost troops arrived just as the townspeople were coming to realize that the Americans had in fact liberated them. The Nazi occupiers had fled so fast they even left some of their equipment, including a large number of the ubiquitous swastikas and even some weapons. The grateful townsfolk planned to welcome the American conquerors in a big way and quickly began to remove overt evidence of the Nazi occupation.

The Ghost Army troops were dumbfounded by the reception they got as they drove into town, and knew they did not really deserve it. Somehow, no large force of Allied troops had been in Torce since the German retreat. The entire town had been ready to be liberated and provide a grand welcome to their liberators. Never mind if the Ghost Army was not a front-line combat outfit. Who knew, anyway? They certainly looked formidable enough. So Torce became the only town officially liberated by the Ghost Army.

Everyone turned out, including all the city officials, a band, and several hundred cheering residents. Some waved the tri-color and some had obtained a few small American flags. The men were delighted by the reception and especially enjoyed the attention of all the pretty young women, some of whom threw flowers. Some kissed GIs on their bearded cheeks. The men tossed them chocolate.

Here is a surviving Ghost Army description:

> Torce was the only town in all Europe officially liberated by the Twenty-third. It was an impressive ceremony. There was a crack American color guard from the Signal Company, a band of French Firemen, a pretty column of schoolchildren with white flowers and leading citizens. Colonel Reeder delivered a gallant speech which ended with a rousing Vive La France! Torceans were visibly moved and their rendition of Le Marseillaise was all the more thrilling after four years of silence.

The mayor and other town officials made long speeches in praise of their liberators. Most of the Ghost troops knew a bit of high school French, although some were fluent. Some had picked up all the words they needed while in Paris. They all listened respectfully. Pretty girls flirted and smiled, accepting chocolate from the troops. The Ghost troops had strolled by accident into their own private Eden.

The first bottle of Cointreau were obtained and Maj. Joseph P. Kelly began making very popular "sidecars," which were one-third Cointreau, one-third cognac, and one-third lemon juice. "Everyone stopped throwing away the lemon powder packets in their K-ration dinners so they could make sidecars," said one soldier.

Some of the men ate at the small restaurants in the town. The French onion soup was a specialty. A favorite place was the Hotel du Commerce in Evron. Any American in uniform was a hero.

One Ghost trooper who asked not to be identified said this was the first city outside of Paris where the young women were really sultry and lovely. He said the girls of Normandy, while pliant and accessible, were usually plump and pink and almost "too wholesome" in a milk-maid kind of way to be sexy. The Germans called the girls of Normandy *"rein und hold,"* which is a line from the German poet Heine: *"Du bist wie eine Blume, so rein und hold."* ("You are like a flower, so wholesomely clean and lovely.")

Troops learned that *"rein und hold"* was almost untranslatable, but meant roughly a very wholesome and pure beauty. At last the local girls were becoming less wholesome and freckled and more glamorous. They wore makeup while the Normandy girls merely scrubbed their faces. But most said Paris was the best of all, with Torce a very, very close second.

Before Bettenbourg, trucks of the Twenty-third roamed around the countryside checking out what the Germans had done. In the town of Les Granges, the men heard that the Germans had stored something in a warehouse. They forced it open and found "an immense cache" of German liquor. It included the finest wines and most particularly, cognac. The men immediately began to repack several of the trucks much more thoroughly and compactly, freeing up space for 520 cases or 6,240 bottles of cognac.

This bivouac area became known as "Cognac Hill." Shortly after the liquor discovery, one officer quipped in a memo, "The Blarney Theater showed the movie 'Ghostbreakers' with Bud Abbott and Lou Costello for four nights running but each night it looked different."

The next destination was Bettenbourg, and it was back to work. Here, the objective was to relieve pressure on the XX Corps' bridge-head south of Metz by preventing the Germans from reinforcing Metz, the historic fortress city. Hitler had personally ordered that every German was to fight to the death at Metz.

This was how important the Nazis viewed this historic fort on the Moselle River. It had never been taken by force throughout its history, which stretched back to medieval times. It was viewed as the key to the Moselle Valley. General Patton was fascinated by it because of its long history in war. It was similar to a German West Point, and was a natural fortress designed by nature.

The American XX Corps was headquartered in a muddy area just west of Metz. It was attacking the fortress city with two divisions from a bridgehead to the south, while the Ninetieth Infantry contained it from the west. Unfortunately, this left only a small part of the Third Cavalry Group to fill a 50-mile gap to the north.

The Twenty-third, in the guise of the Sixth Armored Division, was thrown into this precarious hole. Many of the men still had terrible cognac hangovers from drinking the cache of booze. War was even more hell than usual after the heady liberties in Paris and Torce. Now suddenly they were in a dangerous position. Their safety and the success of the mission depended on how realistically they could bluff the Germans. Had the Germans known the truth, they would have attacked the Twenty-third like lightning. And this late in the war, the Germans had a bad habit of shooting prisoners unceremoniously because they did not have the capacity to take care of them or even imprison them.

The mission of the Twenty-third in this role was to draw enemy pressure from the Metz area and to reinforce the Forty-third Cavalry. Later, the second mission became more important than the first when the Germans attacked the Forty-third. The Twenty-third was first told this mission was to last just 60 hours until more troops could be brought up. Seven days later they were still awaiting eventual relief by the 83rd Infantry. The fighting ability of the Twenty-third was minuscule to nonexistent compared to a normal division or even a regiment. It was stretched thin in this operation.

But the Germans were deceived, and even sent heavy reinforcements to defend in front of the Ghost Army. More importantly, they were afraid to attack what they thought was an overwhelming force. Had they only known, even a small attack here would have cut through the Americans like a hot knife in butter. The Germans used aerial reconnaissance extensively in this operation, usually by a light aircraft, the ubiquitous "Storch" (Stork), at dusk. The camouflage nets and inflatables, along with radio traffic and night sounds of moving tanks, half-tracks, and even swearing of men, were swallowed whole by the enemy. Even the inflatable howitzers were made more realistic by scattering empty howitzer shells on the ground.

Observers in the German light planes returned to report a massive buildup. In actual fact, they would have overrun the Twenty-third with a couple of companies of regular troops. But this allowed the real Sixth Armored Division to move east from Lorient and launch a successful attack.

A recently declassified Army document said, with the usual understatement: "Bettenbourg is believed to have been a success."

It might be held partially responsible for the German nickname for the real Sixth Armored Division—"the Phantom Division." This name did not stick, however, because early on the men began referring to themselves as the Ghost Army. Several of them collaborated on the design of a Ghost patch, the inspiration for the dust jacket design of this book, but they were warned never to wear any such patch.

Chapter Ten

Operation Metz

As any veteran of the Ghost Army's campaigns can tell you, most of France is drained by five large river systems. The Ghost troops traveled across or along all of them. The most famous is the Seine, which flows down from Burgundy, through Paris, and empties into the English Channel at Le Havre. With its major tributaries, including the Oise, Marne, and Eure rivers, it drains most of Upper Normandy and the Paris Basin, and is an important waterway to and from Paris. The Loire River, which has the largest drainage basin of any river in France, rises in the Massif Central.

Tributaries such as the Vienne, Cher, and Sarthe rivers join the Loire before it flows into the Atlantic Ocean below Nantes. The Rhine River starts in the Swiss Alps and enters the North Sea in the Netherlands, where it becomes the boundary between Germany and France. Most of the often-disputed Alsace and Lorraine region is drained by the Rhine and its larger tributaries, the Meuse and Moselle.

The Germans planned to use the natural barriers formed by these rivers as extensively as possible to slow the Allied attacks and give them time to regroup and rebuild. The German high command particularly wanted to make a strong stand on the Moselle and then the Rhine rivers. One place it hoped to slow the Allied advance was at the ancient fortress city of Metz on the east bank of the Moselle, a valuable military fort since Roman times.

The Ghost Army would play a key role in operations around Metz, which is now the capital of the Moselle area in northeast France. Before the war it had a population of about 80,000 people and is still a transportation and manufacturing center for the Lorraine region. There are 110,000 people in the city today.

A Ghost trooper stencils Ninetieth Division markings on a jeep. The Ghost troops had to constantly change the markings on their vehicles, along with their shoulder patches. U.S. Army photo.

Hitler ordered his armies to hold Metz to the last man. During the Roman conquest of the area, it was known as Divodurum and was also the capital of the Celtic's Mediomatrici. Because of its location at the junction of several major highways and on the Moselle River, the town has always had great military importance.

In the year 843 it became capital of the Kingdom of Lorraine, and several diets and councils were held in the city. The town became part of the East Frank Kingdom in 870, and, as part of Lorraine, belonged to France.

During the Franco-Prussian War of 1870-71, Metz was the headquarters of the Third French Army under Bazaine. It was surrounded by troops led by Prince Frederick Charles of Prussia, and Metz was forced to surrender its 6,000 French officers and 170,000 men. By the Treaty of Frankfort, Metz once more became a German city. It had been occupied by either France or Germany in a tug-of-war for centuries. Napoleon III had a circle of fortifications built.

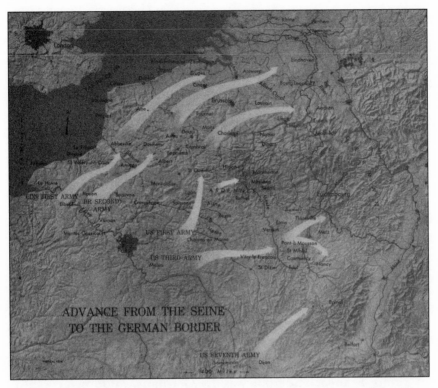

A map showing the U.S. Army advance on a wide front from the Seine River to the German border. The Ghost Army was involved in a number of the actions, including the siege of Metz and the crossing of the Rhine River. U.S. Army map.

When the Germans took over in the late 1800s, they made the strongest part of the fortifications face west. Then after the French took it back they made an effort to connect the ancient city to the Maginot Line. The city itself contained an inner circle of 15 forts. There were heavy guns in fortifications in a circle about six or seven miles outside the city. Each of these mini-forts was designed to be self-sufficient.

Men of the Ghost Army watched as P-47s and even heavy bombers on occasion tried to penetrate the heavy bunkers, to no avail. Frontal attacks on the city repeatedly were beaten back. Patton eyed the city but later was forced to bypass it. His fascination by the fortress city was equaled by Hitler's, who did not want to give it up without a big fight. And the Allies could not simply ignore it for fear of creating a troublesome pocket that could attack rear troops and disrupt communication and supply lines.

The Germans had fortified the city well, viewing it as one of the last strongholds to thwart an Allied push to the Rhine River. It was hoped that the Germans in the city could be immobilized if they were led to believe that they were confronted by a substantial Allied force. This was deemed necessary because of the fear that they might break out of the city and attack Patton or others from the rear, or at the very least cut supply and communication lines. Patton crossed the Moselle between Metz and Nancy. The idea was to envelop the city without confronting its heavy fortifications.

The Ghost Army had two major parts to play in the Allied attack on Metz, which began on New Year's Day in 1945 and was carried out during the next few weeks. The first was to simulate, by special effects, the bumper markings, shoulder patches, signs, and traffic of the Eighty-seventh Infantry Division. The Battle of the Bulge, not yet a sure thing for the Allies, was taking all available American divisions. It was said by the Ghost troops that "the bottom of the barrel had been reached and General Patton was demanding some of the staves." The Ghost Army was to imitate some of those staves.

Meanwhile, the Eighty-seventh had actually moved to the vicinity of Reims, France. The hope was the Germans would make a false deduction as to its location. The area around Metz was known to be teeming with spies among the civilian population, including the usual leftover Vichy French. The operation included the full range of the Ghost Army's talents, including phony radio traffic, inflatables, camouflage netting, tracks in the snow and earth for reconnaissance planes to see, and even well-calculated "loose talk" by men among the civilian population in the area.

The second major part of the Metz operation came later when the Ghost Army simulated the Ninetieth Infantry Division. The Ninetieth, a veteran Normandy outfit that had seen much hard fighting, was holding the Saar line east of Thionville. It was needed for the American drive against the Nazi bulge at Bastogne. The Ninety-fourth Infantry was rushing over from Lorient to take its place but looked like it would be a little late.

The Twenty-third's mission was to hold by simulation alone the Ninetieth in its old location until the Ninety-fourth was securely in its position and also to bring the Ninetieth south to a reserve area in Metz. Eleven Twenty-third radios replaced the existing Ninetieth network for 3 to 18 hours, but there was no message traffic and only the most infrequent callups.

In Metz, the rest of the command set up the normal procedures on division special effects. Shoulders, bumpers, and signs advertised the presence of the Ninetieth throughout the area. It was very cold and the roads were slick with packed snow, but the Twenty-third men and vehicles were kept out of doors during most of the daylight hours. No sonic, dummies, or radio were used in the Metz operation.

In spite of the fact that one Ninetieth regiment had pulled out without obliterating its identity as it should have, the Twelfth Army G-2 spotlighted the secret move as a model and called it a complete success. The Ninetieth did do a splendid job in the Battle of the Bulge. It cut off an entire Nazi paratroop regiment on the first day.

As soon as Metz 2 was completed, the Ghost Army's deception machinery was set in motion to do the same job for the Ninety-fourth Infantry Division, which was going to be relieved by the Bulge-tired Twenty-sixth Infantry Division. By the time the Ninety-fourth network was taken over by the Twenty-third radios, however, the situation had become less critical and Metz 3 was called off.

It was here that the Germans tried to drop a few paratroopers behind American lines to sow confusion, at the very least, and disrupt communication and supply lines. Most of them turned out to be Hitler youth. Gusty winds blew them all over the countryside and the Twenty-third's troops stopped their technical work to help round them up. Most surrendered meekly. One of them ran into a barn.

Enderlein ran into the barn ready to shoot. The youth threw down his weapon and held up his hands, trembling. Enderlein recalled that the young man was anything but the Nazi *"Ubermensch"* of propaganda.

"He had a brand new Mauser 8mm rifle," said Enderlein "It was very nice. I disassembled it, packed it in a box, and mailed it to my dad. Dad assembled it for me before I got home. I still have it and still use it on deer hunts even today. It is a very accurate, nice rifle."

But not all of the Hitler youth were so docile. Some fought fiercely and were killed by the Americans. In one case, the Twenty-third's movements were halted by one machine gun emplacement at a rail line. They checked it out with powerful binoculars and saw what looked like a teenaged German. Because of this, they decided to try to capture rather than kill the boy. When they finally got behind

Men assemble a dummy tank used by the Ghost Army. U.S. Army photo.

the machine gun, they found it manned by a fifteen-year-old Hitler Youth soldier with a long mane of blond hair. They captured him and he was furious, cursing them and acting very tough.

"He was also doing a lot of Sig Heiling," said Enderlein. So the men tied him to a wire-cutter—the angle iron welded on the front of each jeep to prevent decapitation by the wires strung across roads by retreating Germans. Then they took him for a high-speed trip down various country roads.

They had already cleared these roads of wire but the German teenager didn't know this. He thought that one of the wires would cut him in half at any moment. By the time they returned, the German teen was crying and his spirit completely broken. They gave him a chocolate bar and he was completely docile after that.

In the second phase of the Metz operation, a previously classified Army report states: "The Battle of the Bulge was still taking all available American Divisions."

In fact the bottom of the barrel had been reached.

The men of the Twenty-third, to heighten realism, were kept driving around and around during daylight hours. As usual, the trucks had just two men in the back so that a casual observer or Germans with binoculars would think the trucks were full of men. Bill Blass and Bob Tompkins often drew this duty, sitting in the trucks all day on bumpy, icy roads. It was cold and miserable duty, Tompkins recalls, like taking a very long trip on hard seats on bumpy roads. And all the while, they hoped the villagers would not recognize them and discover that the same few trucks were riding around and around, over and over.

Fortunately, to most Europeans by this time, an American GI had become about as indistinguishable from one another as jeeps and tanks. The Ghost Army counted on this.

From Metz, the Twenty-third raced north to take part in another job dubbed Operation L'Eglise January 10-13. On the way up, some members were dropped off in Briey, France, which was to be headquarters of the main body until April. They began to clean out the Caserne Guard Mobile in preparation for the return of the command. Due to some local politics, it was difficult to turn on the plumbing.

The Briey Water Commissioner demanded two dozen bars of chocolate D-rations, a case of soap, and sixteen loaves of white bread. His demands were refused, so the plumbing became very erratic as he attempted to get even.

At this time, the Fourth Armored Division fighting with the 101st Airborne Division at Bastogne was being withdrawn. It was to be used in a new blow east of Luxembourg. The effectiveness of this attack was going to be increased by making the move under secret blackout and covering the departure with the Twenty-third.

By radio and special effects, the notional Fourth Armored was brought back from Bastogne into VIII Corps reserves in the vicinity of L'Eglise, Belgium. No dummies or sonic were used. They really were not needed. The region was swarming with tanks from four armored divisions: the Fourth was blacked out; but the Sixth, Tenth, and Eleventh were everywhere.

It was incredibly cold, but the snow was lovelier than the finest Belgian lace. Everyone was snugly billeted. The fictional headquarters was especially comfortable in a home that turned out to belong to a notorious collaborator. He kept the fires high and served hot chocolate every night.

His duplicity actually turned out to be a bonus, however, because the men never discussed secret business around him—always playing their assigned roles just in case—and he took them at face value. In fact, this was a help as they strove for authenticity. Another advantage Americans had around would-be spies was that their language was so full of idioms that it was hard for a foreigner who had not lived in the United States to follow them precisely.

The Fourth Armored did not attack until March when it broke through to the Rhine. Until that time it remained under a security blackout and its location was not even carried in the Twelfth Army Group G-3 periodic papers. The Twenty-third maintained its ruse for a few days and then whistled back to its new base camp in Briey. The planning staff officers went back to their Italian legation in Luxembourg.

Four days later, the 3132nd part of the Ghost Army drove as fast as possible up the Moselle River east of Luxembourg for a one-night stand involving sonic alone. This operation, called Flaxweiler, was carried out in the middle of January. It was designed to assist the XII Corps Diekirch attack by supporting a river crossing demonstration 19 miles to the south. This division was operated by the Second Cavalry Group. The Cavalry stepped up reconnaissance, displaying bridging material and boats, threw over some artillery fire and smoke, moved some tanks up, and crossed the river with combat patrols.

The 3132nd augmented the deception with a heavy sound play. They set up on a little road 500 yards from the river. The sonic vehicles also raced up and down—always at night—broadcasting the arrival of tank forces using the tank noises and sounds. A decided increase in enemy artillery fires was received in this area the next morning, but the 3132nd had already slipped back to Briey before daylight.

When the Ghost Army signalman reported into the Fourth Infantry Division mess for Operation Steinsel at the end of January, the cook threw up his hands in dismay, crying: "Here come those S.O.B.s who helped get us shot to hell in the Hurtgen Forest." Steinsel was a cover job similar to Elsenborn, but only fake radio traffic was used.

The deception was successful, and later called one of the most economical ever attempted: just 72 men, 4 officers, and 22 vehicles were used in this operation. No mess trucks were taken along. There were plenty of warm messes in this area and people ate wherever they happened to be. The weather continued icy cold and snow still blanked the ground.

Steinsel was a simple matter of infiltrating spoof radios into the Fourth Division network beginning two days before the operation began. It was made easier due to the fact that Twenty-third operators had already worked with the Fourth Division and were familiar with its procedures.

In the big picture, the Fourth Infantry was set to be pulled out of the line at Diekirch-Echternach to swing north for a surprise punch into Houffalize. By radio, the Twenty-third was to show a phony Fourth in XII Corps reserve near Luxembourg until the real Fourth jumped off. Operation Steinsel was probably aided by the simultaneous cross-movements of many real divisions in that general area.

In addition to the secret Fourth, the Seventy-sixth Infantry under a security blackout had just replaced the Eighty-seventh on the right flank; the Eightieth had come down to relieve the Fourth. A little further west the Twenty-sixth had withdrawn to make a secret move to XX Corps. The Ninety-fifth was making a similar move northward. In all, four divisions were tearing around with their bumper markings and shoulder patches removed.

Unfortunately, the anti-visual discipline of the Fourth was not as good as it had been in Elsenborn. The advance party reconnoitered the Houffalize area in full Fourth display, and there were a few untouched bumpers and shoulders in the daylight convoys. Naturally, it does not take many oversights to compromise the secret movement of a division. It irked the Ghost troops when they were so attentive to the smallest details, only to have other units get sloppy.

January, a full and busy month for the Ghost Army, wound up with Operation Landonville, which spilled over into February. Landonville was practically identical to Metz 2, even to the same area. Only in this case the Ninety-fifth Infantry was being replaced by the Twenty-sixth. It had been the Ninetieth and the Ninety-fourth in Metz 2. The Ghost troops played the Ninety-fifth and by radio alone held them in position for two days until the ticklish transition period was over. The phony Ninety-fifth was brought back into reserve east of Metz. Both real divisions obliterated all identifying marks and insignia during the relief.

The fake command post of the Ninety-fifth was in the gloomiest chateau in all of Lorraine, according to Ghost troops. Things brightened a bit when one of the troops received from home a bottle of Southern Comfort, which he shared. The arctic weather finally broke on February 1. The ride back to the base camp in Briey was slushy but almost balmy compared to the weather for the past few months. The most popular food during this operation was a bar of D-ration heated to fudge-like consistency over a pot-bellied stove.

Almost immediately, the Ghost troops were called out to aid in a diversionary effort along the southern half of the Third Army front, Operation Whipsaw. This effort was really two simultaneous operations: one pure sonic and the other pure dummy. No special effects or spoof radio were used, although the signal company furnished its usual straight communication.

The sonic half of the job was carried out in the sector east of Luxembourg. The 3132nd had played there less than a month before in Operation Flaxweiler. This time it projected the sound assembly of three tank battalions in Grevenmacher on the night of February 1 and 2. The following night, it did the same in Wormeldingen. During the third night, it broadcast random tank movements around both areas and then returned to Briey.

Again the sonic demonstration was greatly assisted by real diversionary tactics of the Second Cavalry Group. The Germans reacted to the combined deceptive effort by a generous use of flares to try to see what was going on, an increase in mortar and artillery fire, and low-flying reconnaissance planes.

The decoy operation was not as profitable. This half of Whipsaw centered around Saarlautern 30 miles south of the sonic show. Rubber dummies and camouflage nets were installed in positions formerly occupied by real U.S. batteries. No real guns or flashes were employed as in Operation Dallas. It was just a static representation of two battalions of field artillery.

Sonic deception became more popular as more top officers learned of its effectiveness by word of mouth. About a week afer Whipsaw, the 3132nd was on another mission for XX Corps. They called this one Merzig, during the middle of February. It was an attempt to pin down the elusive Eleventh Panzer Division. The Eleventh Panzers were variously reported all over the front and as far east as Russia, but there were strong indications that most of the outfit was near Remich opposite the U.S. Ninety-fourth Infantry. In this position they were fairly harmless, so the Twelfth Army Group wanted them to stay there. For this purpose, the 3132nd simulated by sound the concentration of American armor in the vicinity of Merzig some 15 miles to the southeast.

Just as the Second Cavalry Group had done in Flaxweiler and

Whipsaw, the Third Cavalry Group did in Merzig. The Cavalry diversionary effort included a real tank buildup, increased fire, and a
smoke screen. Naturally, this flesh and blood deception materially
assisted the more gossamer contribution of the Ghost troops. No
one ever knew exactly what happened to the Eleventh Panzer, but
the enemy certainly acted up locally and appeared frozen in place.

During the two nights of operation, 135 rounds of 80mm mortar
and 28 rounds of German artillery fire exploded in the vicinity. Also,
enemy planes flew over on the hour every hour of darkness dropping flares. This was a clear indication that the Germans feared a
massive attack at that point—one the few hundred men of the Ghost
Army would have been hard pressed to mount.

The Merzig commander was sorry he did not have rubber tanks to
simulate a combat command in a convoy column along the road to
heighten the effect even more.

Operation Lochinvar during the first couple of weeks of March
was rather complicated. It was a little like the old shell game with
someone knocking over the table before the end. On February 28,
the Ghost Army was called in by its best customer, XX Corps, to help
cover the juggling of the three divisions on the Saar front.

First, the tired Ninety-fourth on the north was to be relieved by
the Twenty-sixth, the division on its immediate right. Next, the hole
left by the Twenty-sixth was to be filled by the Sixty-fifth, the fresh
green troops from the states. Other troops said they were so fresh
they still had cosmolene (a heavy preservative oil) on them. This was
the plan, but the Ghost Army was supposed to deceive the Germans
into believing that the Ninety-fourth and the Twenty-sixth were
merely exchanging sectors.

The freshman Sixty-fifth was to be hidden under the veteran man-
tle of the Ninety-fourth. The Sixty-fifth infantrymen were to wear
Ninety-fourth shoulder patches. The Sixty-fifth vehicles were to be
marked Ninety-fourth. Spoof radios that had infiltrated into the
Ninety-fourth radio nets were to move down and play in the Sixty-
fifth area. Meanwhile, the real Ninety-fourth was to go into Corps
reserve and get a good rest.

What actually happened was quite different. When the operation was
only partially complete, the Germans took advantage of what they per-
ceived as an unstable situation and attacked. This threw Operation
Lochinvar into a complete tailspin. The vulnerable Ninety-fourth—half
in and half out of position—returned to its original front-line position.

Two Twenty-third spoof radios were hit by artillery fire, and two others were cut off by the enemy for about 48 hours. The Sixty-fifth continued to relieve the Twenty-sixth, not, however, wearing the Ninety-fourth's identity, but under a security blackout. The visual evidences of the other two divisions also were obliterated.

The Twenty-third furnished only radios and advice in this operation. Fortunately, no dummies, sonic, or special effects were used. Had they been used, it is highly probable the Germans would have discovered the ruse. Also, no division was simulated. The effects of this double-dealing ruse were never revealed, but as one contemporary internal classified report put it, "If the enemy was half as confused as we were, Lochinvar was a glorious success."

From Lochinvar, the Twenty-third stepped right into Operation Bouzonville in mid-March. This operation was conducted in virtually the same area and was the last deception job carried out for XX Corps. Although Bouzonville was one of the shortest of the Ghost Army's operations on record, just 33 hours, it was costly in that 2 Ghost troops were killed and 15 were wounded.

Capt. Thomas G. Wells, an earnest young headquarters commandant, and Staff Sgt. George C. Peddle, an enterprising and well-liked platoon sergeant, were killed in action near Picard, Germany. They were the only Ghost troops killed during the entire war by enemy fire, although others died in accidents. One of those accidents occurred when one of the Ghost troops who was being relieved of duty accidentally pulled the pin of a grenade. Realizing instantly that his carelessness would kill his relief, Henry Rapsis, the trooper fell on the grenade himself, absorbing its full force and shielding his comrade.

Meanwhile, the main effort of the XX Corps was to be between Trier and Saarburg, Germany. To draw attention away from it, the Twenty-third was to show a buildup farther south opposite Saarlutern. For this purpose, the Eightieth Infantry Division was simulated assembling in the rear of the Sixty-fifth. On the morning of the real attack, the Sixty-fifth Division artillery was to put on a demonstration supplemented by the Twenty-third's rubber guns and artillery flashes.

On the night of March 12, the sonic unit played a tank program along the west bank of the river two miles north of Saarlautern. Spoof radio nets were set up for a division, but no heavy traffic was carried. Special effects duplicated all visual evidences of the

Eightieth while the real division attacked on the morning of the 13th under a security blackout.

The specific results of Bouzonville are indicated by a report by the Eightieth of only light resistance in the zone of its advance. The XX Corps was well pleased with the result and thought the Ghost troops did a good job of fooling the Germans.

There was no rest for the Ghost Army during early 1945. It never had R&R, and traveled to more places during the European invasion than any other single military unit, according to Army documents.

Robert Tompkins in a photo taken during the war near a camouflage tent.
Photo courtesy Robert Tompkins.

Chapter Eleven

Bob Tompkins' War Diary

Bill Blass and Bob Tompkins, artists and privates in the Ghost Army, first got to know each other during basic training at Fort Meade, Maryland, in 1943, not long after Tompkins was married. Tompkins, in addition to his other duties, was a driver for Lt. David Gray.

Tompkins stenciled "BUNNY HUG," on the side of his jeep, and it became a familiar icon to Ghost troops throughout his time in Europe. It was a tribute to Tompkins' wife, Bernice Hart, also known as "Bunny" and "Babe"—Bunny to her friends and Babe to her intimate friends. She had been pregnant with their first child when Tompkins left for Europe aboard the Liberty ship *Gibbons*.

"Even today, when I look at my wedding pictures, I don't like to think of the war years because that was such a bad time," says Bunny. She spent the war years worrying about the safety of her handsome young husband.

Bunny Hart had been a pretty high school senior in Bronxville, New York, near Scarsdale when she saw a young man from Yonkers, the wrong side of the tracks. But, never mind, she set her cap for him.

"He didn't have a chance from the moment I saw him," she asserts. And Tompkins took one look at the most beautiful girl at Bronxville High and fell instantly in love, as he will tell you he still is today, more than half a century later. After high school graduation, they were married the following April 13, 1943.

Her father was the first to call her "Babe" and everyone else called her beautiful, including the John Robert Powers Modeling Agency, which asked her to become a model. She elected instead to follow her husband from one army base to another, driving her 1940 beige Chevrolet coupe deluxe.

175

It was on one of those occasions near Camp Forest, at Tullahoma, Tennessee, that Bunny and Bob and two of his Army friends went to stay at a hotel in McMinnville, a few miles north of Tullahoma just to get away from the base for awhile. The friends were William "Willy" Blass and Ray Harford, fellow Army privates. They spent most of the evenings drinking white lightning and chain smoking cigarettes, talking about the war and their postwar futures. The next morning, as they sat smoking in the lobby of the hotel, Bunny asked their friends what they wanted to do after the war was over.

Blass was very definitive, and when he spoke, conviction and certitude rang true in his voice: "I will become one of the world's great fashion designers."

He was so serious that no one dared kid him about it, Tompkins recalled.

Blass also called Bunny "Babe," and in later life, some of the wealthiest and most sophisticated women in the world wondered why he called them all "Babe."

He and Babe Tompkins developed such a good friendship that after Blass and Tompkins were shipped overseas, he wrote her a witty and informative letter each month, with most of it devoted to a description of how her husband was getting along.

Blass often spent money showing Tompkins a good time because he knew that Tompkins was sending all but $5 a month back home to Babe.

When her baby boy was born, Babe sent a cablegram to Bob, but she heard that because of the Battle of the Bulge it probably would not get through. In desperation, she gave the information to the service newspaper, *Stars and Stripes,* and that is how Bob and Bill Blass found that Tompkins had fathered a boy. He was named "Butch," born on December 18, 1944. Blass was named the godfather.

In September 1999,Tompkins took Bunny to Europe on a tour of various Ghost Army bivouacs and operations. He said Luxembourg and Houffalize were particularly nostalgic places to revisit. The terrain near Houffalize when he had last seen it had been a forest literally chopped down by machine gun and artillery bullets.

"That was when we were en route to the Rhine during the war. It had been really torn up back then. Now it was again a green and inviting place," he said.

The old girl's seminary where the Ghost Army had bivouacked for a time had been converted to an office building "It looked like IBM

building or something," he said, adding: "It was here when I first saw
V-1 rockets fly over back in 1944. Then Babe and I ran into some
fellows from the 101st Airborne." They were back visiting
Luxembourg for the same nostalgic reasons, remembering where
they had been during the war.

"We stopped by Monet's home and we walked in the famous garden that was the scene for so many of his paintings. But it was rainy
that day and the light was not good. It didn't look like his paintings,
but it still looked good."

A few of the men kept pocket diaries, although that was strictly
forbidden. In fact, the men were told that anyone in the Twenty-
third caught keeping a diary could be ordered shot on the spot.
The idea was that had they been captured, the diary would have
tipped the Germans to the secrets of the Ghost Army.

Despite this, Tompkins clandestinely kept a pocket diary. He
made sure to work on it out of sight of officers or anyone who might
report him. Blass was the only other soldier in the Twenty-third who
knew Tompkins kept a diary. The diary started off with just a few
dates and times of departure. But it gradually got more and more
complete and interesting, especially considering that he had to write
it on the run, in snow and rain, and under fire.

It captures the immediacy of the Twenty-third's work, especially its
mobility and how often it had to move from one battle area to the
next.

Lieutenant Gray, for whom Tompkins drove a jeep throughout
the war, had been a manager for famed actress Helen Hayes before
the war, and it was a job he resumed after the war. Driving
Lieutenant Gray was among Tompkins' many other duties, which
included changing insignia and signs and setting up dummy tanks
and guns. As his diary shows, he logged 10,000 miles on the jeep in
one year. Soon the jeep bearing the moniker "BUNNY HUG"
became a familiar sight. That was one marking that even spies might
have had trouble deciphering.

Throughout this period, he worried about Babe and their first
child, who was on the way. It is evident from portions of this diary
that a delay in hearing from her because of a delay in Army mail
caused him more stress than the enemy.

In the diary he used a bit of his own shorthand. "Parke" was
Bernard Parke; "Shil" was Art Shilstone; "Sak" or "Sac" was Norman
Sakowitz; "Goozy" was Sgt. Guzik; "Tony" was Tony Young; "Beef" was

Charles Boulliane; "Harf" was Ray Harford, and Grandmother or Gray was Lieutenant Gray. All were fellow soldiers in the Ghost Army's 406th Combat Engineers Battalion. "HEATER" was the signal company part of the Twenty-third specializing in sound effects. Tompkins' diary started off clipped and spare, but became more detailed as time passed.

Here's the diary as it was transcribed into typescript shortly after he returned from the war by Bill Blass's mother, exactly as Tompkins wrote it in 1944 and 1945:

May 2-	Left [Camp] Kilmer to board Henry Gibbons.
May 3-	Left New York for England.
May 14-	Anchored off Cardiff.
May 15-	Docked Avonmouth.
May 16-	4 A.M. left boat and boarded train for Walton Hall.
June 18-	Left Walton Hall and arrived Exeter, 154 miles.
June 19-	Saw hundreds of C-47s leave nearby airport to drop supplies and return a few hours later.
June 20-	Left Exeter, arrived Hursley Camp 115 miles.
June 21-	Left Hursley for Southampton. Boarded the LST No. 335 late afternoon.
June 22-	Laid in harbor off Isle of Wight.
June 23-	11:46 P.M. pulled anchor for France.
June 24-	D-[Day] plus 18, anchored off Utah beach about 11:30 A.M., drove out the big doors about 5:30 P.M. through traffic control area, etc. through Carentan, Isigny, to about three miles north of Treviers. Arrived at camp about midnight. Ecranville.
July 1-	First mission about 2,000 yard from front lines.
July 4-	Returned to base camp. Mission accomplished. Heard one plane shot down about 2 A.M. on first mission.
July 5-6-	Moved to new base camp two miles south of Treviers (Mandeville).
July 14-	Saw first enemy aircraft shot down [by] a P-51.
July 17-	On or about 17th, first alarm of gas, false of course.

July 22- Residue with Willy [Bill Blass with the rest of unit].

July 25- While playing softball saw largest raid on front lines ever attempted—1,500 heavies and 1,500 fighters. Saw two columns of smoke indicating two planes lost.

July 28- Reconnaissance trip—Treviers, Isigny, Coventon, LeHaye, DePuits—turned back on road to Lessey. Too jammed. Returned by vicinity of St. Lo—95 miles. Heaviest AA barrage seen yet about ll:30 and about 4 A.M. in morning, got up and slept under a truck [to avoid falling shrapnel from American guns, which killed and wounded a number of Americans during the war].

July 30- On Guard. 8:30 A.M. [British bombers] Lancasters roar overhead. Hundreds headed due south.

Aug. 2- USO. Not so hot.

Aug. 3- Leave Camp at Treviers for new camp south of here between Priers and St. Lo about six miles north of Coutances.

Aug. 5- Patton arrived Brest two hours ago.

Aug. 6- Reconnaissance to Coutances, Tourville and Agon. Coutance in rubble. Had Calvados in Tourville and Agon hotel. Were told hotel keeper pro-German. Took nine snapshots. Saw first French armored division roaring up with our equipment.

Aug. 7- Reconnaissance for 70th division. Supposed to land at Omaha Beach.

Aug.9- Only A Company, C Company and Signal Corps and 406th moved out tonight for assembly area about 1/2 mile from Avranches. Took Lt. Grey down after chow with stencil men. Saw German horse drawn carts littering the roads, 88s and tanks. Saw St. Michel in distance. Had to drive in pitch dark all the way back. Had a flat about seven miles out of Coutance. German prisoners rolled by us by the truckloads. Coutance looked like a ghost town. Back about 1:30 A.M.

Aug. 12- Heavy raid on. Sounded like Forts [B-17 Flying Fortresses] went overhead this morning. Outfits return. Captured several Jerries. Schraeder missing. Reconnaissance being organized to look for him.

Aug. 13- Colonel Schraeder found. Messages failed to get through. Problem [mission by Ghost Army] reported a big success. Reports from German radio report Second Armored Division on Brittany Peninsula. [This was one of the outfits that the Ghost Army pretended to be on the Brittany Peninsula near Brest]. Aren't we the devils?

Aug. 16- Bombers continue to drone overhead. Just counted 102 Mitchells [American B-25s] headed for that 10-mile gap. Trap should be completely closed by tonight.

Aug. 20- Pulling out on problem. Location Brest. Mop up job. Don't expect to return to this area. News today: we're now in outskirts of Paris. Twenty thousand Jerries trapped in Brest. [Tompkins was in error. There were just under 40,000 Germans holed up in Brest.]

Aug. 21- Sunday—Saw headless cow hanging from a 30-foot tree on hill in Coutance. Must have been a hell of a blast. On our way to simulate artillery fire on Brest— still a hell of a lot of Germans to be cleaned up there. Pass IP at 1:30 P.M. Bivouac in the vicinity of Dol.

Aug. 21- Dol to 10 miles north of Brest. 164 miles. Pulled out 8:10 A.M. 158 miles to vicinity of Lesneven—about 10 to 15 miles north of Brest. Drove most of the way with top and windshield down in driving rain. Would give my right arm to be able sit in front of cozy fire with my little Darling in my arms. Oh, Adolf, you S.O.B. I feel like a frozen, drowned rat.

Aug. 23- Bivouac to front. Left here 2:30 P.M. Arrived 1,200 yards from front lines about 3:30. Have dug in tonight with set up. Two minutes ago one of our artillery observation planes was hovering overhead. All of a sudden German AA opened. Three shells exploded. Plane dropped off to left, flew back out of range. Looks like it will get hotter before it's over.

Aug. 24- Maintained items. Tore them down at 9 P.M. Moved up

500 yards to new area and set up [dummy] tanks. Willy [Blass] and I set up our tent with our feet sticking out in the pouring rain and passed out about 3 A.M.

Aug. 25- Fireworks start. Artillery raising hell. Stood on hedgerow and watched the whole show. Saw shells landing about 400 yards in front of us. Could hear machine guns, rifles, mortars, etc. Saw time firing. Saw four [P-47] Thunderbolts strafing with rockets. They roared over our heads and then dove into the thick of it. Havoc [British bombers] came over and bombed. Couple of mortar shells came our way, landed about fifty yards behind us. Whole front line is one screen of smoke. Twenty 2½-ton trucks burned to shit by German Patrol in our area night before last. Pulling out at 10 P.M. tonight to return to bivouac area. Looks like the battle of Brest is over for us. Thank God! I'm dead tired. Leave front after tough three days to bivouac area.

Aug. 26- Getting everything straightened out today. Will start our drive to Chartres early tomorrow morning. Just beginning to realize how vulnerable we were the last three days as stories came in from various sources. Heavies giving hell to Brest today.

Aug. 27, 1944- Lesneven to Rennes. Left Lesneven, super trip, 9 P.M. Thursday morning. Arrived five kilometer from Rennes about 6 o'clock. Beautiful estate.

Aug. 28- Rennes to Torce near St. Suzanne. Leaving 9 A.M. for Chartres this morning. Arrived just east of St. Suzanne near the village of Torce, supposedly liberated by Reeder last Sunday. Crowds wave and cheer and throw flowers.

Aug. 29-30- Spent night in bivouac. Got drunk for first time since England night of 28th. Roy and I held each other up. Back to camp.

Aug. 31- Torce to Mouny near Sens just about 50 miles east southeast of Paris. Bivouac in woods. Left Torce on 225 miles trip East of Paris to Mouny. Drove all the way. Tired, dirty, no water to wash with. Bivouacked in

woods. Went through Chartres, La Loupe,
Fontainebleau, Port Se Sanne, etc. Things seem more
civilized. People seem very well dressed. Heard Yanks
are in Belgium, Luxembourg, and Patton nearing
border of Germany.

Sept. 1-   Waiting. No one knows what's up. While on move, no
mail service. That's all I worry about.

Sept. 2-   Awakened at 1 A.M. Thompson and I have to take his
truck on convoy for gas. Left at 6 this morning.
Destination Cherbourg. Came by way of Argentan
where German Seventh was trapped. Just one mass of
bomb craters. Just missed going through Paris again.
Traveled 245 miles to QM gasoline dump. Giving us
three or four truck-loads. The rest of us will go on to
the beach tomorrow. Insigny our destination.

Sept. 3-   Awoke at 8. Did a little sketch of a nearby farmhouse.
Heard the Sunday school choir singing in a small
church nearby. Thought of my little darling.

Sept. 4-   Start drive for Mouny at 8 A.M. via Chartres,
Fontainebleau, Port Sur Yonne, etc. Arrived in camp
10 P.M. Monday night after [after trip of] 280 miles.
640 miles round trip.

Sept. 5-   Stay here indefinitely. Rumors we go to Versailles.
Also, [rumor that] we sail on Nov. 2 for states. Sounds
too good. It was.

Sept. 7-   Mouny to St. Germaine— six miles from Versailles
and about 10 or 12 miles from center of Paris. Stucco
barracks. Camp des Loges. What a set up! Leave
Mouny-St. Germaine five miles from Versailles and
eight to nine miles from the Eiffel Tower and Gay
Paree. Left 3 P.M. for Torce. Pick up [rubber tank and
gun] dummies. Arrived 10:30.

Sept. 8-   Loaded. Went to Chateau Dun.

Sept. 9-   Returned to St. Germaine. Everyone gay [the word
simply meant happy and cheerful during WWII].
Wonderful quarters, tennis courts, stadium, swim-
ming pool. Intend to do some shopping tonight.
Spent evening in St. Germaine. Bough perfume. Saw

Bunny "Babe" Tompkins, who turned down a modeling offer to follow her husband to various bases during his Ghost Army training. Robert Tompkins photo.

Chat 14. Visited a couple of dives and drank champagne in very nice outdoor café.

Sept. 10- Sunday. Left in truck and entered Gay Paree for the first time. Truck parked in front of Notre Dame Cathedral and we went inside and then walked around in the department store section. Then walked up Champs Elysees to Arc De Triumph. Took pictures. Two Frenchmen offered to show us around town. Drank beer in open-air café on the Avenue and met Mr. Ross. Returned to truck by way of Place De La Concorde across Seine to left bank and walked down to Notre Dame. Little 16-year-old girl presented me with her personal key to the city.

Sept. 11- St. Germaine for the evening. Had champagne, by the way, while working in the motor pool this afternoon. Bought mom a charm bracelet with all the coat of arms on it.

Sept. 12- Versailles, palace, etc.

Sept. 14- Loges to Chalons, bivouac overnight. Left Loges 4 P.M. on rush alert. 120 miles, bivouac east of Chalons at 1 A.M. Drove black-out for 3½ hours. Eyes puffing.

Sept. 15- Chalons-Bettenbourg. Begin mission, 248 miles from Paris to Bettenbourg. Left 8 A.M. through Verdun into Grand Duchy of Luxembourg. Great ovation. Arrive Bettenbourg about six miles from city of Luxembourg, 12 miles to the German border. Front lines about two miles to east. Might go on mission tonight. Everybody has a cold. Feel . . . ([Drove] 248 miles total. We're the only outfit on this part of front except for one cavalry squadron spread very thinly. No one knows where front is.

Sept. 16—Last night moved up about 1½ miles and pulled into heavy woods about 3 o'clock A.M. Tanks moving all around us. Woke early. Sewed on [phony] patches. Set up [rubber] tanks. Built fires simulating armored infantry battalion. Truck goes out every hour into village on atmosphere [run with just two soldiers sitting in the back to make it appear that it is full inside].

Drank a quart of beer with a German family in
Bettenbourg. Spoke with a woman who had been to
New York and Chicago.

Sept. 17- German soldier in civilian clothes gave himself up this
morning, and Seckel interrogated him. Says Germany
is in a miserable state.

Sept. 18- Report says Germans have withdrawn on Moselle
River. Setting up tank obstacles. German 15th has left
Metz to oppose us. It seems the 603rd has been given
credit for pushing Nazis completely out of
Luxembourg. Reports say we are a terrific success.

Sept. 21- Still continue to maintain fires and general activity.
Small truck came in last night. Only one letter from
Babe but it boosted my spirits as always. Heine patrol
reported about three or four miles away. Platoon of
406th went out to look for them. Civilians seem to be
getting too anxious about our set-up. We should have
moved out a couple of days ago, but attack seems
imminent so I guess we have orders to remain until it
begins. I have exactly one week left on my prediction.
Another problem [mission] immediately after this is
now rumored. Went into Luxembourg this afternoon
for about an hour and 15 minutes. Had hot shower
and managed to get some odds and ends and a glass
of beer. Beautiful city.

Sept. 22- Moving out! Outfit moves back about 10 miles to
Ukange to make room for Eighty-third to move in.
Platoon moved out with rest of Company this evening
at 5 P.M. Bascharage 8 to 10 miles to rear. Lt. Grey and
I remained to check fires and signs. Slept at Mary-
Cort, old Twenty-third command post. Our water
point was sniped and a couple of the wires cut according to report. Three infantry divisions have also been
opposing us. New problem [mission] commences.

Sept. 23- Lt. Grey and I leave to join platoon at Bascharage.
Rained early this morning. Arrived at Company area
at 8:30 A.M. Saw collaborators being marched to work
by Luxembourgers at point of rifles this morning.

Sept. 25-   Into barracks. Seminary in Luxembourg. 4:15 leave
            woods for quarters in a Seminary in Luxembourg.
            Thank God, we'll be dry and able to sleep in beds.
            Arrived in outskirts of Luxembourg at about 5:45.
            Beautiful huge building, B Company [also] residing.
            One squadron to room on top floor. What a haul with
            equipment, trying to get lights fixed. Great commo-
            tion! Jerries pulled all the fixtures out. Bastards!
            Hope to hell we stay here until it's all over! [It was not
            to be.]

Sept. 27-   Have the hives. Oh my Christ, do I itch! Too many
            green plums I guess. Stored dummies in former Nazi
            auditorium. Larger plaster gilt eagle with Swastika on
            stage. Rumors wild again—such as sailing for home
            Oct.15th. Looks like my prediction was all off.

Oct. 1-   Sunday. Had dinner with a wonderful Luxembourg
            family tonight. On our way to a movie when they
            called us in. Home-made ice cream and cake. Wow! It
            was terrific. Sherry, and upper Moselle wine. Getting
            up at 4:45 A.M. tomorrow to leave on a problem near
            Metz. Just taking flash equipment.

Oct. 4-   Yesterday afternoon Lt. Grey and I spent part of after-
            noon at 344 FA HQ. At Coutance until telephone
            could be put through. Had coffee and doughnuts at
            RC. About fifteen minutes after we left village, two
            German shells landed about 100 yards from
            Headquarters. Supposed to set up a couple of batter-
            ies [fake, of course] in front of heavy artillery.
            Tentative problem called approximately Drian on
            Right flank of Metz. We stood on a hill about ¾ mile
            away from fort. Planes came down in long dives. Ack-
            ack all around them. They then would open up and
            we could see their rockets and .50-caliber tracers
            streak out in front of them. Then they would disap-
            pear behind the trees and then roar right over our
            heads and then go back again for another crack.
            Could hear the roar of machine gun fire.

Oct. 5-   Thursday. Six shells landed off to our left flank about
            600 yards away last night.

Oct.6-	Last night 1-2-3 Platoon fired flash equipment [simulating artillery] several times. Had to leave guard 10:30 to go out and pick 3rd Platoon up. Has been continuous thunder of artillery today. P-47s strafed again. Took Lt. Grey down to division command post this afternoon. Going back for mail at Luxembourg with Grey tomorrow morning.
Oct 7-	Successful trip.
Oct. 8-	Watched FA Battery fire German 100mm at Metz.
Oct. 9-	Leave bivouac for Luxembourg 9:30 A.M. Arrive 11:30. Lead convoy home. Had dinner at Hotel Cravat.
Oct. 10-	Week's extra duty for being over the hill. Eating according to rank. . . .runs high. Would like to . . . on every officer in this damned company. Going on reconnaissance with Momma [Lt.] Grey tomorrow.
Oct. 11-	Left 8:30 south to Mars-Letours and then down to Pont A Mousson. Crossed Moselle, came up East bank about 12 kilometers from Metz, then took bridge shielded by smoke screen and returned by way of Belgium. Three countries in one day!
Oct.19-	Stood nine hours straight guard.
Oct. 21-	Saw first robo-bomb [V-1 buzz bomb] about 8:45 A.M. this morning. Just a tiny speck in the sky. Going south-southwest. [Pulse jet] Motor cut off. Heard nothing after that. Whoops! Just heard the explosion. Must have been it. Probably 10 miles away. Another one at 1:45 about same direction. Saw what must have been a Jerry plane circle city twice this noon. Looked like a JU88 [Junkers 88]. Another robo-bomb about 2:30.
Oct. 26-	Two more bombs about 6:30 and 6:45. Seem to be low, noisy as hell.
Oct. 28-	Around 3 A.M. this morning a couple of shells were thrown into town, probably Nazi railroad guns. Hit right next to Heater outfit and knocked out a half track. Two civilians reported killed.
Oct. 29-	Went for walk this morning. Bill [Blass], Paul, Sac took a roll of films and did a couple of sketches. Beautiful

day, first in a long time. 9:30 P.M. Jerry just came over
our building and then a few seconds later we heard
about ten bomb explosions. Couldn't see anything.
Looks like they are gunning for [our] headquarters.

Oct. 30-   Took Lt. Holeman into Verdun for payroll, 110 miles
round trip. Colder than hell. Louis from 3132nd says
push is on. Start within next three days. Hope so.

Nov. 3-   Back at Metz. Line has been so static that they have
set up barbed wire all along front. Put up 105 [fake
howitzer] in old emplacement deserted yesterday. [To
replace a real howitzer.] Setting up howitzer flash
equipment. Ready to fire tonight. Expect long siege.
Six months ago today left the dear old States. It's
muddy by the way and very cold. If this isn't our last
job, I guess maybe then your Butch was all wrong
about [being sent home before] Christmas. Will it
ever end!

Nov. 7-   Election day. Our kitchen is set up in railroad station in
Batilly. We're now eating C Battery about ½ mile down
valley. Squads alternate firing and guard every day.
Rain, wind and mud make for horrible existence. Our
hut is leaking like a sieve. Everything is soaked. Don't
see how attack can start in this weather. Was scheduled
to begin a couple days ago. Hope to God they went for
the mail. That's all there is to look forward to. It would
be great to know that Dewey had won, however, have
my doubts. Probably won't know until at least the end
of the week.

Nov. 8-   Received bad news. Spent horrible night on guard.
Cleared today. Just been stuck for hour and half.
Good news. Leave for Luxembourg tomorrow, thank
God. Soaked to skin. Is pouring again. Thinking only
of my sweet Darling and home. 9:30 P.M. have fired
twice this evening [fake artillery barrages] at 8:40 and
9:27. Can plainly hear machine gun fire, mortar and
rifle fire about a mile away. Artillery shakes the hut.
Must be attempt crossing on the river. Beginning of
large attack to circle Metz. Simulated Ninety-ninth
FA, 20 Corps, 193 FA Group.

Nov. 9-   Arrived back at seminary at 1 P.M. afer tearing down
           dummies and having to push one truck up the hill.
           What a hell of a trip. Terrific gale, cold as hell and
           just a few minutes ago it began to snow. Got back just
           in time. Can be recorded as my most miserable week
           in Army.

Nov. 15-   Luxembourg becoming a living hell at night. Last
           week five GIs were found dead in the Gulch. Shooting
           every night. Boys arriving from front for rest get
           drunk and spray street with machine guns. Five civil-
           ians killed the other night. Still many collaborators
           working under cover of darkness. Several signal men
           and 406th men were awarded the Bronze Star today.
           We paraded down to the field where Gen. Doran
           made awards.

Nov. 16-   9 P.M. Jerry [German planes] just came in over city,
           wandered around. Some flak went up. Sound disap-
           peared then we saw light flash on and off at various
           points around the city. Looked very much like signals.
           All clear 15 minutes later.

Nov. 17-   Robo-bomb just came over very low and loud. Could
           see light of a rocket on tail. Hell of a noise about 9:30.
           At 10 o'clock another raid alarm. Heard no planes
           this time.

Nov. 18-   Two more air-raid alarms this evening about 45 min-
           utes apart. Heard no bombs fall. Probably just Jerry
           reconnaissance.

Nov. 20-   [Marlene] Dietrich put on a show here today. Really
           swell. Nearly knocked her down as I was coming down
           the hall.

Nov. 21-   Several Jerries flew over tonight. Little flak.

Nov. 22-   Parke shoots Bier in Hall of Seminary with Army .45.

Nov. 23-   Thanksgiving Day. Beat A Co. 13-6 [in football game].
           Starred again. Pappy won goose. Luxembourg stadium.

Nov. 24-   Last night about 5:00 robot came over very low, shook
           entire building. This morning about 9:15 another, far-
           ther away.

Dec. 1-   Two years in the Army today. Beat A. Co. again 13-6.
           Feel like I had a steam roller go over me tonight
           [from football aches and pains]. Alerted to go on
           reconnaissance. Won't leave until tomorrow. Only a
           matter of days now until LB arrival. Wow!

Dec. 4-   Three separate air raid alarms this evening. Planes
           droned overhead. Heavy AA tracers lit sky. Went down
           to shelter for ½ hour during movie air raid. Could see
           real AA outside. Movie: "Until We Meet Again."
           Terribly fidgety last couple days. LB due very shortly.
           My Sweet Darling is my constant thought.

Dec. 6-   Have funny hunch tomorrow is the day. We'll see! Air
           raid siren just started. More AA fireworks on display.

Dec. 8-   Lt. Grey and I left at noon on simulated reconnais-
           sance for billeting 75 X-290 [the Seventy-fifth Infantry
           Division], who have supposedly just landed in
           Cherbourg. Actually they are still in England.
           Company still follow to simulate division on Sunday.
           Went over to main road from Arlon, Belgium, then
           cut back Northeast about 15 miles from Luxembourg.
           Went to Junglingster. Grey questioned by a couple of
           Colonels and we had discussion with Eighty-third
           man. Said we should try schnapps and get down to
           Luxembourg some time. Also said that we had missed
           all the hedgerow fighting. Went to see mayors of small
           towns about billeting. Sleeping on top floor of con-
           verted school house in little village near Junlingster.
           Sore as hell because this way there may be added
           delay in receiving word from Babe [about whether
           their child was born].

Dec. 9-   Found billets in Eschweiler about seven miles from
           front. Drove in driving snow this morning. Cleared a
           little this afternoon. Had three cognacs in small café
           few hundred yards from here this morning, and got
           dozen eggs. Rey got stuck with another Colonel this
           afternoon. It's really getting to be a joke. Boys arrive
           tomorrow at 2 P.M. [the rest of the Ghost Army].
           Colonel Schraeder said we'd get mail. Thank God. I
           don't feel quite as fidgety as I have the past week and
           I think it's an indication. Terribly anxious to get word.

Dec. 11- Men arrived yesterday afternoon from 3 P.M. on.
Waited with Grey at fork for three hours. Froze. Went
on mock convoy about 9:30 — snowed hard. Led convoy over route second time around after Robinson's
driver was blinded [snow blindness]. Nearly smacked
into Shil [Art Shilstone] with a jeep. Returned 12:30
A.M. frozen. Eating chow in hall downstairs. Took Grey
down to Division Command Post this afternoon.
Reeder simulating two-star General rides in staff car.
On guard duty tonight. First Platoon put up dummy
artillery. I know for sure that LB has arrived and pins
and needles waiting to get word. No telling when it
will come through with this set up.

Dec. 12- This afternoon went on a reconnaissance for simulated attack with Sac and Grey and went up on hill
overlooking Moselle River and looked through binoculars at Germany of the other side still held by Jerries.
Heard small arms first and then drove through
artillery installations. Cold as a bitch and Lt. Grey
made me furious. Gets more like an old woman every
day. Towns all evacuated in that area. Eerie and ghost-
like. Third platoon killed two deer today. Will have
venison tomorrow.

Dec. 14- No word yet! Yesterday morning drove out to Moselle
again with Van, Roy and Ray, followed Staff with Shil,
LaHive and Goozy. Dropped them off outside
Maternach and they went on for reconnaissance. We
met them on hill overlooking river after they shot
deer. Got word about 5 P.M. that we were leaving to
return to Luxembourg. Took McGill and picked up
fake signs and then pulled out at 8:25, drive blackout
all the day-dead tired when I got back — arrived
about 10 P.M. Went back to Eschweiler this morning to
pick up lister bag. Crossed air strip and saw three-star
generals at a C-47, also a cracked-up P-38 and two
wrecked JU88s. Practically off my nut waiting word
from Babe. Eleven more shopping days until
Christmas. Ha, ha.

Dec. 17- Suddenly alerted about 4 o'clock. Germans reported
counter attacking heavily around Eschweiler area.

[This was the beginning of the Battle of the Bulge.] Reports say three German divisions on this side of river. Supposedly on eight kilometers out of Luxembourg. All trucks have been dispatched to Factory Section loading all special equipment in case we must pull out. On guard at main gate tonight. Worried and really low tonight. No word yet. Nothing seems right. . . .

Dec. 18-   On guard. Last night had about five air-raid alarms. Several Jerries were constantly flying over. Two dove out of flak over our building in power dives. One came in very low over south part of city.

Dec. 20-   Suddenly re-alerted. Told to pack everything - ready to move out. The 80th Division coming into town. Civilians going wild in fear of Germans returning. Loading belongings on trucks and wagons. Bringing out their rifles and pistols again. No news yet from Babe.

Dec. 21-   All ready to leave for Doncourt tomorrow, situated on old French barracks in the Maginot line. Wondering if we'll ever come back here. Several Jerries wandering overhead tonight. Lot AA fire. Still no word from Babe. Got drunk last night. Killed a bottle of champagne tonight but it didn't help.

Dec. 22-   Friday. Left Seminary at 9:36. Arrive outside Doncourt about 11:00. French Army Post. Pink and yellow stucco houses. EM in large building, two platoons to a room. Sixty seven men on guard. About three inches of snow on the ground. Temperature about zero. Maginot pillboxes all around us. Planes overhead at night occasioned by AA fire. Report brought plane down last night. Playing orderly and valet with other jeep drivers to the officers—bastards!

Dec. 24-   On guard tonight, Christmas Eve. No Christmas rations for tomorrow. Several trucks left today, destination unknown. Staff went back to Luxembourg. Hear we are going to Metz area soon. Paul insists I'll get word today. It would be a wonderful Christmas present. Fellows cut big tree for our room.

Dec. 25-   Had a swell little buffet supper last night and a song
fest before going on guard. Had champagne and
brandy but it seemed to help the blues. Clear as a bell
and plenty of air activity—strafing and bombing off to
the East and northeast. Drove fellows to church this
morning and took the rest into Doncourt and gave
villagers our rations. Got pretty tight on terrible
schnapps. Had dinner at 3:00. Feel pretty low tonight.
Reminiscing of last year's Christmas with Babe.
Things look blacker tonight than they have for a long
time. Jerries still raising hell north of here. Can't help
thinking of those poor guys in the fox holes. Moving
over to the barracks in the morning. Still no word
from Babe.

Dec. 26-   Levy, Brogdon and a couple of A Company boys
brought in two escaped Jerry prisoners from out on
the road to Doncourt this evening wearing GI clothing. Seckel first went down to question them. One
had his face bashed in by a civilian. Drove out on that
same road this afternoon in a jeep. Luck I wasn't
picked off.

Dec. 29-   Left camp at Doncourt yesterday at 1:30 P.M. and
arrived in Verdun about 3:15. Cold as a bitch, loaded
tools on trucks. Ate K rations without getting warm.
Left leading convoy at 5:20 for Gravelotte and Metz.
Arrived Metz about 8:00. Briefed by Captain Seale,
simulating Eighth, B Company, 87th QM B, G, D
Companies and Heater making up the Division.
Sleeping on 3rd floor, no heat, no glass in windows.
Temperature about 20 degrees. All bridge blown up
over Moselle and canals. Bailey [Army Engineer pontoon bridges] have replaced them. Outskirts pretty
battered up. All large buildings still intact. Put out
[phony] signs this morning. Will put the rest of them
out tonight.

Dec. 29-   JUST READ IN STARS AND STRIPES IT'S A BOY.
DEC. 18th. WOW!

Dec. 30-   No mail yet from Babe. Possibly today. Feeling greatly
relieved and very happy today. Trucks went out to

secret area this morning then returned. Grey and I
removed signs. Had shower. May move out tonight—
nothing definite as yet. Left Metz at 9 this morning
and returned to Verdun on very slippery road. Light
snow last night caused slippery conditions. Set up
here similar to Doncourt. Two stoves. Stone floor is
pretty cold though. Tonight is New Year's Eve
although you'd never know it. Rumors are that entire
outfit will return to Metz shortly for permanent base.
Six letters from Babe today but all from November.
Still waiting for THAT letter that will give me all the
details. Jerry just came in over town and very heavy
AA barrage opened on him. Looks like hot spot and
these damn buildings are right next to the railroad
yard. GIs shooting it up tonight. Small arms fire all
over town.

Jan. 4-   Received first letters from Babe. Colonel Fitz left
603rd today. Hooper takes over. Certificates of merit
presented to several men today by Gen. Doran.

Jan. 6-   Verdun to Metz simulating 90th. Have two good
stoves in the Fourth Platoon room. Warm and comfortable. Marking bumpers this morning, stenciling
helmets, etc.

Jan. 7-   Left Caserne Rouge 6 P.M. about three miles to
Moselle Caserne. Arrive across from main part of city.
Stood guard. Pull out individually between 8 to 9 on
route from Metz to Ukange to Dalstein to Friestroff to
Metz. About 60 miles Dalstein to Metz closed convoy.
Led convoy all the way. Snowed heavily. Never been so
cold, except G.M. Arrived Moselle Caserne 12:00.
Rumors are we stay here awhile. Continue to simulate
90th, B Company 358th Infantry until the 90th is
committed. What a hole. Get bluer every day. I want
to go home to my wife and baby. To hell with this fool-
ishness. Big attack imminent according to Colonel
Schraeder.

Jan. 9-   Restricted to garrison. Painted out bumpers 2 P.M.
Hiding some vehicles in garages in rear. Problem
[mission] over, don't know when will leave.

Jan. 10-   Leave Moselle Caserne 11:30 arrive Briey about 1:30.
            Billeted in large apartment buildings. Officers living
            downtown. Unload everything. At 7 P.M. told we are to
            leave on problem at 12 midnight. Got Gray then
            orders change. Move out at 5:30 tomorrow morning.

Jan. 11-   Thursday. Move out at 5:28 via Longyon to Arlon.
            Had Willie [Bill Blass] relieve me when we stopped in
            field north of Arlon. So cold I thought I'd die. Snow
            one foot deep. Got warm in farm house at 2:05. Move
            north about 30 kilometers to heavy woods and paint
            bumpers, sew on patches, simulating Fourth
            Armored, B Company, 1260. Going into rest area.
            Drive 20 kilometers to village of Les Bulles. Billeted in
            farm houses with farmers. Bill, Van and I in swell little
            room with stove and real snappy wall paper and elec-
            tric lights. Very tired. Have had two meals in last 48
            hours. Will write to Babe and Little Butch now and
            then bed. Bottle of ink is even frozen.

Jan. 12-   Continue effects. Will be here tonight thank God!
            Living like kings, that is to say we are warm.

Jan. 13-   Saturday. Leave Les Bulles 1 P.M. to woods. Remove
            patches and markings and then returned to Briey.
            Arrived about 5 P.M. Snow now drifting two and three
            feet deep in some places. Problem over. What next?

Jan. 19-   Survey reconnaissance. Gray and Tool Eighth Port Au
            Mousson 35 miles South of Briey. Had lunch with
            Eighth Headquarters and then went to Metz and
            spent an hour and a half eating doughnuts in Red
            Cross and a beer in café. Saw two, two-star generals in
            Red Cross. Had flat tire on return.

Jan. 23-   Tuesday, coal detail to just west of Saarbrucken on
            border 65 miles. Miserable day. Froze, sore throat and
            ear ache on return. Got back after 8 o'clock. Got doc-
            tored up and went to bed. Feel better today. News
            looks good, although Russians seem to be slowing a
            bit, but I think we are on our way very shortly.

Jan. 27-   Sat. Painted trucks all white!!! Coutance out of
            Granville, 175th Co. yesterday afternoon. Will leave

either this afternoon or tomorrow on 95th Division problem area. Metz.

Jan. 25-   Sunday. Corporal of the guard B Company takes over guard. Still await orders to move out on 95th problem. Everyone else will be gone tomorrow.

Jan. 30-   Briey to Les Estanges simulating 95th Division, B Company of 378th Infantry Command Post in major's house. Fourth platoon billeted in attic of farm house. Old lady downstairs is a Nazi.

Jan. 31-   Our squadron moves into café. Have better set up than anyone yet. Guard duty tonight.

Feb. 1-   Snow melting. 406th and Heater moving up to front on another problem. Guard last night. Had wine and spent evening talking to Flauss family.

Feb. 2-   return to Briey.

March 5-   Monday. Leave Briey 7:30 A.M. to Enney. Extremely secret. Will have to wait until problem is over to enter details. I'd be shot on the spot if I were caught with this in my pocket as it is. Return same afternoon and spent two hours in RC. Problem called off.

March 11-   Briey to Ittersdorf, Germany. Simulating 80th Division, 318th 1, 3rd and Fourth Platoon 905 FA. Went to town of Ittersdorf with old artillery position. Set up nets and flash stuff. Flashed 1:59, 4:00 and 5:30, 5:45, and 6:15. Put up dummies in the morning.

March 12-   Artillery all around us living in town at road junction. Saarlautern several thousand yards in front of us. Went back to Itterdorf after show this morning. Shells landed around last night by the way - hit the dirt a couple of times but they landed just over the rise and about 200 yards in front of us. Retired to Artillery area at 5 P.M. Learned Captain Wells was killed by mortar fire this afternoon just up the road a ways. First fatality since we landed. Firing tonight. Have removed dummies. Leave at 6:30 A.M. tomorrow. Returning to Briey. Another problem is pending.

March 13-   Tuesday. Stood guard 12:00 to 1:45 last night. Heavy artillery. Finished firing at Midnight. Came back to

Command Post at 6:30 this morning. Left Ittersdorf at
10:30 arrived Briey 12:30. Late this afternoon got
report that seven men D Company were hit by shells
on the way back, including Captain Ranier. S/Sgt. in
Signal Company was killed this afternoon, too. All
happened on the same road we were on this morning.
It was under enemy observation from opposite site of
valley. Saw Tom Weir's jeep had a hole right through
front panel and steering post. This has really been a
hell of a blow to us all. We just thank God that ours
[number] wasn't up today. We were darn glad to get
out of that hole. Reports are that we move out Friday
to the north near Cologne. Maybe permanently. Just a
little shaky tonight.

March 16- Entire outfits moves to Sittard, Holland. Am remain-
ing behind with 30 M.S. men. Will pick up Grey in
Verdun Monday and leave for Sittard Tuesday. B
Company hauling 170 some odd dummies. Rumors
are that we will destroy men.

March 20- Briey to Dulkens, Germany. 120 troops of the actual
30th Battalion are attached to us. This evening we set
up all our trailers and deuce and one-halfs just north
of Bosheim. Lt. Grey and I put up all signs.

March 21- Put up signs all day. Tonight we put all our own M-4s
and 5s [phony tanks]. Finished about 2:30 A.M. We
also have AA attached to us and they put on a show
tonight. Get up 5 A.M.

March 22- Checked items and then chow. Slept in a farmhouse
for 2½ hours. Took it easy today. Will pull guard duty
at Command Post in town tonight. Have more dummies up now than we've ever had before. Not permit-
ted to speak to civilians. White flags on every door.
Feeling very lonesome and homesick tonight. Got
those wonderful photos [of his baby boy] today.

March 24- Last night removed signs and took down 15 items.
Heard bombing and saw flashes in Northeast about
10:30. Jerries were roaming back and forth all night.
Heard that Patton crossed the Rhine yesterday.
Colonel Schraeder just came in with a report that we

had started heavy bombing and artillery barrage last night in a fake crossing - and British and Canadians crossed at Wesel with hardly any opposition. Generals who viewed our stuff from the air yesterday claimed a great deal of credit for this deceptive move goes to us. Jerry must have copped it all with his cameras past couple of days. Eighty-third Corps really think we're hot stuff. Will take down items tonight and move to rear area. Who knows what's next on the bill.

March 25- Palm Sunday. Slept in town at Command Post, Dulken, last night after taking down all items in record time. Moved into farmhouses in devastated area this morning. Supposed to leave for Briey Tuesday. Rumors have it that a lot of items are being given away. Sounds good. Received batch of mail this morning. Feel much better.

March 27- Tuesday. Leave Dulken 7:15 for Briey. Saw remnants of 21 Sherman tanks near Houffalize. Battle must have been terrific. Forest of trees completely flat from artillery and machine gun fire. Arrive Briey 6 P.M.

April 12- Thursday. Leave Briey 8:45 for Witlick Germany via Luxembourg and Trier. Arrived Witlick about 2—87 miles from Briey, [which is] still base camp. Have job of policing Displaced Persons Camp. Sleep in schoolhouse tonight. Move into two houses across the street tomorrow. May be here a month or more until they hear from Washington. Have five posts, one morning patrol. On 24, off 24 hours. Four Russian girls clean barracks and two boys do KP.

April 13- Our second anniversary and not a very happy one either. I pray that next year will be different. Stood guard last night. KP until 4:30 today. Have heard report of Roosevelt's death. Still a bit skeptical, but it seems to be true. God, what a mess!!! Fourth Platoon begins patrol duty tomorrow at noon. Supposed to be 6,000 Russians and Poles in camp. They've been having a lot of trouble with the Negroes. Most of these people came from Coblenz area—have only been free for two weeks. Steal sheep, raid German homes, throw

*Ghost troops have Thanksgiving dinner in Luxembourg City, 1944. Photo
courtesy Robert Tompkins.*

             stones at the Heinies, and you can't blame them, poor
bastards. They wonder why we don't shoot the
Germans. I wonder myself.

April 14-   Went on raid on Russian barracks about 10 P.M. last
night. Recovered truckloads of clothes. Herded everyone into the building, then MPs searched the rooms.
I guarded latrine exit. What confusion.

April 15-   Rode in on German's milk wagon as guard against
Russian bandits 7 A.M. Russians and Poles stealing
everything they can get their hands on and I don't
blame them. Resented having to guard Goddam
Heinies. Some Russians are hiding in hills with
weapons and raid German homes at night. If we were
smart, we'd turn our backs. German stopped to look
at his watch in street today and a big Russian came by
and took it right out of his hand. It's really a joke.
They steal bikes right out from under the rider.

April 18-   Butch is four months old today. Bless his heart!! Last night six Russians went into a nearby village to buy flour from Heinies. They rang town siren and whole populace came out and murdered two of them and pitchforked the others. There's going to be hell to pay now.

April 19- On guard last night at camp gates. First and Second platoons went on raid in village where Russians were killed. Russians went first and when crowd came out with pitchforks, Jeeps with 50s [machine guns] closed in. Russians choked hell out of Heinies and Tony let loose with 50s to stop Heinies from running away. A Russian hopped a German who was coming at Beef with pitchfork. Six of them were arrested.

April 24- Grey, Harf, Belcher and I go on reconnaissance for kitchen equipment to Kochen. Beautiful trip - scenery magnificent.

April 26- Raid on Russians. Wehrmacht sympathizers who were raiding town. Senat killed two and one was wounded. Messy business. It's one hell of a problem. You don't know what to think. LaHive and I went out this evening to hunt a couple of Russians who were supposed to have kidnaped eight children. No luck. Parked the jeep on hill overlooking countryside and discussed what a wonderful golf course this battlefield would make.

April 27- Go out to local estate to sleep overnight to act as protection from raiding Russians. Four of us, Van, Paul, Masey and I. Woman spoke good English. Four or five babies in the house. One is 3½ months old. God, it made me homesick. Family seemed to be old Germans, but two sons were killed in Luftwaffe. It made me cringe to think we were actually protecting them. I thought of Dick right away. Suddenly called back. Leave Trier tomorrow at 2:30 with Tony. Will stay there at Castle and company will go down Sunday.

April 28- Hear that Himmler has offered unconditional surrender to the States and Britain but not to Russia. It looks like it's all over. At least within the next week anyway. Witlick to Trier and sleeping in castle. Marvelous news. All sorts of rumors. Lt. Grey said today we'd be home by July Fourth. Others say Northern Germany. Being with 15th A of Occupation isn't so good. Getting Eisenhower jackets. Have to wear issue ties now. Things are very composed and no one seems to know were we turn next.

May 2-   Hitler dead! Have transferred 2,300 DPs [displaced persons] into camp. Should have 5,700 DPS by end of week. Running back and forth all day. Rumors have it we leave for Briey Sunday. Rumors very strong for return to States. I think I'm really getting a bit punchy from driving that damn jeep constantly. I guess it must be 'jeep fatigue.'

May 7-   It's a beautiful world tonight, naturally. It's been a long hard road and we thank God it's over. [Germans had formally surrendered.] Let's hope it won't be many weeks before we leave for Utopia and our loved ones, and God bless the guys who are finishing it off on the other side of this messed up world. Got a keg of beer, a bottle of wine from some Heinies, and I drove into town with some of the guys and we raided an empty wine cellar. However, we eventually had champagne, wine and beer. Hear we may leave within six weeks—the sooner the better. Heaven and all that goes with it awaits my arrival.

May 8-   6:01 P.M. Cease firing. Tuesday official. Signed 2:41 A.M. May 7, Monday by German General Jodl, Lt. Gen. Smith, [Admiral] Doenitz, Ivan Susloparaff, French F. Senes in Rheims, France.

May 18-   Butch five months old today, Friday.

May 19-   Got word to be ready to leave Tuesday 22nd. Be ready to leave Europe by June Seventh.

May 20-   Sunday, Luxembourg, all-day pass. Came back in terrific thunderstorm.

May 21-   Monday, Left our palace on the hill in Trier at 12:30 P.M. for Oberstein, East 51 miles. Arrived Oberstein about 3:00 about seven miles outside. Oberstein way up in hills in wide open field. Has been raining all day. We're supposed to be here until the Seventh June awaiting orders from post commander. Will crate equipment, have inspection, etc. Two more stars supposed to be official, giving me 78 points, still not enough. Oh God, will I be glad to see that boat. Yipe!!!!!!!!!

May 27-   Oberstein to Mainz on Rhine sightseeing trip. Mainz in ruins. Saw largest army engineer bridge in world. Went north along river through wonderful, pictur-esque villages. Took four snaps. Saw huge prisoner of war camp just west of Mainz.

June 5-   Oberstein, Trier with Seltzer. Will greets me on return that I've been recommended for [promotion to] Sergeant. What a surprise.

June 6-   What a holiday. Go to Frankfort with Grey, Van, Mo, Welentz, Taffae and Goozy.

June 9-   Official order out. Now Sgt. Tompkins. Will save it to surprise Babe. Have taken over Second Squadron. Guenther, Thompson, Belcher and Martin. Switzer now jeep driver. Quit at 9,973 miles—27 short of an even 10,000.

June 14-   Start trip to LaHavre from Oberstein. Staying in tran-sient camp at Montmedy, France 120 miles tonight. Go on tomorrow to vicinity of Rheims and third day LeHavre and then WOW!!!!!

Montmedy - Soissons - gone on pass after pitching tents, took in movie at Red Cross.

June 16-   Soissons to Twenty Grand Camp. Huge camp - turn-ing everything in here. About 35 miles from LeHavre. If we complete our POM in time, will be on the boat Monday or Tuesday. Otherwise we wait possibly two weeks for another convoy. God, let's go.

June 20-   Sightseeing, town of Rouen. Beautiful cathedrals, con-siderable damage.

June 21-   Alerted to leave. All set to go at midnight.

June 22-   Have chow at 1 A.M., wait for trucks, which arrive about 3:15. Pull into Le Havre about 5:30 A.M. City completely flat. Largest and most devastated city I've seen yet. Trucks drive out on concrete piers. Wait about an hour and a half while preparations are made. Up gang plank about 7:30 A.M. The last European soil has passed under my feet, thank God. Sleep all day. Have first meal at noon on ship. Not bad at all because the Navy runs things here. Name of ship "Leonard O. H. Ernst." Supposed to sail tomorrow the Twenty-third . Rumor is that we land at Norfolk, but are naturally a bit disappointed.

June 23-   This is it! Raise anchor at 7:25 P.M. and get under way. Will arrive July First or Second in Norfolk. Au Revoir France.

June 26-   A little woozy first few days. Today we were called by a Swedish freighter to come and remove one of her officers for an emergency operation. Met in the afternoon and sent small power boat to Swedish vessel to pick up patient. Took us about 60 miles off our course. They asked for blood donors and I volunteered, but they had already picked their man.

June 28-   1,736 miles to go.

June 29-   1,327 miles to go.

July 2-   Happy Birthday honey. USA Virginia Beach dead ahead, 6:45 A.M. Ft. Story 7:45 A.M. Drop anchor off Newport News 10:10 Dock 10:30. Debark 11:45. Board train to Camp Patrick Henry.

July 3-   Processed. Leave Camp Patrick Henry about 6 P.M. for Ft. Dix, New Jersey.

July 4-   Arrived at Dix about 10 A.M. Processed.

July 5-   Called Babe. Receive furlough papers about 5:30 P.M. after waiting in rain for about four hours. Nardiello's drive us to New York. Arrive at [Bill] Blass's apartment about 7 P.M. Wellllllllll - you know the rest!!!!!!!!!!! It was the most wonderful moment of my life.

Chapter Twelve

Battle of the Bulge

Pfc. Bob Van Houten of Fairfax, Virginia, was a forward artillery observer on December 16, 1944. When he peered over the edge of his fox-hole on that fateful day, his eyes widened in fear and disbelief.

"I'd never seen so many Germans in my life, he said later. "There must have been ten thousand of them coming across that field."

It was not through lack of trying by its liaison officers that the Ghost Army was idling away the hours with card games, routine training, and other time-killing efforts during the dull days of November 1944. But the war was to get hot for the Twenty-third soon—very hot. On November 15, the command of the Ghost troops began planning what turned out to be, inadvertently, almost the end of the Ghost Army itself.

For a long time, the Luxembourg sector was the dullest part of the Western Front. It was held lightly by VIII Corps and used primarily as a rest area for tired divisions or as an orientation area for new divisions fresh from the States. Over a period of a few weeks, the Second, Eighth, and Eighty-third Infantry divisions were replaced by the Ninth Armored and 106th Infantry and the Twenty-eighth and Fourth, both weak from the fierce fighting in the forest of Hurtgen. The 106th was brand new.

Robert Tompkins recalled that the Ghost Army was occupying a large thin line in the area where the Battle of the Bulge would erupt: "They were patrolling through our lines all the time, we were stretched out so far. There was nothing we could or should have done about it. Our orders were not to engage the enemy unless it was unavoidable or to save ourselves."

On the other side of the border, the Germans seemed to be using the area as a training ground. They would bring in a baby-fresh Volksgrenadier division or a pea-green "Battle Groupen," permit them to enjoy a short course in sporadic and somewhat leisurely combat, then move them either north or south into the steaming cauldrons of the Roer or Saar, where the fighting was intense and casualties were high. The American High Command did not like to see fresh German troops being trained in and deployed from such a "rest sector," so steps were taken to prevent the enemy from moving its units around at will.

On November 15, the Twenty-third was directed to prepare and submit to Twelfth Army Group a deception plan with the objective of containing the present German strength on the VIII Corps front until December 30. This plan was called Operation Koblenz (sometimes spelled Coblenz on American and British maps) because it intended to poise a phony attack aimed down the Moselle Valley toward Koblenz. This would not only put an end to the training ground, but freeze German units there in place. It was to have been executed in two phases, but only the first one was completed, December 6-14. The second part was interrupted by what came to be called "Operation Grief," December 16, when the Ardennes counteroffensive of Field Marshal Gerd Von Runstedt began, known universally later as the Battle of the Bulge.

Operation Koblenz was beautifully organized in everything but the G-2, the men later joked. While the Ghost troops thought they were having a little fun with weak German units, the biggest counteroffensive of the war was about to erupt under their feet. Two raging Panzer armies drove into the area with a fury.

The Twenty-third did not handle Operation Koblenz alone. It acted in a supervisory capacity for VIII Corps and, of course, supplied its skilled deceptive units. Amazingly, in retrospect of course, the VIII Corps actually drew up plans to attack through Trier to Koblenz. Preliminary air bombardment was to have been started December 9 and last for five days. Corps artillery moved some units into support position using assumed names.

Real infantry patrolling was to have been intensified on December 13, and a feint made by the Twenty-eighth Infantry Division. Engineer and ordnance dumps were to have moved as if in a buildup mode. Propaganda, press, and counter-agents were to spread the word. The Twenty-third was to pretend to be the extra division.

The guise of the Twenty-third was changed so many times the Ghost troops themselves were sometimes confused. The joke was that they had an identity crisis all during the war. The changes were made four times: from the Ninth to the Seventy-eighth to the 106th to the Seventy-fifth. Each time a name was decided upon, the operation was postponed and the real division appeared in person somewhere else along the front.

The Ninth stayed around Elsenborn; the Seventy-eighth went into the Hurtgen Forest, and the ill-fated 106th—destined to be virtually wiped out as it surrendered en masse—took over St. Vith. The Seventy-fifth Division was finally chosen for the Ghost Army's new role because it was moving from England to France and the Germans probably did not know its exact location. A Twenty-third liaison officer was flown from England to help the Ghost troops "type" the Seventy-fifth—or learn its idiosyncracies—and provide shoulder patches and other special effects markings.

On December 7, Lt. Col. Schroeder of the Twenty-third, acting as billeting officer for the fake Seventy-fifth Infantry, reported to the town major and arranged for division billets east and northeast of Luxembourg. This sector was then held by the Fourth Infantry Division. On the same date, the Twenty-third and unit commanders reconnoitered their assigned areas in preparation for bringing in troops. The phony Seventy-fifth moved in over a three-day period beginning December 9. This was accomplished by infiltrating unmarked Twenty-third vehicles into a hidden transit area west of Arlon, Belgium, where the signs, bumper markers, and insignia were applied. Many of the men had become very adept at stitching on insignia and stenciling bumpers.

The freshly disguised vehicles and troops then moved out in Seventy-fifth convoys. These phony convoy movements were reported to the German Signal Intelligence in "Slidex," the code known to have been broken by the Germans. Traffic was augmented at night by the use of vehicle noises broadcast toward the enemy.

Beginning December 11, the commanders began reconnaissance of the forward area as if in preparation for an attack. Beginning December 12, the engineers began preparations for a river crossing. On December 13, some real tanks were moved up to Osweiler and at night were tripled by broadcasting tank noises. On that day, the Seventy-fifth began fading from the area, and fictional columns were reported by spoof radio to be moving north. The ruse was complete about a fortnight later when the real Seventy-fifth came in on the northwest slope of the area where the Bulge was to erupt, near Marche, Belgium.

Operation Koblenz II was scheduled to begin December 21, using practically the same scenario as Koblenz I, but playing slightly to the north. The Twenty-third was destined to act in its advisory role and to again impersonate the Seventy-fifth Infantry Division, which reported into the exact same place five weeks later. Although no formal cancellation was ever made, it soon became obvious that it would never be attempted, especially after the Twenty-third liaison officer with VIII Corps lost his trailer in the quick retreat from Bastogne.

On December 16, 1944, the Nazis launched their famous and furious counterattack in the Ardennes, making a large bulge in Allied lines. While overcast skies grounded Allied planes, 24 German divisions drove this bulge 60 miles wide and 45 miles deep into the American lines. Much of this early success was won by a specially trained unit that wore American uniforms and drove captured American vehicles.

This German unit impersonating American troops made Allied troops nervous and almost paranoid, exactly the effect the Germans wanted. The Americans spent a lot of time checking each other out after this, which made the Twenty-third especially nervous because they usually wore some other outfit's insignia anyway. This also created the chance of a fake German army impersonating Americans capturing a small and equally fake American army impersonating another division. Although it did not happen, the proximity, in retrospect, shows that it could have had just a few small things occurred differently.

The Germans, however, were finally halted by heroic resistance. The First, Second, Fourth, and Ninety-ninth Infantry divisions held the shoulders of the bulge at Monschau and Echternach. Other brave stands were made at St. Vith by the Seventh Armored Division and at Bastogne by the 101st Airborne Division and Combat Command B of the Tenth Armored. On December 26, the Fourth Armored Division relieved encircled Bastogne, ending the crisis. The First and Third armies eliminated the bulge during January. The Nazis lost 220,000 men and 1,400 tanks and assault guns. Allied casualties totaled 40,000.

By February 10, 1945, a long, grinding combat drive through the Hurtgen Forest took dams on the upper Roer River and ended further

Bill Blass, left, and Robert Tompkins stand in the snow shortly before the Battle of the Bulge sent the Ghost Army running for safety in December 1944. Some units of the Ghost Army came close to capture during this time. Photo courtesy Robert Tompkins.

One of the Ghost Army's dummy jeeps. U.S. Army photo.

danger of flooding the troops below. The First Army promptly attacked and reached the Rhine at Cologne March 7. The same day the Ninth Armored Division captured the Ludendorff bridge intact at Remagen. This action breached the last natural German defensive position. In the meantime Patton's Third Army swept the Nazis from the Saar and the Palatinate and unexpectedly crossed the Rhine near Oppenheim.

By March 31 all seven Allied armies were smashing deep into Germany.

After crossing the Rhine, the Americans sprang a gigantic trap on the defending Germans. North of the Ruhr the Ninth Army drove straight east while the First Army broke out of their Remagen bridgehead and struck east and north. The two columns joined at Paderborn on April 1, cutting off the Ruhr in the largest pocket envelopment in the history of warfare. While the Fifteenth Army held the west face of the pocket along the Rhine, units from the First and Ninth drove in to crush the enemy in 18 days. They took more than 300,000 prisoners.

The Canadian First Army routed the Germans in the Netherlands, and the British, Americans, and French swept through Germany. On April 25, the Sixty-ninth Infantry Division met Soviet forces advancing from the east at Torgau on the Elbe River. This sealed the fate of Germany. Meanwhile the Third and Seventh armies plunged into Czechoslovakia and Austria.

Total German casualties after June 6, 1944, on the Western Front were 263,000 killed, 49,000 disabled, and 7,614,794 captured. But the victorious outcome seemed very remote on December 16 when the massive German attack began. And the Ghost Army happened to be in the wrong place at the wrong time.

Supreme Allied Commander Gen. Dwight D. Eisenhower had halfway expected it—perhaps not on such a massive scale—and had even warned his subordinates about it from time to time. Eisenhower knew that the Germans would not continue to give ground without a major counteroffensive, perhaps on the Meuse or the Rhine, or, as happened, with their backs to the Maginot Line.

In fact, in some strange way, he looked forward to it because he thought it would give the Allies a chance to pinch off the German salient, when it came, and capture so many German troops that the entire Axis would be demoralized and crippled. His plan was to immediately strengthen the shoulders in an area of Allied troops

A dummy reconnaissance plane used by the Ghost Army. U.S. Army photo.

adjoining each side of any breakout, then close them completely, pinching off a large number of German troops. The one thing Eisenhower did not anticipate, nor did American G-2, was the scope and strength of the counteroffensive, nor did they anticipate the place or the vigor with which it was pushed.

For one thing, American military intelligence was convinced that the Germans could not muster enough divisions to make a meaningful counteroffensive. The conventional wisdom also said there simply was not enough gasoline for an extended German push. This was true, but German generals later said the plan, straight from Hitler's high command, anticipated capturing American gasoline and supplies, particularly at such large fuel and supply dumps as Liege and Antwerp.

Meanwhile, at SHAEF (Supreme Headquarters, Allied Expeditionary Force), Eisenhower also felt comforted by Allied air superiority. But a thick overcast kept American and British airplanes

A dummy Sherman M-4 tank deployed in France, loaned to the British by the Ghost Army. U.S. Army photo.

A dummy, inflated artillery field piece used by the Ghost Army hundreds at a time. U.S. Army photo.

grounded for several days in the beginning of the German breakout. This also prevented aerial reconnaissance, which left the Allies guessing about the total German strength.

If one would consider the German attack area as a large target, then the Ghost Army was sitting near the center, although some of them had already begun the trip back to Luxembourg City and some were there already. For a brief time, under orders from Eisenhower himself, consideration was given to staying and fighting, despite their thin ranks, even as cooks and clerks and medics were fighting a rear-guard action elsewhere to help slow the breakout.

But it was quickly decided that the specialized value of the Ghost Troops was too great to risk having them obliterated and their secret equipment captured and examined.

It is now known that the German high command thought that the Seventy-fifth would not be as effective because it was just moving in and getting set up. They thought they would be attacking through an area held by 17,000 newly arrived green troops. In actual fact, there were fewer than 1,000 Ghost Army troops deployed over a front of many miles and the Seventy-fifth Infantry was enjoying the green peace of England.

Meanwhile, in greatest of secrecy, the Germans had begun withdrawing armor from many places on the front and concentrating it in preparation for the breakout offensive.

Eisenhower and General Bradley were meeting at Eisenhower's headquarters on Saturday, December 16 when, Eisenhower later related in his report to the Joint Chiefs:

> We received word that some penetrations of the American line had been effected, with the enemy using tanks. Sensing that this was something more than a mere local attack, I immediately advised Gen. Bradley to move the 10th Armored Division from the south and the Seventh Armored Division from the north, both towards the flanks of the attack. Army commanders on both flanks were directed to alert what divisions they had free for instant movement toward that region if necessary. My own staff acted at once to move our reserve divisions forward. Of these movements, the most significant and important was that of the 101st Airborne Division, which was in SHAEF reserve and which was directed to Bastogne.

The next day, the 17th, General Bradley returned to his own headquarters to keep a close eye on the big German counteroffensive. During the next two days it became clear that the Germans were making an all-out effort to split the Allied army and throw the campaign into fatal disorder. They had done it before against battle-toughened Russian troops and Hitler thought it would be far easier against the Western Front, where he routinely underestimated American resolve and fighting ability.

"The enemy's general plan," Eisenhower said,

> as we initially analyzed it and as events subsequently confirmed, was to break through our thin line of defense in a sudden blitz drive to the Meuse in the Liege-Namur area. Having seized Liege, which was our key maintenance and communication center feeding the Twelfth Army Group from the north [under which served the Ghost Army], the enemy hoped to drive rapidly and with as much strength as possible to Antwerp, our great port of supply.
>
> Seizing or destroying this, he would have made our supply position practically untenable and would at the same time have split the British armies, together with the American Ninth Army and part of the First, in the north from the American and French forces in the south, isolating them and making possible their destruction in detail by attacks from Holland in the north and by his striking force in Belgium. The attack upon Antwerp itself would probably have been coordinated with an assault by paratroopers and infantry from Holland.

Some 200,000 German troops in white snowsuits, including crack Panzer divisions spearheaded by Tiger tanks, swept toward Bastogne, until then only an obscure small town in Belgium. Although the German tanks were superior, fortunately there were many more M-4 Sherman tanks.

In all, the Germans ordered three armies into the battle, the Fifth Panzer Army and the Sixth Panzer Army supported by the Seventh Army, totaling some 14 infantry and 10 Panzer and Panzer Grenadier divisions. It must be noted however, that the German divisions were often as few as seven to eight thousand men and sometimes as few as four thousand toward the end of the war. Eisenhower said he liked to keep American divisions at about 17,000 men, but most of them were closer to 15,000 men. Still, the Allies were shocked to see such strength from a foe they thought they had on the run and virtually defeated.

Field Marshal von Rundstedt was in personal charge, and captured field orders confirmed Ike's early conviction that this attack was in the nature of "a final, desperate blow into which every available reserve was thrown." Eisenhower was particularly disturbed by the Panzer brigade that operated in American equipment with the mission of spreading panic and confusion in and immediately behind the American front line.

This unit had approached American troops with little notice. Soon the GIs were startled to see Sherman tanks and what appeared to be American troops, even down to American small arms and machine guns, firing at them at point-blank range. To Eisenhower, there was just something beyond the limits of modern war in this treachery.

Because of this German brigade, much extra care had to be taken. Roadblocks were set up behind American lines and special passwords were issued. The especially trained Germans chosen for this deadly ruse often spoke good English and were up on American idioms and even American slang.

But Bill Enderlein of the Ghost troops said there were several ways they could be caught, aside from passwords and the familiar questioning about American sports figures. "They held their cigarettes in a funny way, a European way. They cupped them and you could tell from the way they smoked that they were not Americans," he said.

Also, parties of paratroops were dropped throughout the battle area, particularly in the Malmedy area, where about one battalion was employed. Meanwhile, small paratroop units and agents who had remained behind during the American advance were active in attempting to sabotage key bridges and headquarters as far to the rear as Paris. For the first time also since D-Day, the Luftwaffe, thought to be moribund, showed up in surprising strength to give active combat support to the ground forces, and attacked the airfields and installations throughout Belgium as well as U.S. ground troops.

On January 1, 1945, the Luftwaffe attacked U.S. airfields in Holland and Belgium with the largest concentration of planes employed since American troops hit the Normandy beaches. Some 800 sorties were flown in an all-out air attack. American losses of planes on the ground were so high the Allies concealed the number until after the war, although on this one day alone German losses amounted to 200 aircraft.

The Ghost Army not only watched much of this from near Luxembourg, but some of their troops manned anti-aircraft guns from rooftops in Luxembourg to fend off German ME-109s. Some of the Ghost troops said they enjoyed this actual fighting as a contrast to their normal role of play acting.

The full brunt of the enemy assault was met first, Eisenhower reported, by the four divisions deployed along the thinly held Eifel-Ardennes sector: the Fourth [which looked in vain for help from the Seventy-fifth Infantry Division being simulated by the Ghost Army], Twenty-eighth and 106th Infantry Divisions. In spite of being bypassed and divided by the penetration, these forces slowed the enemy thrust and the Seventh Armored Division denied him the important area of St.Vith during the critical early days.

The Fourth Division tried in vain to make radio contact with the Seventy-fifth Division, which they counted on for flank protection. Even most of the officers of the Fourth were unaware that there was no Seventy-fifth next door—that the few troops there were play acting and had been ordered to retreat.

The town of Bastogne, centerpiece of the Bulge, was bombed by the Luftwaffe from December 18 through the 21st, and encircled from the 20th of December onward until well into January. For the first six days, Bastogne underwent an intense and terrible bombardment, and in some places there was hand-to-hand fighting. On December 22, the Germans asked for the surrender of Bastogne. And there was bad news in many other areas of the Bulge.

Col. Clifford Simenson was in General Middleton's headquarters when Middleton heard some bad news about the 106th Infantry Division. The division had been moved into an area near the heaviest part of the Bulge attack shortly before it began. Since things were relatively quiet, supplies and ammunition had not yet been hauled in with the troops. Through a mixup for which the army is famous—giving rise to the word SNAFU (Situation Normal, All Fouled Up)—the 106th was sent to the front with scarcely any ammo, food, or communications equipment.

Normally, this would have been remedied in a few days, when supply trucks caught up with them, but they were sitting there when the ferocious German attack began the Bulge breakout. After a soldier fired the little ammo he had with him or in his rifle clip, his Garand suddenly became as useless as a club. If he had a bayonet, he affixed it, but he would likely be killed long before he had a chance to use it.

The Ghost Army at one time had been prepped to simulate the ill-fated 106th Division. This is why Simenson was in General Middleton's headquarters acting as one of the liaison and planning officers for the Ghost Army. He was present when Middleton was told that the 106th was about to be overrun like sitting ducks, without supplies or ammo. He was told the horrible facts: most of the troops had the ammunition in their weapons and that was all.

To let them stay there would mean annihilation if they tried to fight. The field commander said he would surrender his men rather than have them slaughtered. Middleton agreed with the surrender, with great pain and visible anguish, Simenson recalled, and it became one of the most ignominious episodes of the war. Many of the 106th were killed before the surrender, and although some of them escaped, some 9,000 men were surrendered.

Despite the crippling loss of the 106th and other tragic fiascos, the momentum of the breakthrough was further reduced by the arrival in the battle area on December 18 of the 101st and Eighty-second Airborne Divisions—some of America's best fighting troops. They were moved from reserve in the Reims area to the command of Twelfth Army Group. The 101st Airborne Division, reinforced by armor, then held the vital road center at Bastogne although completely surrounded for five days and under constant attack by forces many times superior in strength. The fierce commitment of these divisions, however, removed the last Theater Reserve, and the Eleventh Armored Division, newly arrived from England, was directed to assemble rapidly in the Reims area to protect the center and to meet a head-on attack on the Meuse, if necessary.

The Seventeenth Airborne Division was also ordered over from England to help the Eleventh Armored Division secure the Meuse line south to Givet. To reestablish and maintain a reserve, additional infantry divisions then in England—including the falsely maligned Seventy-fifth Infantry Division—were brought to the Continent weeks in advance of schedule.

Until this day, said Ghost Army vets, most of the Seventy-fifth Infantry Division's surviving vets probably do not know that their division was simulated just days before the Battle of the Bulge by a Ghost Army. Many were unfairly reviled as cowards, an accusation they found infuriating and bewildering. The real Seventy-fifth went on to heroically acquit themselves for the remainder of the war.

"As the week wore on we succeeded in bolstering up the northern shoulder of the penetration," reported Eisenhower,

> at the same time collecting a U.S. Corps under Gen. Collins for use in counterattack. From the south, Gen. Patton began a transfer of six divisions to the north of the Moselle. The 21st Army Group likewise collected reserves and placed a corps under Lt. Gen. Horrocks in

the Brussels area. The flanks of the penetration at Monschau and Echternach were held and the salient gradually stabilized by these measures. However, the penetration directly westward was still moving and while on the north it had been possible with the 17th Airborne Division and the 11th Armored Division to cover the Meuse bridges adequately down as far as Givet, south of that the crossing remained alarmingly weak. To defend them I directed that all available rear-echelon troops and service units as well as six French infantry battalions be moved to the Meuse to protect the crossings at all costs and in no event to permit any bridge to fall intact into the hands of the enemy.

Because of the terrible situation in the Bastogne area where the 101st Airborne Division and other elements were bravely holding out against greatly superior German forces, General Bradley felt that he should start General Patton's Third Army attacking to the north from the Arlon-Luxembourg area no later than Friday, December 22.

General Patton was authorized to begin the attack, but prior to launching it he was instructed to make absolutely certain of the safety of his right flank in the Trier region from which a new offensive by the German Seventh Army still threatened. He was also to attack by phase lines, holding all forces carefully together in order to avoid any risk of dispersion or wastage of strength before Field Marshal Montgomery was in a position to join the attack from the north.

Prior to the 22nd, the weather had been cold, overcast and miserable—one of the coldest winters in years, making for even more misery on the front lines. From the 16th to the 22nd, the Germans used their advantage of being able to attack under cover of thick ground fog, which deprived American troops of practically all air assistance apart from limited and extremely hazardous missions. German ground troops were able to attack U.S. defending forces with maximum surprise.

On the 22nd, however, the weather began to improve, and American aircraft began paralyzing attacks upon enemy communications, supply convoys, and trains at the same time that Patton's Third Army attack was launched northeastward from the Arlon-Luxembourg area. Because the Germans had initiated the attack, prior planning of air operations (such as the set-piece effort for the Normandy invasion) was impossible.

The object of U.S. air attacks against the German rail system, carried out in spite of the bad weather (both in the target area and over the bases in England), was to force back the German railheads. The

German attack and the continued supply of the German forces were largely dependent on rail communications.

The heavy bomber attacks achieved their object and made the closer-range attacks against road movements all the more effective in helping to strangle von Rundstedt's efforts. Unfortunately, many French and Belgian civilians were killed in this air battle. Throughout the period, America's Strategic Air Forces—then under the Army as the Army Air Corps—battered marshaling yards east of the Rhine and blocked centers of movement such as St. Vith. Meanwhile, medium and light bombers of the Tactical Air Forces destroyed bridges, headquarters, dumps, and other targets in the battle area.

Ghost vets said they were vastly cheered by the sight of American planes attacking the German breakout. The fighter-bombers ranged far and wide in and beyond the battle area, creating havoc in enemy road and rail movement, starving the German troops who could not be supplied. Many who surrendered cited this as one of their reasons for surrendering.

A concerted attack on the German airfields on December 24 helped to reduce the activity of the enemy fighters. It also afforded U.S. fighter-bombers greater opportunity for concentration on ground targets rather than on dog fights, which up to this time had been as intense as any the enemy had proved capable of offering since D-Day.

The Fourth Armored Division of the Third Army, attacking northward against heavy resistance toward Bastogne, was able by December 26 to make firm contact with the defenders of the important road net there. The defenders had been supplied by air and checked the German advance on that flank. This attack also drew strong German troop strength away from the north of the salient. Additional reserves had been so disposed along the Meuse as to relieve anxiety over this sector. It was then clear that the Germans had failed in their main effort, although there was still a lot of savage fighting left in the war.

By the time the German drive was halted, they had breached a 45-mile gap in U.S. lines from Echternach to Monschau and had penetrated over 60 miles westward to within 4 miles of the Meuse near Celles. The Ghost Army anxiously watched these developments and saw much of the action, although they were behind the front lines near Luxembourg City.

"As soon as the enemy's advance had been checked," Eisenhower reported to the Joint Chiefs of Staff, "my intention was to cut his lines of communication into the salient and if possible to destroy him by launching ground attacks from both north and south in close coordination with continued heavy air attacks designed to extend paralysis of movement and communication."

The counterattack from the north, aimed at Houffalize in the center of the German "bulge," was launched by the First Army on January 3 on a two-corps front, with a corps of the British Second Army forming on the west flank. On January 9, the Third Army, which had been maintaining strong pressure in the Bastogne area, launched a fresh attack also directed toward the Houffalize road net. Both these attacks were hampered by more terrible weather over snow-covered minefields and were met by stubborn German fighting.

Slow progress was made, however, and the gap between the attacking armies had by January 10 been narrowed to some ten miles. By this time, the Germans had begun to withdraw from the western tip of the Bulge, but still strongly opposed Allied pressure against their northern and southern flanks. Nevertheless, on the 16th, attacking forces of the First and Third Armies established firm contact at Houffalize and turned their full strength eastward against the retreating Germans.

St. Vith fell to the First Army forces on the Twenty-third, and by the end of the month the U.S. line was approximately what it had been at the beginning of the breakthrough, while advance forces attacked beyond this in the direction of Bonn. Unfortunately, Eisenhower's pincer trap was too slowly executed to capture a large force of Germans in this operation, although a few thousand were captured. Most of them escaped the pincers.

In an evacuation hospital a few days after the German counteroffensive began, a soldier from the Fourth Infantry was heard to remark: "I'd like to get my hands on those elusive bastards of the Seventy-fifth." It was generally assumed by units adjacent to the phony Seventy-fifth that they had turned tail and run at the first sign of the big Nazi counterattack, the last great counteroffensive on the Western Front.

Many troops in the Fourth thought it was just pure cowardice for an entire division to simply disappear in the face of the enemy. After all, they had seen their distant tanks and halftracks, heard their radio traffic every day, seen their artillery flashes at night, and even chatted with some of their soldiers. But they had no inkling that it was all a tactical charade.

Also during initial days of the Bulge, a prisoner of war from a German detachment in Echternach told interrogators he thought he had been captured by troops of the Seventy-fifth Infantry Division. He went on to say that the American army radio operators were very sloppy in their radio traffic, and then he added that German intelligence had cracked the Allies' battlefield radio code. It never occurred to him nor to any other German, said U.S. intelligence, that all of that radio chatter could have been phony. Germans thought Americans were too open and forthright, like western cowboys, to be duplicitous and clever. This proved to be an advantage for the Ghost Army throughout the war.

On December 16, the Battle of the Bulge came close to netting a key part of the Ghost Army—the sonics section—it had moved so fast. Although the massive German counterattack was launched after much of the Twenty-third had returned to its Luxembourg City base, there were still many straggling key elements, like the sonic section, that were perilously close to capture.

As the official chronology of the Ghost Army asserts in its typically understated language:

> Organization alerted, documents and records placed in vehicles under guard for immediate departure. Rubber items and special equipment prepared for fire. Guard doubled. Machine gun nests set up for defense of sector surrounding billets. Attacked by air. The Twenty-third gunners fired at enemy planes during entire night.

Enderlein said some of the Twenty-third, a little slow in getting back to Luxembourg, came close to being completely obliterated as a functioning unit by the racing Panzer tanks. In fact, parts of the Twenty-third were actually in danger of capture or worse when they were bailed out at the last minute by an American column of Sherman tanks.

Ghost Army vets said they had a lot of respect for American tank troops because the worst of the German tanks was better than the Sherman in thickness of armor and the size of the main turret gun. It usually took two or three Shermans to knock out one of the three German models of tanks, the vets said, although the Sherman was more maneuverable and had a far more reliable engine. Toward the last days of the war, a larger gun was put on Sherman tanks that was capable of penetrating German armor. During the Battle of the Bulge, however, most were not so equipped, and many brave young men died in their burning tanks.

Some railroad guns launched huge shells that landed very near the Ghost Army troops. Some vehicles were hit, including a half-track that virtually disappeared because of the explosives already under its front seats. Fortunately, it was unmanned at the time because its crew, at the sound of the first few artillery rounds, left the vehicle and took cover. Throughout this time of the Bulge breakout, everyone marveled that the Germans could scrape together so much equipment, aircraft, troops, and supplies. It was demoralizing to many Americans back home who saw it incorrectly as an ominous sign that the war might last for several more years.

The danger to Luxembourg City was not great enough to force the further retreat of the Twenty-third beyond this point, but the arrival of thousands of fighting reinforcements necessitated the evacuation of all Twenty-third units. By December 21, the city housed four major headquarters: Twelfth Army Group, Patton's Third Army, XII Corps, and the Eightieth Infantry Division. The Fourth Infantry was less than a mile outside of town.

On this date, the Ghost Army's columns were streaming ignominiously westward to some cold, dirty flophouse barracks in Doncourt near Longuyon, France. Only Twenty-third Headquarters top brass remained behind, and they decided to stick it out in the Italian legation building.

A previously classified Army report said the Ghost Army apparently played a key role in enticing the Panzers into the first hours of the Battle of the Bulge. The Germans, according to interviews after the war, were surprised at the very light to non-existent resistance in the area of the American Seventy-fifth Infantry Division. Although they knew the troops were green and fresh from the United States, they expected at least some opposition. Prisoners later expressed surprise at the easy advancement in this sector.

The American Fourth Infantry Division later officially complained that the adjacent Seventy-fifth, whose vehicles they had seen and whose radio traffic they had heard, seemed to have vanished shortly after the heavy fighting began. They groused about it for the rest of the war. They were not told the truth for secrecy reasons—even in postwar years.

At this time, vets later related, the daytime temperature averaged 15 degrees. It dropped to zero or below every night. Storms were routine. American riflemen kept one pair of socks in their helmets, put one under their jackets, and wore one pair.

Although they moved to safety, under orders to get out, those front-line troops who were in the Bulge area or moved into the vacuum had one of the toughest, most savage fights of the war.

Daily combat and frostbite were companions for 40 days and nights. Fingers froze to triggers of M-1 rifles. It was a miserable, snowy hell, yet part of what Winston Churchill called "the greatest American victory" of World War II.

It was in this kind of weather when Pfc. Bob Van Houten peeked over the lip of a fragmented concrete bunker on Dec. 16, 1944, and could not believe what he saw. There were Germans everywhere.

The huge German counteroffensive was so advanced and so close that the only thing Van Houten could do as a forward artillery observer—under radioed orders—was "get the hell out of there." He radioed his artillery, who at first were incredulous of his report. "There's not enough artillery anywhere to stop this," they responded.

Ghost Army veteran Ed Biow said, "I'll never forget at that time, a few days after the battle started, seeing Sherman tanks bumper to bumper as far as the eye could see. It was Patton's Third Army going to the relief of Bastogne. It was quite a sight and I thought, seeing that, that things would turn out okay."

Bill Simpkins of Baltimore was a member of the 510th flying P-47s from a field about 10 miles away when his men began daily attack missions—when the weather cleared—in support of General Patton's Army.

"We carried two 500-pound bombs and 3,360 rounds of .50-caliber machine gun ammunition, eight machine guns, two wing tanks, and a main belly tank," he said. On one of his missions, a German tank rolled into a ditch to get an angle and fired, hitting his belly tank. Miraculously, he said, the tough P-47 was still flyable and he returned "with a ringing in my ears that lasted for days."

Eugene Drouillard was commander of a rifle company known as the "diaper division," because most of his troops were teenagers. He lost more than 30 of his command in a few minutes as the furious battle began.

"It was so cold that we would take our corpses and lean them against fence posts so they could be found," Gen. Bruce C. Clark told this writer.

And Clyde Boden of Arlington, Virginia, said one of his strangest memories was playing poker three nights in a row before the Battle of the Bulge, then watching as his poker buddies were killed in the pitched battle hours after the attack. Boden added, "Patriotism, heroism, loyalty, and bravery were taken for granted every day."

Soon, said Bill Enderlein, part of the Ghost Army, the 3132nd Sonic, in charge of the big speakers, was surrounded on a small hill. Enderlein recalled that the men got ready to set the fuses and blow up all the secret equipment when someone saw a column of American armor headed their way. The Germans gave way and the 3132nd was rescued.

"We were just a few seconds away from blowing up all of our equipment," Enderlein said. "We thought we could escape on foot through some of the forest paths. We had been in this area for awhile and we knew the trails pretty well."

Later, German Field Marshal Gerhard von Tebbe told General Clark he learned the hard way that reports about poor fighting ability of American troops were absolutely false. Von Tebbe said determined pockets of Americans fought fiercely and stalled the attack, the last gasp of the Third Reich.

Enderlein said the men later joked that perhaps they provoked the Battle of the Bulge—that this time they were "too darned good and realistic for their own good." Later, when adjacent American units who actually thought they were next to the Seventy-fifth Division ran into the real Seventy-fifth's troops, fistfights broke out as the veteran troops, badly bloodied by the German breakout, accused the Seventy-fifth troops face-to-face of cowardice. Although the Seventy-fifth was not even present, other American troops had bought into the deception so thoroughly they called the Seventy-fifth troops liars and cowards.

"Perhaps only now will survivors of the real Seventy-fifth learn that they had been represented at the front before they arrived by the Twenty-third Headquarters Special Troops," said Colonel Simenson.

German POWs, captured by the Fourth Infantry Division, also told interrogators that they wondered why the American Seventy-fifth Infantry Division seemed to have disappeared.

Albert Speer said after the war that Hitler had confidently predicted that the Allies would fold up under such a massive attack, and that the

German troops could divide the Allied army and re-capture the vital port of Antwerp. This would be so demoralizing, Hitler told his subordinates, that the Allies would seek peace at any cost. The Wehrmacht could then devote all of its attention to defeating the Russians on the Eastern Front. Speer said Hitler had begun living more and more in a fantasy world. The Ghost Army, of course, also lived in a fantasy world—but by its own design.

When its troops and equipment got back to the vicinity of Luxembourg, it could still have been overrun by Germans had it not been for the snag at Bastogne. General Middleton told Eisenhower this would be a good place to bring in reinforcements. To Middleton's credit, he ordered Bastogne, where he personally had reconnoitered the terrain, to be held at all costs. He told Eisenhower at the time that Bastogne might very well be surrounded or cut off, but he said it would be a pocket of resistance that could slow the German advance.

Von Rundstedt said after the war that the decision was made to "mask" Bastogne by leaving it surrounded so as not to slow the attack. But he admitted that it was such a good fighting unit that it did slow the advance.

General Middleton saw the importance of the area and its defensive terrain. The Eighty-second Airborne Division was diverted to Stavlot in the north and the 101st, with detachments of VIII Corps, became the famed defenders of Bastogne.

Their famed heroism so slowed and disrupted the German advance that Allied troops were able to regroup. When the weather cleared, Allied aircraft began attacking the German columns virtually at will and with little opposition except for ground anti-aircraft fire. General Patton began an attack on the Bastogne area with three divisions on the morning of December 23, 1944. That was the beginning of the end of the German highwater mark on the Western Front. And it was a trauma the Ghost Army would never forget.

It was also a time that Charles R. "Chuck" Cuppet, a radio operator, would not forget. Cuppet narrowly escaped being assigned to a front-line unit because of a vacancy in the Ghost Army for another radio operator. Cuppet, who lives in Twain Harte, California, said:

> I joined them at the time of the Battle of the Bulge—just after it began. At that time the battle was raging and the Army needed every able-bodied soldier they could get their hands on to plug into the line to

stop the German advance. I was sent to a replacement depot to be assigned to an infantry unit on the front lines when a call came in with a higher priority for a radio operator. It was the luckiest day of my life, as I'm sure had I been sent to the front at that time, I would have little chance of survival. When I got to the replacement depot, there was a steady stream of trucks taking troops to the front and then putting Red Cross signs on their canvas tops and returning with casualties.

I was told to go out back and pick out an M-1 rifle and be sure and check it to make sure it worked. [Many were recovered from the dead and wounded on the battlefield.] I had to try three rifles before I found one that would work. It was scary. After I returned with the rifle to the office, I was told to return the rifle to the pile that I got it from, as I was being sent to the 3132nd Signal Service Company in the Twenty-third Headquarters Special Troops as a radio operator. The sergeant said, "You're very lucky."

When I arrived at the Signal Service Company I was assigned to the communication platoon as a radio operator within the company. The way we operated was so different from anything I was used to in the Army. When we went on a mission we were given X number of hours to get to our rendezvous and they didn't care how we got there or what route we took as long as we arrived on time. We never went in a big convoy as long as I could remember. It was great, especially when we had two or three days to arrive. We could do a lot of sightseeing, which we did.

One time we were given a mission and had two days to arrive at our destination. We had been eating K-rations and were getting tired of them when we came to a little village in northern France. There was a little restaurant but they didn't have much on the menu, which was understandable at the time. They did have some fresh French bread and the makings of a tossed salad and red wine. So we bartered with them, trading cigarettes and candy bars for the best salad and French bread I have ever had.

Another time when we were on reconnaissance we were on a back road which was dirt and full of mud holes which were quite deep and long. We came to this one which was quite wide and about eighteen inches deep so we stopped to check it out as we didn't know at the time how deep it was. Our sergeant decided to sit on the front of the jeep and hold on to the wire breaker that was attached to the front of the jeep and direct the driver from there.

Our driver was somewhat of a character who meant no harm to anyone but always managed to bungle things up. The sergeant told him to drive into the mud hole slowly and to be sure not to stop. The driver's idea of slow and sergeant's idea of slow were different. The driver put the jeep in low gear and stepped on the gas and the jeep lurched forward into the mud puddle.

He got about halfway in and the sergeant was screaming for him to slow down when he hit a large obstacle. The jeep came to an abrupt halt. The sergeant flew head first into the mud and came up wiping mud off his face and cursing the driver at the same time.

The driver then stomped on the accelerator. The jeep leaped forward and out of the mud hole to the other side where he stopped, leaving the sergeant standing in the middle of the mud hole cursing the driver. The driver sat calmly in the jeep listening to the sergeant and never said a word. When I saw that the sergeant wasn't hurt I couldn't help laughing so much I almost wet my pants.

A Christmas Story

It was during this depressing, bitterly cold time in December that Sergeant Henry Rapsis and his buddies were sent to stay in an old school near the village of Malmedy. Rapsis, a sergeant with the 3132nd, the sonics part of the Ghost Army, said one of his strongest memories was the Christmas of 1944 at Malmedy. His outfit was staying in a barracks improvised from a former school. He recalls:

> We were all pretty down and depressed. It was the Christmas season and it was cold and the war had been going on and on and we were not in the Christmas spirit. In fact, we were all down in the dumps. But all of that changed one night. I heard a noise and saw movement out of the corner of my eye in the mess area. I ran there and caught a Polish boy. His name was Joseph. He was a hungry waif, with big blue eyes. A sad but very likeable little kid. He was trying to find something to eat in our garbage cans.
>
> I could speak a little Polish, so I talked to him and found that he was trying to find something to take back to his people. The people were hungry and had it real bad because of the war. The Germans had been rough on them. They were practically starving and dressed in tatters, he told us.

Rapsis and the rest of the troops practically adopted Joseph. He became, during the few days before Christmas, a combination mascot and adopted child of the entire outfit. They fed him and gave him new clothes, including some altered GI-issue clothing, and chocolate and all but spoiled him.

"So we got in the spirit of Christmas through him," said Rapsis, now a retired Coca Cola executive living in Atlanta.

We decided to bring a lot of stuff and gifts to his people. We used Christmas wrapping paper we had got through the mail from back home. We had a lot of extra clothes and food, chocolate, pocket knives, and all kinds of gear—but mostly food and clothes. We wrapped it all up and we drove in a little convoy to this Polish community. Joseph wanted to ride in the lead jeep like the conquering hero, of course, and we let him.

Well, the people were overwhelmed, so grateful and so happy. And that in turn made us all happy. It was a very spiritual thing. It was one of the best Christmases ever, and it was all because we were doing something for them. And all of this right in the middle of the war.

Chapter Thirteen

Lonnie Gault's War

Lon "Lonnie" Gault, an eighteen-year-old army private from Clinton, Iowa, mentioned previously in the Ghost Army's participation in the Brest Operation, kept a memoir of his Ghost Army experiences. Some of it is poetic and haunting. Some of it is routine observation about life in the Ghost Army. He also kept his Boy Scout card and a copy of the Boy Scout oath in his wallet, which went with him across the channel when the Ghost Troops followed the invaders.

Gault landed at Utah Beach and kept a detailed memoir, even in dangerous areas. He had been sent to radio school in Camp Crowder, Missouri. When his test scores were found to be exceptional, along with his IQ, he was later tapped for the Ghost Army, where a high IQ was a must.

Most of his pocket diaries concerned his day-to-day life in the Army, but his observations became of special interest when he arrived in Normandy within a couple of weeks after D-Day. This is his story as he recorded it:

———◆———

Truck after truck rolled out of the LSTs and up the beach. It was very foggy and the trucks and jeeps and other vehicles just rolled into the fog. Roads leading from the beach were posted with hundreds of signs warning the soldiers of the dangers of mines, unexploded shells and booby traps on either side of the road.

Every few yards there were shell holes, bombed-out places,

Corporal Lonnie Gault on guard duty at Trier, Germany, in April 1945.

dead animals, horses and cows, trenches and fox holes dug by the men who had preceded us during the worst of the fighting, barbed wire by the mile, smashed and burned equipment everywhere. The strange stench of war hung over the whole area. Buildings near the beach were shot up and destroyed by artillery. It was very strange going into the fog to face an unknown and dangerous fate.

Up the road we continued until we reached a large area miles inland from Utah Beach where we halted and awaited further orders. Nearby was an exploded, burning truck, having only the twisted frame left to show what it once was. It made everyone realize how close we were to the war. We could also hear the sound of artillery and machine gun fire not far away.

Orders finally came and the convoy proceeded along dirt, graded and macadam roads for over thirty miles until the Twenty-third was again complete. Many villages and towns were just remembrances of what they were shortly before. It was early seen that warfare of modern kind leaves the land struggling for supremacy. So much new to all that books could be written on oddities of France in relation to America. The Twenty-third was attached to the Twelfth Army Group and later assigned under the Twelfth Army Group Special Troops.

Several trips were made down the highway through Granville and Avranches on false runs. After being close to the point of operations the "problem" [mission] was called off. Then the unit drove back through the sniper-infested ruins of the cities to the apple orchard. The apple orchard had foxholes near the tents of the men in case of strafing or bombing. At night on guard duty the distant rumble of artillery could be heard all night long. Flashes from the artillery also could be seen. Also the "bed-check Charlie" German planes made [their] nightly appearance with typical sounding German motors. Our search-lights tried to pick them out. Flashes of our anti-aircraft fire searched for the bombers and shrapnel rained down around us. We had to take cover from our shrapnel.

At last the companies drove down along the coastline to the Brittany area where an overnight stay was spent before going to Brest, the surrounded seaport. The next day the organizations of the Twenty-third camped back ten miles from the front lines, leaving part of our supply and mess trucks back while we went forward to the front on August 21, for the first time for most of us.

The Second, Eighth, and Twenty-ninth divisions were the main forces surrounding the thousands of German in Brest, including paratroops, marines, etc. Germans from all parts of the peninsula retreated to their stronghold at Brest for a big last-ditch fight. Under a continual torrent of heavy artillery, constant bombings, Brest managed to survive somehow.

Rubber dummies were placed near the front to fool the Germans as was the use of the exact sound recordings in moving battalions of tanks and companies of trucks. The signal company kept the air filled with fake messages of the Ninth Armored Division. All of our trucks carried phony markings and we had phony insignia, patches and bumper markings on everything that moved. The Germans then shifted their guns to meet the threat of the impending American attack, but the real units attacked in the wrong spot [where the Ghost Army had been demonstrating], losing many men and tanks. Brest had proven to all that the Twenty-third's deception had proved its right to be used in the field.

Some artillery fire directed against the deceptionists came close enough for the men to pick up bits of shrapnel from the German 88s. Americans fired into the city of Brest day and night with guns up to 240mm, hitting several oil tanks, making the fire visible for many miles. Fires within the city burned day and night. Large fires out of control burned and warships in the harbor fired tons of shells into the city while American and British bombers dropped tons of bombs, flares and propaganda leaflets telling the Germans that further resistance was futile.

We were doing what we could to have the Germans surrender before the harbor facilities were ruined for Allied use during the rest of the war. The flares lit the countryside bright enough that newspapers could be read even though we were several miles from Brest. Sharp brilliant bomb bursts were seen all throughout the air raids. Brest was literally a glowing city. We wondered how any Germans could survive there, but as it turns out, they did.

The boys of our air corps strafed the Krauts all during the daylight hours, and the Germans fired back. Some of this seemed almost at ground level and some of it was from several thousand feet in the air. The Pilots of the P-51s seemed to disregard all of the flak coming up at them from Brest, and some of our P-51s were shot down by the German anti-aircraft fire. War seemed different to everyone than we fellows had expected. No longer did it seem so glorious to most of us— just dirty, hard, unpleasant work—work whose results were not always readily apparent or visible. For the first time I realized that all nations propagandize their young men into believing that war and combat are glorious and courageous and that this is all part of being a patriot.

But when you see a body half sticking out of the mud, whether he is a GI or Kraut, you know that war is really a nightmarish, grimey business totally devoid of glamour, a business of seeing which side can kill the most of the other side. Never mind that these young men who are dying, like our P-51 pilots I saw shot down over Brest, had mothers, sisters and fathers who loved and doted on them, who prayed nightly for their safety and well-being; men with pals back home they played baseball or went hunting and fishing with or shared a Coke or soda with, people who will now have a bleak and mournful hole in their lives all because the leaders of nations filled with hubris and strutting pretensions want the territory of some other nation.

I guess I am just now beginning to understand the universal truth of war and its real face as young men have for a thousand years. I will say this to anyone who will listen: It is not the war of the movies or the war of the recruitment posters back home; it is not the war of the knights in armor; it is not the war of Churchill's stirring words; it is not the war to preserve our way of life in the shining and glorious future. What it is is a group of human beings acting out the savagery deep in their breasts left over from prehistoric times. Only now instead of a few bows and arrows and spears, there is the robot buzz bomb and the .50-caliber Browning machine gun.

War is an ugly and depressing business, the lowest impulse of mankind. My heart aches knowing so many of our young men are dying, young men who could do something wonderful with their lives—write a great book, compose great music, discover great cures in medicine, live lives of meaning and purpose. Well, I guess I sound kind of corny as I write this note to who knows who— and it probably will never be read by anyone—as I sit scrunched up in a muddy fox hole wondering how long this stupid war will last, but most of all, whether I will be around after it's over.

But back to reality: Part of our Signal Company was fixing radio pictures at Lorient. Part of the 3132nd was at St. Malo broadcasting propaganda to the besieged Germans surrounded there, and trapped on an island.

Heater unit crossed the Luxembourg border, a marked difference in the countryside was noticed. It was not just the contours of the land, but the farms also looked different. The Houses had a much neater appearance in Luxembourg than in recently defeated France. This was another country added to the list of the Twenty-third and its travels.

On this Autumn day of Sept. 15, the world was beautiful, shining sun, dreamy clouds, cool playful breezes. Americans were chasing the Nazis; the war would be over soon, we thought—maybe even before Christmas is what many of us guessed if the present pace continued. We thought we might be home soon. Little did we know what the months ahead had in store for our American armies.

Cheering, waving, dancing, joyful people greeted the convoys as the Twenty-third dashed into Luxembourg and other small farming communities, and the industrial cities Kail and Esch. Hundreds of people were on the streets, a cheering-madly happy crowd, honoring the liberators.

Into the bivouac area 1.3 miles north of Bettenbourg, the Twenty-third slowly drifted in during the night and day. The Twenty-third was simulating the Sixth Armored Division in a preparatory camp for their attack while other American divisions tried to go through the lines in the far north. Paratroopers had attempted to bend the Siegfried Line before winter. Radio traffic of a division was sent on the airways; dummies were placed in logical gun positions and tank harboring locations. Heater [the 3132nd] projected sound throughout many miles of the surrounding countryside, all adding the impression that a large striking force was on hand and ready to move.

The half-tracks, jeeps, $2\frac{1}{2}$-ton trucks, ambulances, etc. patrolled the roads as normal divisional traffic, showing anyone who might be interested the fake bumper markings and shoulder patches. We also drove around in a big loop to make our numbers appear much larger than they actually were. The sonic effects were carried on just before midnight for the benefit of the Germans and any German spies in the area. Sounds came from the woods from land near Bettenbourg and one night was aimed back at the cities.

Our inflatable tanks were put in sheltered areas and a few

real tanks were put in plain sight of everyone who moved by on the crossroads. This had a carry-over effect on the slinking local people who prowled around the area, many of whom we knew to be German spies or sympathizers. The overall effect of fake radio, fake tanks, tank tracks, some real tanks, fake insignia and fake markings was very convincing and fooled other American troops all the time.

Trips were made into Luxembourg City for what we called "atmosphere," or a chance to let the civilians see our markings, insignia and hear some of the stories we were told to tell civilians when they inquired about us. Newspaper correspondents were amazed upon seeing the 6th Armored Division here so they stopped one of our lieutenants for questioning. Stories were written concerning the outfit as the Sixth, then orders came from General Bradley to cancel the story. Correspondents were amazed and didn't know what to think.

A problem [mission] has been requested by the 20th Corps for a few days but such a fine job was done the 20th retained our people for over a week. Only a few tanks actually patrolled the west side of the river separating Luxembourg and Germany. This was a very precarious position for all of our troops in the southeastern part of Luxembourg. If only they had known, a few German combat patrols could have smashed through the southern part of Luxembourg with ease. But we played our bluff well.

Large artillery flashes from the south near Metz were seen nightly indicating a titanic struggle going on there. The dense forest covering the bivouac area seemed to hold all the moisture collected from heavy rains making the roads a pool of mud besides making sleeping in our pup tents a miserable experience.

Rumors seemed strong that the Twenty-third would leave for the port soon to prepare for doing what we do in the Pacific. Days were anxiously counted, with the men hoping that the unit would pull directly back through France to Cherbourg. Next area is eleven miles away, one mile east of Boscharge, Luxembourg and was another damp woods. The entire Twenty-third camped for a few days together. Miserable rainstorms prevailed. In the daytime, men spent the day chopping trees down for firewood. By the fires we all huddled under extra dirty shelter halves, talking and shooting the bull. What else could we do?

At night the fires had to be extinguished so the woods seemed barren. German planes were busy at night, particularly the odd-sounding planes that swooped around all the time. A few German bombers appeared also. We all laughed about what Eisenhower had promised us—that any planes we saw after D-Day would be Allied planes.

A few generators ran to supply power for lights in the special laboratory vehicles where they transferred sounds from records to the wire recordings. That was the only sound to be heard other than the continual patter of rain on the leaves of the trees.

Orders from the Twelfth Army Group came in telling us that the unit will be sent once more to the City of Luxembourg. The new center of our operation will be in Luxembourg City, one of the most charming cities in Europe, and a very pleasant place for American Army troops. Various companies were spread throughout the city. Heater had a former college for a barracks.

This was a real home compared to the barracks in the U.S. As the place began to show the marks of being clean once more, orders came through to leave for another school on the other side of town. This other former school had been occupied by Germans as an officers' training school. Wreckage and trash littered the halls and all of the rooms. Filthiness to Nth degree was present within the small confines of the school area. Huns had left the place in a hurry for their homeland, leaving everything— even their mess kits with food. The basement was later found to contain a lot of live ammo, grenades and anti-tank weapons.

The first school used by Heater had several floors more than the surrounding buildings thereby giving us a magnificent view of much of the city from the upper stories. A fine scene was offered overlooking a valley and out as far as the rolling hills of nearby Germany.

Children hung about the guard posts most of the day chiseling candy, gum and chocolate candy from our generous American guards. Few of the ruffians knew more than a few words of English. But English words were rapidly absorbed and learned by the youngsters and unfortunately not all of it included the choice words of our language.

Winter wasn't far away and the days were getting chilly at night. This spot looked like the spot we'd stay in over the win-

ter awaiting spring before starting another offensive compa-
rable to the big breakthroughs in France.

Some of the other units spread the word and the blarney that
we the Twenty-third would be one of the few units stationed
within the city. Invitations were extended by the citizens to
many of the men, inviting them for an off day in their homes or
a meal at least. Some of the men said the hospitality was very
good and the scarce food most generously shared. The people
seemed grateful that we were here. Others say there are still
plenty of German sympathizers in the area, despite the gen-
erosity. We all had to be careful about what we said.

Orders came to clean the other school house in preparation
for moving back into it. Details every day tore into the piles of
debris, attempting to clean the premises before we moved in.
Bunks, desks, tables, chairs, mirrors, wash pans and so forth
were brought from the supply depot at the Maginot Line. Loud
speakers were connected in every room for music and talking
and communicating with each other.

When the clean-up details returned from dinner they'd bring
back Luxembourg ice cream, cookies, pies and other goodies
bought at the stores or given to them by citizens. The ice cream
had a peculiar flavor as well as the pies, which was as we later
learned a result of lack of proper ingredients. Sugar was in short
supply everywhere, for one thing. I wonder what they substituted.

But still it wasn't too bad and the treats helped alleviate the
homesickness we all felt. Months had passed since we had been
able to buy the sweet stuff anywhere. Pastries came in by the bag-
fuls to supplement our mess hall food, which was unappetizing.

Upon our entrance into this fair city little did we suspect
our unit would spend so much time here. Months rolled by
with the war in progress and us either in the city as stationery
troops or rolling through the woods and hills to the front to
handle a problem. Luxembourg City is located in the southeastern portion of the Grand Duchy of Luxembourg and was
the capital of this tiny European province. One of the most
pleasant cities of six thousand or so I've ever been in. The air in
the city was so similar to the air in the country hamlets, pure
and unadulterated with the thick smoke of busy industries so
commonly noticeable in some cities and in the United States.

People of the country speak several languages, as a rule; English is spoken by many; German by many, French by many, Flemish by some, besides a few other languages of the minority foreigners. Cleanliness and courtesy were typical of the people we met in Luxembourg, the city and country.

The business section had a modern appearance similar to a typical American city of the same size as Luxembourg. Most of the store attendants spoke excellent English: a result of hearing English vacationers during the pre-war years perhaps. Many of the businesses had fine displays tempting a person to buy the merchandise shown. Some of the stores had rounded corners complete with curved and streamlined chromium bands to give a distinctive air to that particular building. Naturally most of the printing on the windows was Letzenburg. The remainder was either in French or English.

One of the most popular stores in Luxembourg for battle-tired soldiers was the ice cream parlor and pastry shop. A continuous line of soldiers crowded this establishment from opening until closing. Although neither ice cream nor pastry was very good because of the lack of proper ingredients, it sold because it had a different taste from the rations we ate every day, and anything that didn't taste like Army food was good to us. Besides, the soldiers like to be able to use our foreign money purchasing articles to defeat their perpetual hunger.

Pastry was rationed to the civilians. The Luxembourg government abandoned the rationing from time to time because of the GIs. Luxembourg had been treated better by the Nazis than some of the other conquered nations. You can understand the bad position national affairs were in throughout the capital city. As in all foreign countries, the soldiers furnished some sort of material for the black market. Cigarettes, candy or some form of clothing seemed to be the most popular articles.

A series of hills and valleys formed the ground beneath buildings, parks and city streets of Luxembourg. Rolling hills and not steep inclines were the rule. Beautiful views were visible when you strolled along the winding pathways overlooking parts of the city located across the valley. Shade trees bordered the paths adding quiet beauty to the serene land. Memories of home could be very haunting as you walked through the peaceful city. I had fleeting mental glimpses of home, especially the imaginary glimpses of the one left behind and loved.

Ancient remains of castles were scattered over a series of a few miles facing the national approaches from Germany. [Luxembourg was known as a fortress city long before the Middle Ages, and sprang up at the cross section of roads built by Roman conquerors.]

Viaducts with their many supporting pillars were numerous, adding to the quaintness. To gaze across the valley floor with a river flowing through and notice the picturesque bridge spanning the valley was a sight that always impressed a person. Autumn changed the vegetation like in the states until the former green stuff had an appearance similar to a rainbow of colors. It was gorgeous to an unbelievable degree.

Melodies of the people of Europe might be heard during the evenings while strolling through the parks. All of the great masters might be heard. Even if no bands were present, the melodies sprang into the minds of those promenading through the parks.

Sweets helped maintain good feeling between the GIs and the Luxembourgian. Rationing was so strict there that chocolate, candy and cigarettes could be used to bargain for anything. Many horse-drawn carts are used in the city, as well as small cars powered by an engine that uses gas given off by burning charcoal. An electric trolley line furnishes transportation to the middle of Luxembourg. By our standards back home, the trolley is almost an antique, but it works. It has square corners and little comfort on hard seats inside.

Luxembourg uses the Belgian Franc or the Luxembourg Franc as their standard of exchange. The franc in both cases has a value of 2.23 cents in American money. Many difficulties were frequent in money exchanges. It was easy to lose money in a merchant exchange when buying something if you were not alert.

The first American troops to arrive in Luxembourg used the German Mark instead of Luxembourg money. From September 1944 until our departure in June of 1945, a marked difference in the price of articles sold to GIs was noticed. This was also true in England and Scotland as merchants tried to make money off of us. Fortunately for Luxembourg, there was little war damage in the city. Most of the bombing raids by both sides were at the railroad yards.

Bed check Charlie appeared nightly over Luxembourg, the observation flight by a German reconnaissance plane. It flew each night despite an intense anti-aircraft barrage by our artillery, some of which were atop flat roofs. His first appearance every night signaled the air-raid sirens throughout the city. People turned out all the lights and went to a spot of safety.

A droning, strange-sounding motor was heard by most of the population before 90mm, 25mm, 40mm, .50-caliber and 20mm guns banged away at the invisible scout plane. Streaks of fire marked the supposed path of the plane; tracers pointed their probing marks all about the night sky. After half an hour, the all-clear was signaled and people could then resume their pre-blackout doings.

The next visit came several hours later after people had gone to bed. Same antics would be followed by waking up the entire population of the city. This second flight would be at 2 A.M. usually. Many times a third and fourth raid would follow before dawn. It was hard to get a good night's sleep. And occasionally we could hear our planes chasing the Nazi planes.

Flights of fifty or more American planes appeared almost daily over the city headed to some unknown target. The flights would be a few minutes apart. Invariably there would be flights of ten, usually more. These were American bombers on to their rendezvous with targets somewhere in Germany. Smaller and faster dots could be seen slashing across the sky around the bombers. These would be the fighters like P-51s sent along with the bombers for protection against German fighter planes.

On October 6th, 1944 the Twenty-third was ordered to a location near Wiltz where elements of the Fifth Armored Division were bivouacked. Tanks, half-tracks, scout cars, jeeps, trucks, guns, materiel, and men abounded within the area.

At the first sign of darkness, fires were extinguished, leaving the men without warmth on the chilly evenings. The weather was cool, misty and occasionally rainstorms blew in. Mud, a particularly clinging, darkly clayish mud, clutched at every moving object. Mud splattered all over everything, including all of us and all of our vehicles.

The second platoon of the sonic outfit, Heater (the 3132nd) had a mysterious connection discernible to the real Fifth Armored boys, but what our connection was they didn't know even though our bumpers were marked showing Heater assigned to this combat command. After establishing local security and pitching our pup tents on the oozing muddy land, the second platoon turned in for the night. It was a miserable night.

Meals were obtained from a mess truck on top of a hill several miles away. During the early breakfast hour the combat command drove away, leaving only the Twenty-third. While pulling away down the muddy road, one tank with two fellows standing inside the turret with heads, shoulders and hips exposed slithered off the road, turning over on its top after hurtling down with all of its many tons of weight for at least fifteen feet. How many deaths? We were surprised to learn there were none somehow, miraculously. The men inside the tank immediately ducked inside when the tank began slithering. Hard to believe something that big and heavy could slide around like a toy sled.

In a few more hours, the Second Platoon packed its belonging and headed on to another sector several miles away. Our route took us through the mountainous terrain of the Ardennes Forest. Signal Company started the airways humming with orders, sharing air traffic the Germans would interpret as a military movement in the locality. Heater played the sound effects for hours during the night. The 603rd inflated the dummies while the 406th furnished much of the local security.

During the day, vehicles toured the Luxembourg countryside, creating what we call "atmosphere" of a real armored division. Patches worn on our uniforms helped the snoopers guess wrong as did the false bumper markings seen by the populations of the countryside. All roads were traveled, making sure everyone noticed the insignia and markings. We pretended to have motor trouble when we saw a lot of people, stopping to check under the hood and let all of our play acting sink in among the locals. Road directions were asked every few miles for the same purpose. Who could ignore our convoys of deuce and a half and half-tracks, a few real tanks, scout cars and jeeps?

Real tanks of the Fifth Armored Division were detached from the main force to add to the realistic touch of thousands of men with complete division equipment. The tanks rumbled through the villages during the day and night to make sure the people saw the real article before making their imagination work too hard. Tank tracks were plowed through the fields over and again for the spies and the airplane observation. During the night, the tanks were left in the open purposefully for German planes to photograph. In the day time, they were left in the open fields for the passerby to see.

Every night a guard was maintained throughout the area to prevent local prowlers trying to learn our true strength. All vehicles were halted at the entrance to the camp area to prevent close-up inspection of the sound of the tanks, although glimpses at a distance of our rubber tanks were allowed. The overall effect was extremely convincing.

The only daylight mission of Heater was accomplished here. In the afternoon, the sonic sections of the crews alternately operated their big loudspeakers from different sections of the woods. It was a success. In the village, it sounded like real tanks grinding along the forest lanes and rough roads.

We were pretending to be a buildup for a big attack against the Siegfried Line area. But no one seemed to know exactly where the enemy lines were, whether the unit was near the Germans or too far away. This is where we first heard of the Ninth Army and that we would have a tie-in with them. We were then working with a couple of divisions, one of which was the Fourth Infantry Division.

After projecting our sounds into the forests, placing dummies in the area, real tanks roared through the countryside to help the many German sympathizers get a further dose of our play acting. Most of our speakers were mounted on half-tracks. Heavy security was maintained. For some reason, the problem was called off after awhile and we were sent back to Luxembourg. We went on a training schedule. Equipment was maintained and repaired. Our Twenty-third liaison officers were out discussing the next problem.

Another break in the routine came when the 90th and 95th Divisions needed to cross the Moselle to outflank the German-held city of Metz, an old inland fortress. A party of the Twenty-third traveled south 40 miles to a place close to Metz and Rondeaux, France, behind the 90th Division and elsewhere near the 95th. Radio traffic was simulated and the unit bivouacked in a valley of terrible mud several miles from the front. We could hear the artillery barrages from where we were. We began simulating the sound preliminary to an attack.

We also pretended to build a bridge, complete with bridge-building sounds at night, the sounds of motor boats, cranes, and in the daytime we displayed some real bridge-building equipment. Meanwhile, the divisions actually attacked at another spot and it was successful because of our efforts, which had drawn the Germans to our area.

We were told to be on the alert for German paratroops in our area. And there were some nearby, many of them young Germans in their teens. We also heard the terrific din of machine gun fire and the sound of artillery and mortars and thousands of artillery shells during the real attack. Some of the men captured a young German boy manning a machine gun.

Having no more work to do in this area, we drove back into Luxembourg City and tried to get all the mud off of us and our equipment. We had a good Thanksgiving meal, including turkey and the trimmings. That was a pleasant surprise.

Only 15 miles away we went on our problem of simulating the Seventy-fifth Infantry Division newly arrived from England. This was next to the Fourth Infantry Division, which had the real strength in the area. They were resting there from the bloody battle of the Hurtgen Forest. Some companies stretched out and we tried to present a miles-long division, the Seventy-fifth. We put the Seventy-fifth bumper markings on our vehicles and put "75-X" on everything that needed it. We put on Seventy-fifth patches. All of this was done by about one thousand of us and our equipment and some borrowed equipment. Sonic projections were carried out each night to convince the populace that most of the Seventy-fifth tanks were moving in under cover of darkness.

Colonel Railey visited the 3132nd and this helped morale a

lot. Dummies of all known types were used to bring our fake division to full strength. Signal company did the radio traffic and made it sound like a full division moving in. The Seventy-fifth appeared to be ready to back up the Fourth Infantry Division soon.

A few days after most of us pulled out and headed back to Luxembourg, the Ardennes breakthrough began. This was von Rundstedt's last big push [beginning of the Battle of the Bulge].

Soon Luxembourg City was full of troops and tanks from all over moving in to try and stop von Rundstedt. On the 21st of December, the bulk of the Twenty-third left for Doncourt, France, a position normally occupied by Free French at the Maginot Line. For a week, the Twenty-third stayed here while the clouds cleared off Europe for awhile and the Allied air force smashed at the thrusting Jerries. Here the half-tracks were posted on the main roads as anti-aircraft security with .50-caliber machine guns. We saw the German aircraft strafe our truck convoys at night.

The Twelfth Army Group main headquarters at Verdun felt the German might come through in an effort to seize the big store of supplies the Allies had there. All troops not occupied were ordered to form a perimeter of defense around Verdun and to guard against sabotage and possible attack. A small element next to Metz was guarded by the Twenty-third . Some of us saw and heard the first jet plane we'd ever seen in this area.

On December 23 the company left the Doncourt camp at seven o'clock in the evening. Half-tracks were sprinkled throughout the columns to afford anti-aircraft protection. German planes had frequently attacked Allied convoys lately during the day and the night. Germans were smashing through the American lines north of Luxembourg in the last desperate attempt to win the war. In support of the ground forces, Germany somehow found a lot of planes to send aloft to harass our supply lines. We all kept an anxious eye on the skies.

The fifty miles we traveled, however, turned out to be uneventful in spite of the bright full moon that illuminated our procession almost like daybreak. Winding roads, bumps, coldness made the trip unpleasant. Road blocks were set up at the entrance of Verdun after an identity was established, allowing our convoy to head for the billets. The road blocks were another precaution against fifth columnists, Germans dressed like Americans and speaking English and using captured American trucks, tanks, jeeps and other equipment.

The complete Twenty-third finally shut the truck engines off and found a place to sleep for the night in one of the many old French barracks, or Caserne Garde. The barracks were old brick and concrete structures of the First World War surrounded by a brick wall. It was not only very cold, piles of dirty and torn German uniforms lay on the ground there when the Wehrmacht hastily fled from Verdun several months ago.

The advance party to Verdun, having traveled in the day time, had a chance to see the many interesting objects along the road. They saw many cemeteries of German dead, crosses marking the dead from the last world war, and the old battlefields of 1914-1918, with the depressions in the ground grim reminders of trench warfare, rough fields torn by the murderous hail of artillery barrages. Hard to tell whether it was from the Germans or the Allies. Only signs in French warned the traveler of the dangerous ground caused by the old trenches and battlefields. We understood there were still some live shells, grenades, etc. in the ground from that war. Ironic that we are fighting another war across the old battlefields of 1918.

On the 28th the fourth platoon of 3132nd plus much of the rest of the Twenty-third went to Metz for another military operation until the end of the year, while the rest of the Twenty-third went on defensive guard posts throughout the city.

Chapter Fourteen

Triumph on the Rhine

The Ghost Army's finest performance of the war came near the small German town of Viersen on the beautiful Rhine River, where it was so convincing that it tied down about 30,000 German troops and kept them out of combat as the real river crossings were made.

Years later, when Robert Tompkins and his wife, Bunny, visited Luxembourg and Germany, he was struck with the beauty of the places he had been. But during the war, there was too much stress to enjoy the vistas, especially if you were in the Ghost Army. He found the Rhine River was such a place.

The busiest waterway in Europe, the Rhine River has played a major role in shaping European history. From its source high in the Swiss Alps, the Rhine flows 820 miles through widely varying terrain from Switzerland northward and westward to its North Sea outlet in the Netherlands. The Rhine runs through the most populated part of Europe, and its steamers and barges carry a steady flow of cargoes.

The Rhine begins in east-central Switzerland at the juncture of a pair of mountain streams near Chur, the Vorderrhein and Hinterrhein. Their combined flow bends northward to form the western boundaries of Liechtenstein and part of Austria. The Rhine then turns westward through Lake Constance, northward to form part of the boundary between France and Germany, and westward through the Netherlands. There it branches into many arms that form a wide, flat delta on the coast of the North Sea.

It moves through a narrow valley to Cologne and through a great plain to the North Sea. The German part of this plain is laced with industrial cities. Some of the major cities are Schaffhausen, Basel, Mannheim, Worms, Mainz, Wiesbaden, Koblenz, Bonn, Cologne,

Dusseldorf, and, in the Netherlands, Rotterdam. The largest tributaries include the Neckar, Main, and Ruhr on the right bank, and the Aare, Moselle, and Erft on the left bank.

Canals link the Rhine with the Rhone, the Marne, the Danube, the Ems, and other navigable rivers, providing transportation and an extensive river trade to ports in Germany, France, Belgium, and the Netherlands. Many barges sail from various North Sea ports to Basel, the head of Rhine navigation. Barges carry raw materials that the Swiss use in manufacturing as well as coal, iron ore, petroleum, and grain from the Ruhr valley. Some barges can sail up the Rhine as far as Cologne.

Magnificent falls near Schaffhausen, Switzerland, generate electricity that powers a large aluminum plant. The Rhine has carved a beautiful 90-mile (145-kilometer) gorge from Bingen to Bonn. Many legends, such as "The Lorelei" and "Song of the Nibelungs," were inspired by the river's wooded banks. Splendid castles on the rocky heights draw many visitors.

From earliest times the Rhine has been a path of conquest and trade. Prehistoric peoples were thought to have followed its course, and it later became the frontier of the Roman Empire and then the gateway for the onrushing Germanic tribes. In the Middle Ages the Rhine was the route for the profitable overland trade between Central Europe, Italy, and the Far East. The river served as a major line of German defense during World War II.

Hitler and his high command had high hopes that they could use the Rhine for a ferocious last-ditch defense that would cause the Allies to sue for peace. At the same time, Eisenhower, Bradley, Patton, and Montgomery all were worried that the broad, fast-flowing river could help the Germans win a stunning, high-body-count victory. It was with great apprehension that the Allied troops approached this natural barrier.

General Simpson, commanding officer of the Ninth Army, decided to seek the assistance of the Ghost Army in making an effective Rhine crossing.

This last operation of the war was considered spectacularly successful, and drew commendations from high up, including Simpson. The Twenty-third used all of its skills and all of its equipment in this big show. It was conceived and planned by Lt. Col. Merrick Truly, a liaison officer for the Twenty-third attached to the G-3 Section of the Ninth Army.

The Ghost troops immediately began to patch their rubber dummies and change the markings on their vehicles, set up their radio and broadcast equipment, and tend to the thousand little things that would help them deceive the Germans. Across the Rhine River, several divisions of the enemy waited to catch the Allies in the vulnerable position of trying to build portable Bailey pontoon bridges. It could be slaughter and the Allies knew it.

But aside from the use of Ghost Army troops, the Allies pulled out the stops on their plans for a broad, overall assault across the Rhine at many points.

By the time the Allies were ready to cross the Rhine, the overall troop strength under General Eisenhower, including the British under Montgomery, had reached four million men. Although this sounds like a formidable force, it included support troops, troops in Italy and other areas of Europe, and troops still in England, along with supply troops strung out over France, the Netherlands, Luxembourg, and Belgium.

What was left was stretched for hundreds of miles, from the North Sea to near the headwaters of the Rhine. A favorite German tactic was to find a thin spot in such a long line and counterattack with massed troops and armor. Eisenhower was far from complacent. The Battle of the Bulge had taught the Allies that Germany had remarkable recuperative powers and could still be as ferocious as a cornered predator.

The Allies and the Germans both knew that a successful crossing of the Rhine at many points would probably be the beginning of the end for the Third Reich. The Ghost Army was ordered to ready itself for its biggest, most thorough, and most dangerous mission to date. Its task was no less an undertaking than assisting the Ninth Army by deceiving the Germans into thinking the actual crossing would come near the small German town of Viersen.

American armies had been given fresh divisions from the States. To the Twenty-first Army Group had come British and Canadian reinforcements from the Mediterranean Theater. The combined Chiefs of Staff had decided at their Malta Conference in January 1945 that the Italian Front had eased enough to allow the transfer of as many as five divisions from the Eighth Army to the Rhine front.

The move of three divisions began right away, and two more followed as soon as the fighting in Greece stabilized. Also, a near equal number of troops were transferred from the Twelfth Air Force. One big problem was transferring all of these troops without alerting the Germans. The operation—code named "Goldflake"—was carried out without the Germans knowing the Italian front had been drastically weakened.

In some ways, on a far larger scale, it was like Robert E. Lee detaching Stonewall Jackson for a lightning campaign up the Shenandoah without Northern generals realizing he had weakened his own army near Richmond. But it was on such a grand scale it is a miracle that the Goldflake operation was not detected.

During the feigned river crossing of the Rhine, Capt. George Rebh said he took a few men on an armed patrol to add realism to the fake crossing. They drove to a point across the river that dropped off steeply. Rebh left his jeep on the plateau above the river and joined his men on foot as they walked down the steep embankment. Suddenly they came under fire from Germans across the river. The fire was too intense to remain in such an exposed position, so Rebh and his men returned fire to cover the men as they scrambled in small groups back up the embankment to safety.

But Rebh said he is fully aware that, because of its special mission, men of the Twenty-third were far safer than those in front-line combat units. He said being assigned to the Twenty-third may have saved his life, noting that his West Point class had the highest percentage of men killed during the war.

By the time the Twenty-first Army Group offensive across the Rhine was ready for launching, all of the units had been transferred. The Ghost Troops were nervous and apprehensive. A lot was riding on their skill. Many thousands of GIs could be killed if they somehow tipped off the Germans through some unforeseen ineptitude. Any little thing could do it, from a rubber tank being blown over by the wind to a mistake on the phony radio net to a breach of security by a German civilian.

Already the bridge at Remagen had been seized in the north, but it was hardly sufficient for launching a large-scale offensive whose chief aim was encirclement of the Ruhr, the throbbing heart of Germany's industrial might. Also, it collapsed a few days later.

Code-named "Plunder," the overall Rhine operation would use three Allied armies. Under the command of Montgomery, the U.S. Ninth Army on the right and the British Second Army on the left were to attack over the river between Rheinberg and Rees. The plan was to capture the Nazi communications center at Wesel, then

Some of the Ghost Army's tanks inflated and on display, probably near the Rhine River. Photo courtesy Robert Tompkins.

expand on the east bank southward to secure the roads through Wesel, northward to help a bridge crossing at Emmerich, and eastward and northeastward to secure a strong bridgehead from which a major offensive effort could be launched.

The Ninth Army's assault was to be launched south of Wesel, with its main bridging area near Rheinberg, and its chief task in the beginning was to be the protection of the Army Group's right flank. The Second Army was to carry out an assault north of Wesel and to concentrate first on the capture of Wesel to enable the Ninth Army to cross there. The Second Army also was to bridge the river at Xanten and the very well-fortified town of Rees, where the Allies were to suffer some of their heaviest casualties.

All of this was to be coordinated with a large parachute drop by the First Airborne of the Army's XVIII Corps, also including the British Sixth Airborne Division and the U.S. Seventeenth, north and northwest of Wesel. This big parachute drop was code named "Varsity." It was timed to immediately follow the ground assault to add still another element of surprise.

Eisenhower and his staff felt that cutting communications from the Ruhr was a mater of paramount importance and made that a prime objective of the bridgehead on the east bank in the industrial area.

Roosevelt, Eisenhower, and Churchill were particularly worried at this time about great advances made by the Germans in jet aircraft, and it was hoped that destruction of the Ruhr area would put a major crimp in jet production. Air reconnaissance also had revealed that the Luftwaffe had moved many jet aircraft up to the Rhine battle area in preparation for the Allied Rhine crossings. A campaign of bombing the longer airfields needed by the jets, and the jets themselves, was begun with good success. Jet fuel dumps also were hit with rocket attacks from P-47s, stubby but powerful aircraft nicknamed "Jugs" by Allied pilots.

Ghost Army officers were told that March 25 was the target date. Operations were stepped up accordingly. An indication of Allied air strength during this time is shown by this simple fact: During the four days from March 21 to 24, Allied air forces flew over 42,000 sorties against Germany, trying to soften it up for the Rhine crossings.

Eisenhower said that the assault across the Rhine was the largest and most difficult amphibious operation undertaken since the landings on the coast of Normandy.

But there was one last trick. Eisenhower and his staff decided on a diversionary attack on Berlin by air from bases in Italy to coincide with the actual attempts to cross the Rhine. The hope was that this would occupy German fighter aircraft and prevent their attacking Allied troops in mid-stream. Had not all of these operations been carried out, Eisenhower said in his report to the Joint Chiefs of Staff, "the success of the crossing might well have been a matter of doubt." He, too, however, was bound by secrecy in outlining the role of the Ghost Army in these preparations. In fact, the Ghost Army itself was still top secret when Eisenhower and Churchill died.

It was during this juncture that Eisenhower also had to put up with and fend off a constant effort by Montgomery and Churchill to confine most of the Rhine-crossing operation to Montgomery's thrusts north of the Ruhr area.

Churchill and Montgomery, perhaps still traumatized by memories of Dunkirk, when the Germans came within a hair's breadth of capturing more than 300,000 British troops, were fearful that a double thrust with the goal of enveloping the Ruhr was just too much. In one of the ironies of the war, the twin thrusts later resulted in the capture of more than 300,000 German troops, about the same number that milled about on the beaches of Dunkirk and awaited the miraculous transport back to Britain on several hundred British boats and ships of every description.

When the plan to cross the Rhine was reviewed at Malta, Montgomery and Churchill argued for a single thrust of great force north of the Ruhr. After all, intelligence reports said Germany had about 82 divisions along the Rhine—about the same number as the combined British and American armies. Churchill and Montgomery thought that by concentrating on one huge thrust, the Ruhr could be cut off without a second pincer underneath. But Eisenhower, showing his usual restraint, pointed out that the German divisions were usually under strength at about 8,000 men each during this stage of the war.

Montgomery had reason to like this alternative idea. A man of incredible ego and ambition, it is clear that he did not want to share the glory of conquest with generals Bradley, Simpson, Patton, Middleton, et al. A second pincer underneath the Ruhr area, as suggested by Eisenhower, would make it less a British victory and more of a joint effort. It also would lessen his chances of a single dash to Berlin.

Eisenhower was disgusted with Montgomery and also, as much as he admired Churchill, a bit tired of Churchill's meddling in tactics. It was a bit like a CEO working for a board chairman who had been the CEO and who now wanted to micro-manage the company, bypassing his new CEO. After all, Churchill had insisted on the Anzio landing and that had nearly been a disaster as the Allies bogged down before Monte Casino.

Then Churchill had done his best to overrule Eisenhower's plan to launch a second landing on the French Mediterranean coast after the Normandy invasion—Operation Dragoon—on somewhat similar grounds: that it would not be as effective as concentrating all resources in the Normandy thrusts. Churchill was wrong on both counts. As great a man as he was—and many consider him the greatest person of the last century—Churchill could become very petulant and insistent when military leaders ignored his advice. He often would try to enlist the support of a number of generals in order to help persuade Eisenhower.

Eisenhower, a man of considerable character and stubborn persistence, did not cave in when Churchill wanted to block Operation Dragoon, and he didn't cave in on the Rhine operation either. He insisted that the original plan be carried out with two pincer thrusts around the Ruhr just after successful crossings of the Rhine at a number of points. The reason for multiple and near simultaneous Rhine crossings was like shooting a large and mean man with a shotgun instead of one shot with a small caliber rifle.

Eisenhower wanted to overwhelm and shock the Rhine defenders with many bridgeheads and attacks to use the Allies' superiority in supplies and battle-hardened troops as a shock to the entire Wehrmacht system on the Western front.

When Churchill pushed hard, Eisenhower asked his number one aide, Gen. Bedell Smith, to make the argument for the twin pincers. Smith crisply outlined the well-thought-out reasoning. He said although on the surface the Germans appeared to have parity in divisions and men, the men were short of supplies, included many old and very young troops, and had no petrol and very little food and morale was very low.

To Montgomery, Eisenhower's plan meant shared glory and the terrible chance that perhaps Patton or some other American general might make a dash for Berlin—a dash he alone wanted to make. Montgomery had continually tried to get Eisenhower to grant him supreme command of all Allied troops. Eisenhower wisely and tactfully resisted, despite a steady drumbeat of suggestions that he do this from the British press. Sometimes Montgomery succeeded in enlisting Churchill in an effort to intercede with Eisenhower.

Churchill, not unaware of Montgomery's incredible ego, also felt a great debt of gratitude to him for the victory at El Alamein. Churchill had sacked several generals before finding someone with the backbone—egocentric or not—of his pal "Monty."

In his book *Closing the Ring,* Churchill wrote:

> We had reviewed the plan at Malta with some concern. We doubted whether we were strong enough for two great simultaneous operations and felt that the northern advance by Montgomery's Twenty First Army Group would be much more important. Only thirty-five divisions probably could take part, but we held that the maximum effort should be made here, whatever its size, and that it should not be weakened for the sake of the other thrust.

It would perhaps be injurious to Anglo-American relations even today if Eisenhower's and Bradley's private conversations about this near impasse could be known. Even from what is known, it is clear that Eisenhower developed a strong dislike of Montgomery's self-indulgent pursuit of the war in his northern sector of the front. Eisenhower did relent somewhat and give Montgomery temporary command over General Simpson and Simpson's Ninth Army, which led to the Ghost Army's assignment for the Rhine crossing under Simpson's command.

Montgomery ordered Simpson and his army to attack north from the Roer River and join Montgomery's force before getting in position for the Rhine crossing attempts on a broad front. Simpson complained to Bradley—and to a far lesser extent to Eisenhower—about the transfer to Montgomery's command. Simpson also chaffed under Montgomery's acerbic, self-important persona and could not wait until he was on his own again.

The Rhine operations began with massive air drops. Churchill had journeyed to the front area across the Rhine and watched with binoculars as the tiny parachutes in the distance filled the sky on the opposite side of the Rhine. The air drops began at 1 A.M. and continued until 1 P.M. The operation involved almost 6,000 Allied aircraft. That figure included 1,326 gliders and 1,253 fighters. Just 46 Allied aircraft were destroyed by the Germans. Eisenhower called the figure "remarkably low considering the fact that, to insure accuracy of dropping and landing, no evasive action was taken." In all, 22,000 troops were delivered on the west side of the Rhine by gliders alone.

Eisenhower also watched much of this, later getting together briefly with Churchill and Montgomery at a sandbagged redoubt. Eisenhower noted the courage of transport pilots flying relatively slow aircraft steadily along their allotted routes in spite of heavy flak barrages. Ike said the timing of the attack had achieved the element of surprise which had been planned, and the rapidity with which the forces reformed and established their positions after landing also resulted in the casualties being extremely low.

When Patton got across the lower Rhine and turned left, he began a scythe-like operation that rapidly paralyzed and cleaned out resistance on a huge section of the Rhine from Frankfort to the river itself.

The beauty of Ghost Army's Rhine operation lay in three facts: 1. The contribution of the Twenty-third was just part of a giant spectacle involving practically all of the real Ninth Army. 2. The Twenty-third had reached its highest state of efficiency and all of its tricks were used. 3. The results were plainly due to the Ghost Army's skill.

Late in February, the Ninth and First armies had finally broken across the Roer River to the west bank of the Rhine, about the time Montgomery asked Eisenhower to loan him the Ninth Army. By an audacious dash, the First Army then crossed the Rhine at Remagen, but the Ninth Army was held on the river line. The Ninth had three corps, from north to south, XVI, XIII, and XIX. The latter two were heaviest, with three infantry and one armored division apiece.

XIII had the Thirtieth, Eighty-fourth, and 102nd Infantry and one armored division apiece. The XIX had the Twenty-ninth, Seventy-ninth, and Eighty-third Infantry, plus the Second Armored.

However, the XVI zone was the most advantageous for a river crossing, so this was the corps and zone that the Ninth chose for the Rhine assault of March 23. It was just south of Dusseldorf. Two crack infantry divisions were taken from the other two corps and added to the XVI's 35th Infantry—the Seventy-fifth Infantry and Eighth Armored Division.

The Ninth Army made every effort to conceal the fact that the Rhine attack was to be made by the XVI Corps. From north to south, this is what was done by each of the three corps to conceal or exaggerate their intentions:

XVI Corps: The assault buildup was done under absolute security. Divisions (Thirtieth and Seventy-ninth) coming into the zone moved in darkness and remained visually hidden or mostly hidden. Artillery positions and engineer parks were either hidden or carefully camouflaged by Ghost Army experts. Artillery registration was done by battery fire on normal harassing missions only.

XIII Corps: It prepared all evidence with Ghost Army personnel for a river crossing operation, the maximum effect to be attained about April 1. The corps and division artillery guns stepped up fire and spread out installation by the addition of more than 600 rubber dummies from the Twenty-third. The Corps of Engineers established new parks and paraded with real bridge-building equipment. Preparations were supplemented by dummy items, installed and maintained by personnel from the Eighty-fourth Infantry and 603rd Engineer Camouflage Battalion. Artillery was built up with sixty-four 40mm and sixteen 90mm rubber guns furnished and manned by the Twenty-third. On some nights on small pretexts, the anti-aircraft sent up fierce demonstrations of firepower that rivaled their activity on Normandy beaches.

Infantry patrolling was intensified to a point 50 percent greater than that by XVI Corps. The two divisions (Thirtieth and Seventy-ninth), which had actually transferred to the XVI Corps, were notionally assembled in the XIII Corps zone by Ghost Army troops. Two battalions of real infantry (from the Eighty-fourth and 102nd) were attached to each of the phony divisions to help add realism, scope, and scale.

XIX Corps: Artillery leaving the corps zone (to support the XVI) was required to leave positions intact and well camouflaged. Phony emplacements were added. The Eighty-third Infantry Division dropped back to the Maas River area vacated by the Thirtieth in the rear of XIII Corps.

The Ninth Army air support given by XXIX Tactical Air Command flew reconnaissance over the XIII zone on the same scale as over the XVI. Army medical installations gave the impression that the attack would take place in the XIII Corps zone. Only one evacuation hospital was installed in the forward part of the XVI Corps zone. A spoof Army Traffic Control Net operated by the Ghost Army's radio operators brought radio attention to the XIII Corps by reporting large vehicular movements and supply trucks pouring into that area.

The Twenty-third's notional divisions were brought up from the old areas and displayed to the east and west of Viersen. All means of deception were employed: sonic, dummies, radio, and special effects. Each phony division had 400 extra rubber vehicles, including 5 phony liaison planes. Aerial photos of these installations showed a layout so authentic that even Allied photo analysts were fooled. It was the first time in the war that every single piece of equipment was used by Ghost Army troops.

The real troops engaged in the Rhine crossing found virtually no opposition. The Thirtieth's G-2 said the attack "came as a complete surprise to the enemy with a consequent saving of American lives." The Seventy-ninth G-2 captured a German overlay of the American Order of Battle just prior to the attack. It had the Seventy-ninth placed approximately where the Twenty-third had portrayed it—where the Germans had massed troops and equipment for an attack that never came—and had lost the Thirtieth's real position altogether.

The Ninth Army G-2 stated that the Germans expected the main Allied effort to be made north of Wesel, with a minor crossing opposite Krefeld.

"There is no doubt," he said, "that operation Viersen materially assisted in deceiving the enemy with regard to the real disposition and intentions of this army."

Lt. Gen. W. H. Simpson, despite the risk to security, couldn't help himself. He was so delighted that he wrote the Twenty-third a letter of commendation. There had been a standing policy of never referring to the Twenty-third in writing. Simpson's commendation stated, in part:

> The unit was engaged in a special project, which was an important part of the operation. The careful planning, minute attention to detail and diligent execution of the organization reflect great credit on this unit. I desire to commend the officers and men of the Twenty-third Headquarters Special Troops, Twelfth Army Group, for their fine work and to express my appreciation for a job well done.

There were just 32 casualties in the real crossing. It had been estimated that, had the Germans been ready as they were just opposite the Ghost Army demonstration, casualties would have been in the 12,000 to 17,000 range.

On the day of the Rhine offensive, as the Ghost troops continued to pretend to be on the verge of a crossing, Eisenhower and General Simpson watched some of the attacks together, and Ike was very pleased with the precision and execution of the Rhine crossings.

Here is the way Eisenhower described the overall effort in his official report:

> The task of the armies assaulting across the Rhine represented the largest and most difficult amphibious operation undertaken since the landings on the coast of Normandy. The width of the Rhine and the nature of its currents indeed were such that, without the operations already mentioned which were to reduce enemy resistance on the far bank to a minimum, the success of the crossing might well have been a matter of doubt. The variations in the river level also presented unusually difficult problems for, apart from the seasonal fluctuations, there was a danger of artificial floods being created by the enemy's ability to demolish the dams located on the eastern tributaries. A special flood-warning system was instituted to guard against this threat.

> It was therefore necessary to treat the assault as an amphibious operation in the fullest sense, involving naval as well as military forces, since the equipment available to the engineer elements of the armies was alone insufficient to cope with the task. Months previously, exhaustive experiments had been carried out on rivers in Britain giving bank and current conditions similar to those of the Rhine in order to determine what ferry craft were most suitable and what loads they could carry.

The LCM and LCV craft were chosen for the purpose and these were transported to the Rhine partly by waterway and partly overland on special trailers build to stand the great strains involved in transit across roads ravaged by war. The immense difficulty of this feat may be judged from the fact that the craft measured as much as 45 feet in length and were 14 feet wide. British and American naval forces were built up to operate the ferry services and valuable experience was gained when some of the craft were used in the Remagen area early in March. The fact that an LCM could take such loads as a Sherman tank or 35 men may serve to indicate their value in the initial stages of the main Allied assault in the north.

The offensive was heralded at 2000 hours on March 23 with a great artillery barrage of one hour's duration, directed against the east bank of the Rhine and extending through the zone where airborne forces were to be dropped and landed the next day. Much of this barrage was directed at the area of the Rhine across from the Ghost Army to add verisimilitude to the fake demonstrations under way.

This led the Germans to assume with even more certainty that they had pinpointed the place of the advance. After all, radio traffic, artillery, tank buildup, tracks, and vehicles from the air, and extensive bridge-building efforts had been seen. Even boat motors were heard at night as the engineers scurried about in the river. Yet all of this was fake. The big loudspeakers broadcast the sounds of bridge-making. And the sounds of the motorboats, recorded from actual army river craft, were so convincing that other GIs who were not in on the plan, and most weren't, made the same assumptions that the Germans massed on the opposite bank had made.

At the same time, assaults were made at a great many locations on the Rhine. A British commando brigade began an assault on Wesel. During the night, the main attacks included the Second Army's Twelfth Corps assault near Xanten, and troops crossed near Rees. South of the Lippe Canal, the Thirtieth and the Seventy-ninth divisions launched the Ninth Army assault under the command of the XVI Corps.

Even the official record regarding the Ghost Army, despite its military brevity, cannot mask the drama of the master deception:

> Objective: a coordinated plan of Ninth U.S. Army to deceive the enemy as to the actual Rhine River crossing area, strength of the crossing and time of the crossing. The mission of the Twenty-third was to simulate the Thirtieth Infantry Division and the Seventy-ninth Infantry

Division in an assembly area of the XIII Corps zone while actual divisions were assembling int the zone of the XVI corps. The mission also included furnishing advice on Army cover plans as well as techniques of deception to the commanding general of the XIII Corps.

During the first week of March, 1945, after the Ninth Army had decided to use a deceptive plan to facilitate its crossing of the Rhine, Lt. Colonel Merrick H. Truly, of the Twenty-third, was called to that headquarters for consultation.

Truly, working with the G-3 of the Ninth Army, prepared a cover plan, "Operation Flashpoint." It consisted of a simulated buildup of forces in the general area west of Dusseldorf and the Erft River to indicate an assault crossing in the Dusselforf-Uerdinger zone.

Effort was made to lead the enemy to believe that the Ninth U.S. Army was not prepared to cross the Rhine River prior to April 1, 1945.

The XIII Corps was charged with the mission of conducting a demonstration in the Dusseldorf-Uerdinger zone. No unit was to cross the Rhine River. The XIII Corps was to continue this deception even after Flashpoint began so as to immobilize enemy troops on the east bank of the Rhine River.

A real radio net for the XIII Corps was made on the same scale as that in XVI corps. Radio silence was maintained by all orders of the Ninth Army not in contact with the enemy. Special attention was given to complete camouflage of artillery weapons and ammunition, and to engineer supplies in the XVI zone. Upon displacement of artillery from the Zone of XIII Corps and the XIX Corps, the previous positions were made to retain their normal appearance.

Movement of the artillery units to new positions was made at night. Dummy Engineer parks in the zone of XIII Corps were created so as to support the false crossing date of April 1, 1945. Engineer preparations included the building up of approach roads to the crossing sites in the Zone of XIII Corps equal to or greater than those of the XVI Corps. Patrolling was approximately one-half greater in the zone of XIII Corps than that in XVI Corps. The actual river crossing training of the Thirtieth and Seventy-ninth Divisions took place on the Mass River under XVI Corps.

Upon completion of this training and prior to their movement to assembly areas, vehicle markings and shoulder patches were removed and not replaced until H minus 12 hours. All movement was at night. No unit identification was used, either code names or road signs.

Movement of individuals and vehicles in the assembly area was held to an absolute minimum and maximum camouflage discipline was imposed. The XIX Corps conducted river crossing training on the Erft River and canal.

The basic purpose was to conceal concentrations of troops and supplies in the XVI Corps. The buildup of a simulated attacking force in the XIII Corps zone and Medical Installations in the Army area gave the impression from the air that the attack would take place in the XIII Corps zone. Attached to the Twenty-third Headquarters Special Troops for the duration of the operation were the Second Battalion, 405th Infantry; the 102nd Infantry Division of XIII Corps; First Battalion of the 334th Infantry; the Eighty-fourth Infantry Division of XIII Corps; and the 430th Anti-Aircraft Battalion of XIX Corps.

The Twenty-third (Ghost Troops) divided in order to simulate both the Thirtieth and Seventy-ninth Infantry Divisions. The Twenty-third moved these two divisions notionally into the XIII Corps zone at the same time that the real divisions secretly moved to concealed assembly areas in the XIX Corps zone. The occupation of the simulated division in the XIII Corps zone was accomplished by the following means:

Billeting parties operated prior to the move. Convoys, with the proper bumper markings, supplemented by night sound effects, moved into the division areas. MP traffic control by radio was broadcast. Activity was carried on in an area by personnel wearing shoulder patches of the represented divisions.

Command Posts were installed with the proper Command Post signs and road markers. Normal traffic circulation was simulated as if supplying the installations and the XIII Corps. Some 318 rubber dummies were installed for the simulated Thirtieth Infantry Division and 300 were set up for the Seventy-ninth Infantry Division. Simulated with some real anti-aircraft strength was build up in the XIII Corps zone.

The signal picture followed the normal pattern for any Corps about to engage in an operation such as a major river crossing. Camouflage netting and assault boats were placed along the edge of the water, and at night sonic equipment was used to play motor boat noises to indicate river crossing practice. Signs were placed throughout the areas to indicate a river crossing demonstration area. A landing strip was laid out and marked with two dummy air planes set up by the runway.

Results: this operation was the most extensive and most satisfactory in which the Twenty-third Headquarters Special Troops has participated. It was felt that this operation was very successful from the intelligence reports, and from the low casualties [34] suffered by troops engaged in the real crossing.

Chapter Fifteen

Japan Looms

After Germany surrendered, the Ghost Army offered its services in any capacity to its parent Twelfth Army Group. It should have known that you never volunteer for anything in the Army. The command was split four ways and given some strange assignments.

Some of the Signal Company went to First Army to act as a monitoring unit for the corps. It nearly reached Czechoslovakia. The wire platoon worked for the Third Army in recovering its expensive "spiral-4" communications wire. In five weeks, this energetic platoon rolled up 800 miles of wire worth $500 per mile, saving the American taxpayer $400,000.

Still another part of the Signal Company was ordered to serve in the Twelfth Army Group code room and on May 7 got to hear before anyone else of Eisenhower's plans to send many troops home.

The rest of the Ghost Army was loaned to the Fifteenth Army, which in turn loaned them to the XXIII Corps to ride herd on 100,000 hungry, homeless, and often dangerous displaced persons.

This was no small task, as bitter feelings among the displaced persons ran high. Former Russian and Polish prisoners often robbed and killed German civilians or each other. Various ethnic groups attacked each other over scraps of food or women. Many armed themselves with weapons salvaged from the many battlefields. Feeding, clothing, and sheltering the thousands became a logistical nightmare, even for an army used to logistical nightmares. The situation bordered on anarchy from day to day.

The Ghost Army began its DP (displaced persons) assignment on April 11 in a dual capacity. One was as actual camp managers; the other was as DP staff section to the XXIIII Corps. No one had ever

Some of the thousands of displaced persons under the care of the Ghost Army after the German surrender. Photo courtesy Robert Tompkins.

come close to handling such a demanding job. For one thing, among the 100,000 under the care of the Ghost troops there were found to be 26 nationalities.

Five swarming camps in the Saar-Palatinate were taken over by the Twenty-third: Bauholder, Trier, Bitburg, Wittlich, and LeBach. The Twenty-third staff took over the Hotel Hermes in Idar-Oberstein, which was also the headquarters for the XXIII Corps. The only good thing about it was that the shooting war had stopped, and the Twenty-third was able to stay in one spot for awhile.

"After the German surrender, we had to ride herd on the Russian and Polish group of DPs," said Tompkins. He said the former slave laborers

didn't like each other. And *both* hated the Germans. Everybody hated everybody. I recall one morning I was asked to drive up to a farm house and escort a farmer in a wagon. He was a German dairy farmer with cans of milk. This was because the Russians and the Poles would attack these guys. I had a little a submachine gun. I could spray machine gun fire if they attacked the farmer. After this duty with the Russians and Poles, we later moved to Trier above the Moselle, where we were in charge of an Italian camp of POWs. They were friendly and would jump on the hoods of our jeeps when we drove up. They were happy fellows.

The Twenty-third was not used to this kind of duty, but it finally helped get the thousands of displaced persons housed, fed, and calmed down. But it was not without some violent episodes and a lot of stress. All of this came, too, at a time when all the men could think of was when were they going back to the States and would they then go to the Pacific, where the war still raged. The Japanese became more intense the closer the Americans got to the Japanese mainland, introducing kamikaze raids on American ships.

"Eisenhower had ordered that any German prisoner who was not in the SS or other elite unit and who was a farmer should be returned to his farm to start helping Germany get ready to feed itself," said Lieutenant Syracuse.

So one day we were ordered to take this German kid back to his farm. He didn't know what we were doing or going to do when we ordered him to get in a jeep and go for a ride with us. We had got directions to his farm, which was not too far away. He was very scared because I think he thought we were going to kill him. But we drove to his family farm and his wife and children were on the front steps when we arrived and we told him he was free to resume his life as a farmer. He began crying and said in bad English, "God bless America." It was very moving.

Eisenhower had defined a displaced person as a civilian outside the national boundaries of his or her country by reason of war who was desirous but unable to return home or find a home without assistance, or who was to be returned to enemy or ex-enemy territory.

Hundreds of thousands were quickly evacuated. These were in addition to prisoners of war and were those civilians who had homes somewhere in Europe and desired to return to them at once. Eisenhower ordered that camps be organized to take care of these classes temporarily and feed them while transportation plans were worked out. That was the duty assigned to Ghost Army troops, some of whom said this duty was preferable to going back into another war zone in the Pacific.

Eisenhower wrote that the truly unfortunate were "those who for one reason or another no longer had homes" or were "persecutees" who dared not return home for fear of further persecution.

Other groups Eisenhower called unreturnable included former citizens of the Baltic States—Estonia, Latvia, and Lithuania—which had been incorporated into the Soviet Union. Thousands of the Balts found in western Germany were classified as stateless. Also in the camps were Ukrainians, Rumanians, Yugoslavs, and others.

To make matters worse, the Ghost troops learned that as soon as word spread about humane and nurturing treatment, the ranks of the displaced persons mysteriously began to grow. Facilities were always crowded, and food could be issued only at a subsistence level for several months. The Ghost troops said they felt bad because they were being fed well by comparison to the people in their charge. In some cases, they said, they were tempted to look the other way when some of the Germans who were well off were stripped of food and other goods, but they had to enforce order.

Some of the Ghost troops griped that they were protecting German citizens from people they had enslaved and brutalized, but no one shirked his duty. Eisenhower himself visited the camps often to see that treatment was as humanitarian as possible.

Unfortunately, there were a number of killings among the DPs, usually someone who had collaborated with the Germans. The Ghost troops would find a large crowd gathered and someone in the middle of it usually had just been killed. The group would then explain that the person deserved his or her fate because of collaboration with the Germans. Rarely could a perpetrator be found.

Charles Cuppett recalled:

> These displaced persons were Polish and Russian and they did not get along at all. I was up on a telephone pole stringing wire for communications when I noticed a large group of Poles milling around and shouting. A young Polish boy of about fifteen came up to me and motioned for me to follow him into the crowd, which I did. When I got to the crowd, they parted and I walked into the center and a person with a uniform on came up to me and saluted. I returned his salute as I didn't want to offend him.

> Lying on the ground was a man with his head bashed in and a tent pole lying next to the body. I raised my rifle and fired three shots into the air to scatter the crowd and call attention that I needed assistance. Some MPs happened to be passing by and came over to see

what the trouble was. I turned the matter over to them, as it was in their jurisdiction.

As I was waiting around, one of the Poles who could speak some English explained to me that the man was an informer and was recognized by some of the people there. Their justice was swift and without formality.

Some of the Russians somehow obtained firearms and began raiding the homes of the Germans, taking all food and brutalizing their former captors. This was stopped with force whenever possible, and arms were confiscated, although most Ghost troops said they sympathized. Feelings still ran high against the Germans among the Ghost troops, as with all GIs.

One day, recalled Art Shilstone, one of the DPs somehow got a gun and climbed a tree. "He started firing on our guys. So one of our guys shot and killed him. It was sad. Here he was about ready to go home after enduring all of that."

As soon as the surrender was signed, men of the Ghost Army began paying more attention to the points they had accumulated under a plan to set priorities for early discharge. This elaborate system took into account such factors as length of service, marital status, time overseas, decorations, parenthood, age, combat duty, and many other factors. But hanging over all of this was expectation, soon confirmed by leaders of the Ghost Army, that it would be headed to the Pacific after its work with the hundreds of thousands of DPs and slave laborers was done.

There also were many thousands of American and British soldiers who had been captured, some of them dating as far back as Dunkirk in 1940 and for the Americans, Tunisia in 1942. These men, many of them just skin and bones, shocked the Ghost troops who saw them, particularly later at Le Havre. The Army doctors had a hard time preventing these men from overeating and also banned spices and even salt and pepper from their diets until it could be very gradually reintroduced.

The Ghost Army took pride in their work with the DPs, noting that they had maintained up to 100,000 men, women, and children in 13 camps. It had consolidated the group by nationalities in separate camps, which halted rioting. It entertained a host of temperamental repatriation officers. It demonstrated the proper uses of modern latrines to about 43,000 middle Europeans.

Capt. George Rebh was placed in charge of 16,000 of the DPs, most of them Russians, along with a few thousand Poles. He said his men constructed latrines of large wooden supply boxes, cutting holes in them to make outhouses. But he said such hygiene was not something the people were used to, and it took some persuasion to get them to use them properly.

Although Rebh was just 22, he became a judge and jury for those DPs under his care, holding unofficial courts to resolve disputes. But the hardest part was getting the Poles and the Russians to live in relative harmony. He said he called the leaders of the Poles and Russians to a meeting and told them they would remain with him until they worked out a plan for getting along with each other. Many hours later, in the early dawn hours, the two men finally reached an agreement, Rebh recalled.

Sergeant Rapsis said his strongest memory of the DP part of the Ghost Army's work was of an eighteen-year-old Polish girl. He said she was one of the most beautiful women he had ever seen, with light brown hair and blue eyes and she had a very vulnerable, almost translucent beauty. "Because of this, the others huddled around her and protected her," he said.

> Her name was Mary, of course pronounced quite differently in Polish. The others took care of her because they knew she was beautiful and somehow, as I said, very vulnerable and even innocent. I wondered how in the world she had survived the forced labor camps and all of the hell they went through. I kept thinking about her and later I went back to see if I could find her. But they said she had gone away. But in reality, they had hidden her away, trying to protect her. Maybe they thought I was too interested in her. Did I think about taking her back to the states? Well, crazy things like that do go through your head, I guess. But I never saw her again after that.

After a few weeks of DP duty, the Ghost Army was ordered to return to the United States for brief R&R before heading to the Pacific to work its same magic against the Japanese. This caused great apprehension among the Ghost troops. Bill Blass, among many others, said he doubted that they could fool the Japanese as easily as they had the Germans. There was something about the Japanese character, the men thought, that would make it far more difficult. The Germans had been given to underestimating the Americans, even to the point of disdain. This made the deception easier. The men thought the Japanese would figure things out quickly.

The troops were told that most of their work would probably come shortly after the invasion, on mainland Japan. It was depressing news. Rumors were rampant about the danger and the numbers of casualties expected against a last-ditch, all-out Japanese defense of the mainland. The brass stressed that neither the nature of their work nor their destination was to be mentioned, under severe penalty, while they were on furloughs in the U.S., not even to closest family members. They had been denied leave and furloughs before sailing to Europe for this same reason at the start of their war experience.

Shortly before leaving for America, Lieutenant Syracuse went to the Army payroll office to collect the $30,000 he had won in poker games. He was a shrewd and capable poker player, but the Army forbade troops carrying money in combat areas. So he had placed his winnings with the payroll office, as per regulations.

Some of the men in the payroll office had heard the Twenty-third was to be shipped out to America, and thence to Japan, the next day. So they decided to stall Syracuse with loads of red tape so that he would be shipped out without getting his poker winnings, which they planned to keep for themselves. Obviously they didn't know much about this tough officer.

When he went to claim his money, they told Syracuse it would be several days, maybe weeks, before he could get the money. They gave him a huge stack of forms to fill out.

"But I'm shipping out tomorrow," he protested.

"Yes, we know," they said with a smirk as they shoved the raft of forms at him, assuring him that the money would be mailed to him.

He knew what they were planning. It had been done to other GIs. Also, the savings of some GIs who died in battle had disappeared in similar fashion. The Army was a tough environment quite aside from combat. If a mess cook didn't like you, he could give you short rations. If you angered someone in finance, then your payroll records could disappear and you wouldn't be paid for months.

Syracuse shocked the men in the finance office when he pulled his .45 automatic and stuck it into the face of the officious payroll clerk.

"You can either give me my damned money now, or you can die now," he announced.

The clerk meekly "found" the money and handed it to Syracuse. No report was ever made of the incident. It is one of the first stories that any veteran of the Twenty-third will tell you, even before they relate their own narrow escapes in combat. Syracuse is still a hero to many of them, even after all these years.

"Yep, that's the way the Hubba Hubba Jab Kid handled it," said one of his many admirers, Bill Enderlein. "He was one hell of a man."

The rest of the story was almost a happy one, with the exception of the ominously looming trip to fight against and use deceptive tricks on the Japanese. The entire Twenty-third assembled late in May 1945 to make their preparations for the trip home. Everyone slept in tents for the first time in many months. The rain, purges, inspections, and training schedules could have been agonizing had it not been for the bright spring sun.

It took about three days for the happy Twenty-third convoys to motor from Idar-Oberstein to the staging areas for the trip home near Rouen. The distance was 350 miles and France never looked so beautiful. The wheat was ripe and mixed with poppies and blue bells. To men dizzy with the thoughts of home, every field could have been a rippling flag or the neon lights of Broadway.

At one point, Art Shilstone said, a farmer plowing in his field struck a German mine and was fatally wounded, losing a leg, his sight, and not long afterward his life. His family rushed into the field. He was taken to a convent hospital by the Ghost troops but it was hopeless. It was an ugly remnant of an ugly war.

"I still remember those nuns with the big white hats hovering around him like angels," said Shilstone, "but a doctor said he would not live."

The Twenty-third rolled into Camp Twenty Grand on June 16. It was a rocky place but there was a lovely view of the Seine. Showdown inspections were required every thirty minutes or so. People who carried more than one gallon of wine or liquor had to declare it but no one seemed to know how to judge a gallon. A quantity of liberated goods was packed, along with German Luger pistols, Walther pistols, and all sorts of other war souvenirs. Much of it was packed in with the trucks and half-tracks for recovery after crossing the Atlantic.

The ship, the *General O.H. Ernst,* sailed for America on June 13, 1945. Eisenhower had recently issued one of his most popular orders of the war. He said if the men eligible to return home did not mind "hot bunking"—taking turns sleeping in the same bunk in shifts—then he could double the number of men going aboard troop ships. No one objected and soon the troop ships back to the United States were jammed with men. Photos of such ships show no exposed deck: there is a man taking up all available deck space.

The men crowded onto troop ships for the voyage home, some

even sleeping on deck all the way under orders from Eisenhower. They did not care about the discomfort, which was not too bad compared to foxholes.

The *Ernst* sailed for America alone and with lights. Although there was no submarine danger any longer, many men still looked at the sea with a bit of foreboding, knowing that they would not be so complacent on their voyage in the Pacific.

The voyage was smooth, the quarters clean, and the food good. The ship was a Navy transport, and the Army passengers were impressed by the efficiency and good spirit of the Navy crewmen. Cpl. Teddy Katz led an impromptu orchestra, and Sgt. Seymour Kent produced a number of extravaganzas built around participation of two much-admired and sought-after Red Cross girls.

The ship's newspaper, the *Ernst Enquirer,* printed a nice vague history of the Twenty-third, which did not violate its top-secret security classification but would serve to quiet some of the curious folks back home during the thirty-day furloughs.

Here is an excerpt from the ship's newspaper, which was saved by Lon Gault:

> The Twenty-third Hq Sp Trps has probably been associated with more Armies and been to more places than any other unit aboard ship. Some of its members landed on D-Day with the First Army. Later, part of the command participated in the Brittany campaign with the Third Army. When Field Marshal Montgomery crossed the Rhine in March, the Twenty-third was attached to the Ninth Army. Finally, when the war was practically over, this versatile outfit took charge of 100,000 milling Displaced Persons for the Fifteenth Army.
>
> The itinerary of the Twenty-third sounds like a roll call of famous place names, although modest members of this unit will be the first to admit that they were not entirely responsible for publicizing those once-quiet little towns. They watched the liberation of Cherbourg, drove through the rubble of St. Lo, could have been cut off by the German counter-attack at Mortain, helped put the squeeze on Von Ramcke at Brest, took the cheers and kisses of frenzied Parisians, were second into Luxembourg after the Fifth Armored Division, shared the cold snows south of Bastogne with the Fourth Armored Division, (but don't let a Twenty-third-er tell you he relieved the 101st Airborne), hung around the dreary Saarland with XX Corps, gaped as the 17 A/B flew over to secure a bridgehead on the lower Rhine. One detachment even got as far as a few miles from Czechoslovakia.

Almost any man in this peripatetic unit can toast in six different languages and talk knowingly of the ETO campaign from the beaches to the Elbe [where the Allies linked up with Russian troops].

Naturally there have been some exciting moments. For instance, last summer one column was temporarily mislaid near Lorient; or when one December 16 the cooks and KPS of the Fourth Infantry Division held the Germans just east of Luxembourg's Twenty-third Hq; or when the Displaced Persons rioted at Trier because one nationality thought another nationality was borrowing its water while actually stealing its women.

After a month or so of such sweet place names as Boston, New York, Denver, Phoenix and Kalamazoo, the Twenty-third Hq Sp Trps will possibly down a series of Oriental sourballs including Chofu, Uchidonai, Tomigusuku, Hakonegaski and Fuchu. "Igaga desu ka!" ["How are you!" in Japanese]

This newspaper article made many of the other servicemen on board curious about how one outfit had such a hand in so many parts of the war, and the Twenty-third troops had to be especially careful about security.

On the morning of July 2, Tompkins and Blass, Syracuse, Enderlein, Arnett, Gault, Katz, Shilstone, Lieutenant Gray, Ed Biow, and the rest of the Twenty-third crowded the railing as the ship slid by the buoys near Fortress Monroe.

The men will tell you today that they unabashedly choked up at the sight of the United States of America again, one of them stating: "The U.S. shoreline looked like something one could eat. All of the buildings were clean and whole. There were shiny cars on the highway. The harbor did not wear bunting or toot a welcome but we could feel the celebration in our hearts."

The Twenty-third debarked at Newport News, Virginia, just after noon on a wharf full of smiling WACs, who just happened to be there to help direct traffic. The Red Cross was there, and the Twenty-third vets said they got their first glass of fresh milk in 14 months, along with doughnuts, in the buses pulled up at the wharf.

The buses then drove to Camp Patrick Henry, which many of the men said seemed to turn into one giant telephone booth as the Ghost troops queued in long lines to call loved ones. Tompkins called Babe right away. He was looking forward to seeing his son, Butch, for the first time. He had named Bill Blass as Butch's godfather.

Processing at Patrick Henry involved changing their olive drab European wools for tan tropical clothing. It was a very hot day, but anyone who complained was immediately offered a return trip to cool Germany by the officers.

The Ghost troops then began moving to various reception centers around the nation starting the next day, July 3. The trains were all day coaches but no one seemed to mind. The furloughs were called, on the orders, "temporary duty for recuperation, rehabilitation and recovery." To most, it was mostly reconversion. Japan and the Pacific were the dark clouds looming on the horizon, but the men tried not to think about it.

Tompkins had a joyful reunion with Babe, and promised to drive back to Manhattan on the last furlough day and pick up Bill Blass at his mother's New York City brownstone for a trip to Fort Dix before shipping out to Pine Camp, then to Oakland, and then to the Pacific.

Bob and Bunny "Babe" Tompkins say, even today, that their reunion was the happiest single day of their lives. Here is the way Bunny described the days before their reunion and the reunion:

I remember my birthday, July 2, 1945. My folks had a few of my girl-friends over for cake and were driving them home. I was all alone except for Butch, who was about seven months old. The phone rang and it was Western Union with a telegram. He said "Happy Birthday, Babe," and I didn't hear anything else. He was so nice he read it twice and then decided he better send it because I wasn't listening. No one was with me but a sleeping baby.

I called Bob's folks and then at 11:30 I had to call Ethel and Ginna Blass. They were still up waiting for my call. They had heard from Bill in the afternoon. Then Mom and Dad got home and it was some birthday.

I was at his [Bill Blass's mother's] home on July 5, 1945, waiting for a call from Bob at Grand Central Station. I was going to drive there to meet him so that Bill and his mother and sister could see him alone.

We heard the elevator door open and someone cleared his throat. Ethel said, "That's Bill." There was a knock on the door and they were both there. I thought back on that moment later and realized that it was the very best moment of my life. What makes it even better, Bob decided that was his best also.

But their happiness was under a dark cloud. All of the newspapers, magazines, and radio commentators were predicting a long and costly war with Japan. The news was gloomy. Somehow it didn't seem fair that the Ghost troops would leave one war and then be shipped to another.

Enderlein, Blass, Tompkins, and others said they had an ominous foreboding. They felt they had used up their rabbit feet—all of their luck—against the Germans. But while they were preparing to ship out as a preliminary to going first to Oakland, California, and then to the Pacific, two atomic bombs were dropped on Japan, one on Hiroshima and the other Nagasaki, ending the war a few days later. Bob Tompkins recalls the electric moment:

> Bill Blass asked me to pick him up at his mother's home in New York City for our trip to Fort Dix, New Jersey. From there we were to go to Pine Camp and prepare for the Japanese voyage after our furlough. Babe and I and a friend drove to his mother's place in New York. I'll never forget that day when he came running down the steps, carrying his duffel bag. He was all blustery and shouting.
>
> He kept saying, "Did you hear? Did you hear what happened? We dropped some kind of big bomb on Japan. Just heard it on the radio. It just about destroyed the whole country."
>
> Babe and I just laughed. I thought maybe we had dropped a few 500-pounders on Tokyo or something. We kidded him. Bill did have a tendency to exaggerate sometimes. I turned on the car radio. We were driving through the Jersey Meadows. I remember it was a foggy night. We could smell that peculiar smell of the Jersey Meadows. Then we heard the radio newscaster, Gabriel Heater. He was talking about this new "atomic bomb."
>
> Neither Bill nor I had ever head of anything like that before. But we wondered if it meant the war would be over soon. We agreed that it sounded good to us. We sure hoped so. Later on we were at Pine Camp when we dropped the second one. We knew the war would soon be over.

The atomic bomb was completely new to the Ghost Army, just as it had been to Harry Truman when he succeeded to the nation's highest office on April 12. Secretary of War Henry Stimson, the man who ordered the Ghost Army created, asked to see Truman on April 25. He said he had some important secret information for him.

Stimson had been at the top of the Manhattan Project hierarchy and had routinely kept Roosevelt and Marshall informed, but oddly enough not Truman. His last report to Roosevelt on the atomic project had been on March 15.

On April 13, Truman's appointments included meetings with Secretary of State Stettinious, General Marshall, Admiral King, Admiral Leahy, Stimson, Secretary of the Navy James Forrestal, General Giles, and James F. Byrnes. Byrnes first learned of the atomic project when he became Director of War Mobilization. Although Truman did not say so in his memoirs—he was not the kind of man who would—he probably was a bit miffed that so many intimates of FDR had known of the bomb project while he, holder of the nation's second highest office, did not.

Was it because FDR knew Truman enjoyed playing poker with his old pals from Capitol Hill and might let it slip? Many of the leaks in Washington did—and still do—occur when a congressman or senator— proud of knowing some top-secret tidbit—confides in a top staffer. The staff member in turn confides in other staff members or perhaps friends, and soon everyone in Washington learns of the secret.

The atomic bomb was one of the best-kept secrets of the war. It was so secret that only those with a genuine need to know were in the loop, and that excluded Truman. Byrnes gave Truman the overview, then W. Vannevar Bush, head of the Office of Scientific Research and Development, filled him in on the details of the new weapon.

No wonder most Americans were surprised when they heard the news. But nowhere was it more welcome news than among those who were preparing to go and fight on the Japanese mainland. And that included all of the Ghost Army.

Tompkins said the bomb hastened his exit from the Army:

> Because I was married and had a child, under the point system— after the Japanese surrender a short while later—I was discharged. The war was over for me. Bill Blass had to serve a little bit longer, but not much. And Bill and I have remained good friends ever since. He's one hell of a great guy and deserves all the success he's had.

When the word got out about the surrender, some of the Ghost troops were already in Oakland. Some were passing through the Panama Canal. Some were still in Pine Camp. But all began to whoop it up and celebrate. Art Shilstone was sent to Mississippi's Fort Shelby, and then on to Camp Blanding in Jacksonville, Florida, where he was later mustered out.

Cpl. Lonnie Gault of the Ghost Army says goodbye to Col. Howell Railey at Pine Camp (now Fort Drum) just a few weeks after the Japanese surrender. The Ghost troops had prepared to use the same deception on the Japanese, but the atomic bomb made this unnecessary. Photo courtesy the family of Lonnie Gault.

On August 14, the Japanese high command and the Emperor, Hirohito, accepted the Potsdam terms and the Twenty-third began a wild celebration, along with the rest of America. The 406th Engineer section of the Ghost Army marched in the Watertown VJ-Day parade. They looked like the toughest of veteran troops because most of them had terrible hangovers.

Because the Army moves slowly, the Ghost troops found that their readiness training continued even after the war was over. In fact, officers said a date for shipping out to the Pacific had been set for February, causing the men to look at each other in disbelief. But soon they learned it was a mistake, and by the end of August the Ghost troops learned that the entire unit was to be deactivated by September 15. Some got out a bit earlier due to the elaborate point system.

Robert Tompkins makes a nostalgic return visit to Utah Beach in September 1999.

After the war, the Army deliberately dispersed the Ghost Army personnel among many units shortly before deactivation to aid in keeping its mission secret during postwar years. The goal was to so disperse it that its cohesion would be undermined and the men would be therefore less impelled to tell their unusual, secret history.

Some of its technical experts became part of what was to become the Central Intelligence Agency, the postwar Office of Strategic Services. But despite this, many of the Twenty-third's vets organized and held annual secret meetings after the war. They were distressed because they could not receive medals and could not tell anyone—even loved ones—what they had done.

They suffered in silence. Until now.

A group photo of some members of the Ghost Army. The man third from the left on the first row is Lt. Dick Syracuse. U.S. Army photo.

Chapter Sixteen

Epilogue

As of this writing, Col. Clifford Simenson is retired and living in Boulder, Colorado. He still attends reunion meetings of the Ghost Army when they gather from time to time. He is 90, and his daughter looks after him. He and Maj. Gen. George Rebh stay in contact. Both are concerned that the Army may not fully appreciate the value of Ghost Army-style deception in future conflicts.

Bill Blass has sold his fashion empire and lives in New York City. He and his pal Bob Tompkins stay in touch. Bob is in Gardnerville, Nevada, where he and Bunny live the life of retirees, trout fishing and relaxing. Blass is the godfather of their children.

Grant Hess is retired and lives in Arizona. Dick Syracuse has not been in a hospital once since the war and still smokes and drinks and is robust and healthy. He is an attorney in New Rochelle, New York, and just as tough and cantankerous as ever. Thomas Winfield lives in Stratford, Connecticut, with his wife, Mary.

George Rebh lives in Arlington, where he retired as a major general but still keeps an office for various projects. His sons are successful businessmen.

Bill Enderlein and his wife, Kathy, live in Johnstown, Pennsylvania. He is active in trying to get the medals won by Ghost Army troops, medals the Army still doesn't want to shake loose, not even the Purple Hearts. One reason is that there is still a lot of classified paper hovering over the Ghost troops, virtually all of it ancient and brittle, but just enough to frighten Army bureaucrats.

Lonnie Gault, Hilton Railey, and Walter Arnett died, but fortunately left memoirs and papers used in this book. Colonel Railey's grandson and namesake, who lives in East Falmouth, Massachusetts, provided material for this book. Colonel Reeder and Major Williams are dead. Ed Biow lives near Portland, Oregon, and remains active in affairs of the Twenty-third. Art Shilstone is still an artist and illustrator in the New York area, and makes his home in West Redding, Connecticut. Henry Rapsis lives in retirement in Atlanta, Georgia.

From June 1944 through May 8, 1945, when the Germans surrendered, there were 135,576 Americans killed and 451,052 wounded. This does not include the staggering total of dead and wounded among the other Allies.

Although there is no way to accurately determine how many lives the Ghost troops saved, it is fair to start with the 12,000 to 15,000 Army intelligence said it probably saved in the Viersen operation alone. One could perhaps add about the same number of German troops to this Viersen total. That would make 24,000 lives.

It is not much of a stretch to say that its other 20 operations could have brought the total to about 40,000 Allied lives alone. Each time German divisions were frozen in place, it meant that they were not killing Americans elsewhere. It also meant they themselves suffered fewer casualties.

Although almost 10,000 Americans were lost at Brest, had von Ramcke broken out of this fortress the toll would undoubtedly have been much higher. One reason he did not was the Ghost Army, just a small part of the 80,000 Allied troops there, but a noisy and high-profile part. Metz was a successful operation, probably saving several thousand lives. It is fair to say that the Ghost Army earned its keep and deserved its reputation as a highly effective outfit.

Ironically, many of the Ghost troops felt guilty that they had not been in as much combat as front-line troops. In truth, they were far more valuable, man for man, in the role they played. And it was a role.

The Ghost Army was just a small unit of 1,100 men among 5,412,219 Allied troops under Eisenhower during the war in Europe. But they projected the work of thousands. But that was what they were trained to do.